Toward the Recovery
of Wholeness:
Knowledge, Education
and Human Values

Toward the Recovery of Wholeness: Knowledge, Education, and Human Values

DOUGLAS SLOAN, Editor
Teachers College, Columbia University

Teachers College, Columbia University
New York and London

Published by Teachers College Press, 1234 Amsterdam Avenue, New York, N.Y. 10027

Grateful acknowledgment is made for permission to use the following previously published material:

pp. 34, 45. Figures from K. P. Popper and J. C. Eccles, *The Self and Its Brain* (Berlin-Heidelberg-New York: Springer-Verlag, 1977), pp. 229, 375.

pp. 37, 38. Figures from J. C. Eccles, *The Human Mystery* (Berlin-Heidelberg-New York: Springer-Verlag, 1979), pp. 100, 143.

pp. 40, 41, 46, 47, 48. Figures from J. C. Eccles, *The Human Psyche* (Berlin-Heidelberg-New York: Springer-Verlag, 1980), pp. 18, 19, 36, 45, 66.

p. 74. Extract from THE FAMILY REUNION, copyright 1939 by T. S. Eliot; renewed 1967 by Esme Valerie Eliot. Reprinted by permission of Harcourt Brace Jovanovich, Inc., and Faber and Faber Ltd.

p. 81. Three lines from "Ash-Wednesday" in COLLECTED POEMS 1909–1962 by T. S. Eliot, copyright 1936 by Harcourt Brace Jovanovich, Inc.; copyright © 1963, 1964 by T. S. Eliot. Reprinted by permission of Harcourt Brace Jovanovich, Inc., and Faber and Faber Ltd.

Library of Congress Cataloging in Publication Data
Main entry under title:

Toward the recovery of wholeness.

   Papers presented at a symposium held June 1980 at Woodstock, Vermont, under the leadership of the Charles F. Kettering Foundation in cooperation with Teachers College, Columbia University.
   Originally published as Teachers College record, v. 82, no. 3, spring 1981.
   Includes index.
   1. Education, Humanistic—Congresses. 2. Education—Aims and objectives—Congresses. 3. Moral education—Congresses. I. Sloan, Douglas. II. Charles F. Kettering Foundation. III. Columbia University. Teachers College.
LC1011.T69   1984   370.11   83-18071

ISBN 0-8077-2758-X

Manufactured in the United States of America

89 88 87 86 85 84   1 2 3 4 5 6

CONTENTS

ACKNOWLEDGMENTS

I want to express my appreciation to Robert F. Lehman, Esq., Vice-President and General Counsel of the Charles F. Kettering Foundation, who first conceived of the Woodstock Symposium from which this book evolved and provided the leadership and guidance that made the symposium possible; to Huston Smith, Hanna Professor of Philosophy at Hamline University, who chaired the symposium; and to Carol A. Farquhar, Program Specialist of the Charles F. Kettering Foundation, on whose acumen, care, and hard work the organization of the symposium depended.

A version of this volume first appeared as a special issue of *Teachers College Record* 82, no. 3 (Spring 1981). I thank particularly Frances B. Simon and Glorieux Dougherty of the *Record* staff for their indispensable work in editing and preparing the manuscripts for publication.

Grateful acknowledgment is made for permission to reprint the following material:

pp. 72-73. Extract, reprinted by permission of the Bodley Head, Ltd., from *The King of the Castle* by Gai Eaton.

pp. 108-09, 110. Extracts from *Dibs: In Search of Self* by Virginia Axline. Reprinted by permission of Houghton Mifflin Company and Victor Gollancz Ltd.

pp. 115-16. Extracts from an unpublished autobiography by Jacqueline Langlois. Reprinted by permission of the author.

pp. 117-19. Extract from *An Autobiography* by Edwin Muir. Reprinted by permission of Gavin Muir and Chatto & Windus, Ltd.

pp. 149-58. "Limits in the Use of Computer Technology: Need for a Man-Centered Science" by Joseph Weizenbaum, from *Toward a Man-Centered Medical Science*, edited by Karl E. Schaefer, Herbert Hensel, and Ronald Brady, 1977, pp. 83-97. Reprinted by permission of the author and the Futura Publishing Company, Inc.

DS

Introduction

DOUGLAS SLOAN
Teachers College, Columbia University

In June 1980, under the leadership of the Charles F. Kettering Foundation in cooperation with Teachers College, Columbia University, some fifty prominent representatives from the worlds of academia, business, the foundations, and government met in a symposium at Woodstock, Vermont, to explore the topic "Knowledge, Education, and Human Values: Toward the Recovery of Wholeness." More than one-fifth of the participants in the symposium had extensive backgrounds in the sciences, including neurophysiology, medicine, quantum physics, cell biology, and computer science. Among the other participants were philosophers, sociologists and anthropologists, psychologists, educators, businessmen, foundation executives, and government officials.

They came together because of two fundamental concerns. The first concern was for the relation between education in its broadest sense and those dimensions of experience that give value, meaning, and purpose to human life. This concern with the relation between education and the problems of meaning and purpose was, of course, not peculiar to the symposium but one that is currently drawing widespread attention. Programs for moral education and citizenship training, for example, proliferate in schools and in departments of education. General education, ignored for some years, is once more a burning issue as leaders in higher education seek ways of reconciling the sciences and humanities and of introducing questions of value into the curriculum. Moreover, consideration is being given as seldom before to the college-wide teaching of ethics; increasing numbers of institutes and research programs are devoting themselves to the teaching of ethics in the undergraduate curriculum and in professional education. The pressing problems of modern life that threaten the future of the earth have turned many to look to education for help, calling for broad biological, ecological, and agricultural education—for peace, world order, and disarmament education. The symposium, therefore, represented an effort to address what are widely agreed to be among the most important and crucial issues facing modern society.

The second impulse for the symposium stemmed from the conviction that no genuine and enduring relationship can be established between education and values apart from our underlying conceptions of knowledge and ways of knowing. There has arisen in the modern world an increasingly dominant view that we can know only that which we can count, measure, and weigh. In this view—and it often dominates modern education in the schools and in the

1

media—feeling, imagination, the will, intuitive insight, are regarded as having little or nothing to do with knowledge, and are frequently even disparaged as sources of irrationality. In this view of knowledge and knowing there is no place for purpose, mind, meaning, and values as constituent of reality. Humanist educational reforms have time and again foundered on failure to engage the issue of what counts as genuine knowledge about the world. Indeed, humanists have often been enthusiastic collaborators in their own undoing, at one moment seeking to out-science the scientists, and at the next acquiescing in the view that they deal only with inspiring and entertaining fancies. In consequence our conceptions of knowledge often give rise to views of the world that provide little support for human values and for an education in which persons and the values of persons remain central.

Thus a major impetus behind the symposium was the recognition that to examine our understanding of knowing and knowledge is to consider education and human values at their most fundamental level. The main speakers at the symposium—representing natural science, philosophy, philology, sociology and anthropology, religion, and education—were persons whose life-work has been to show that there are ways of knowing and thinking about the world that do, indeed, make meaning, purpose, and values central, and that require a radical new look at education in all its dimensions.

Although there were important differences in viewpoint and emphasis among the main speakers, there was firm agreement among them on the need for an adequate conception of knowing and of our knowable reality. Each made a unique contribution to the transformation of our ways of knowing: David Bohm—in his notion of passionate Insight that penetrates beyond the fixities and particulars of the given to an underlying wholeness that is the source of all genuine new knowledge; Sir John Eccles—in his insistence as a neurophysiologist that mind and brain are not only not identical, but that mind is prior and primary; Owen Barfield—in his demonstration that one crucial way to recover the objective as well as the subjective reality of qualities and values is by attending to the actual meanings and changing meanings of words, and thus to the larger matrix of meaning from which human language springs and to which it gives testimony; Huston Smith—in his elucidation of the "forgotten truths" of other cultures; Kathleen Raine—in her eloquent argument from tradition that the banishment of Imagination creates a dead universe, but that the reinstatement of mind, encompassing nature, restores it to the living; Peter Abbs—in his demonstration of the cognitive value of the imagination and the emotions and in his affirmation of an authentic self-identity behind the social appearances; Joseph Weizenbaum—in his urgent warning of the apocalyptic consequences of permitting our technology to define the human rather than to serve the human; Robert Bellah—in his search for living cultural traditions that contain resources for communal vision and commitment; and Hubert Dreyfus—in his plea for a knowing that proceeds from deep participation in experience. Each supplied a dimension and an emphasis to that of the others.

There was also unanimous agreement among speakers and participants that modern science, technology, and culture are not as such to be rejected, but that the task is to realize fully their potential for human and humane purposes. Three broad possible approaches were explored in the course of the symposium. One approach would be to accept our present situation as basically sound, but in need of some streamlining and readjustment. From this point of view our culture is somewhat out of kilter, needs an infusion of good values, requires more committed people manning the levers, but at bottom requires no radical revisions. Almost every participant agreed that our problems are more serious than such a view would imply. A second approach would be simply to abandon our modern culture as utterly decadent and beyond redemption, and try to return to the traditional wisdom of a pre-modern, prescientific age. This did not present itself as a meaningful possibility to the participants; even those most appreciative of the traditional wisdom stressed that merely to try to return from whence we have come is neither possible nor desirable. The third approach, for which there was broad agreement, begins with the awareness that there have been real gains in the modern world—specifically, in the emergence of the individual and self-conscious identity. With individuation has come the possibility, if not always the reality, of genuine freedom. And, as an expression and instrument of this freedom, technological reason has emerged in all its power.

Each of these—the person, freedom, and reason—is a real achievement in the human being's evolutionary development and carries potential for further achievement yet unrealized. Yet each, if cut off from its grounding in a larger meaning and purpose, becomes, as only a moment's reflection will demonstrate, aberrant and destructive. The task then becomes one of finding and struggling for ways that will maintain the achievements of the modern world while at the same time recovering the sources of meaning in the primordial traditions that prevent these achievements from becoming aberrant and destructive. It is at this point that the deep Imagination—Insight—central to all of the speakers at the symposium, but explored particularly by Bohm, Barfield, Raine, and Abbs, can become the bridge between our modern individual freedom and reason, on the one hand, and the deep resources of meaning and reason contained in the cultural and spiritual traditions of mankind, on the other.

Meeting in small working groups, the participants sought to explore the concrete implications for education of the new connections being made between knowledge and values. Time did not permit the spelling out of specific educational implications in great detail. Most important, however, the call for a change of premises, of basic assumptions, was so fundamental, so thoroughgoing, that it precluded any quick-and-easy move from theoretical reflection to detailed practical application. Any demand for a ready kit-bag of teaching techniques would have missed the significance of the symposium. And, yet, more was being called for than a mere general change of attitude, however "value-laden" such change might be. A truly fundamental change of premises would have truly specific and detailed implications for curriculum, pedagogy, and educational practice. But what would be required in such a restructuring could reveal itself fully only in the process of being lived into and worked out.

Nevertheless, in discussions in the small groups, at the dinner tables, and during free time, some intimations of specific educational import of the symposium began to emerge:

1. The crucial role of Insight in knowing suggested the possibility of a genuine integrating principle for what is widely acknowledged to be a fragmented modern curriculum. The deep Insight present in scientific discovery is the same activity at work in art, poetry, and in the perception of ethical vision. A fundamental unity joins scientific Insight, artistic Insight, and moral Insight. Here lies the possibility of a unified cross-fertilizing curriculum that promises to go well beyond the vagaries of so-called interdisciplinary courses without losing the conceptual power of the individual disciplines.

2. Once the primary importance of Insight in all knowing is recognized, the way is opened for a reinstatement in the curriculum, and in their full right, of those subjects—philosophy, literature, art, religion—that deal with meaning and value as providing genuine knowledge about the world. A conception of rationality and of knowing that takes into account the qualitative dimension of reality will not consign to second place (and see them the first to be chopped off in years of financial adversity) those fields whose primary concern and domain is quality.

Indeed, recognizing the role of Insight in knowing will lead to a corresponding recognition of the role of the arts as revealing, par excellence, what is fundamental to all knowing—scientific, philosophic, religious, and practical—as well as in achieving the basic goal of all knowing: to discover intrinsic meaning.

It will also mean paying heed to those philosophies of science that consider wholeness, life, quality, and mind as much a part of nature as quantity.

3. At the level of pedagogical and classroom practice an awareness of the important role of Imagination, of Insight, raises a multitude of questions—negative and positive—requiring substained attention.

For example: Negative—How destructive to their intellect and character is the unrelieved pressure on pupils to acquire narrowly conceived analytic, mathematical (now add computer), and reading skills at an ever earlier age? What serious and permanent harm do we cause inadvertently (but with the best of intentions) by introducing into the earliest school years electronic teaching technology without providing for the nourishment of words, colors, dance, and the engaged presence of living persons? What possibilities for growth and capacities for caring and commitment do we shrivel by enveloping students with a vision of the universe as dead and finished, a place where life, meaning, and quality have but an ephermeral and quirky existence?

Positive: How can we best foster Insight and the imaging capacities? What should be the place in early education of storytelling, fantasy, daydreaming, fairy tales, myth, painting, dance, and movement? How essential is early involvement in these, as some claim they are, to the development in later life of sound analytic abilities and healthy character? How important to the development of Insight is the existence for children of an aesthetic, warm, and calm architectural and natural learning environment? How do we begin to put together a holistic and rhythmic curriculum in which, over the school year, the various parts interact in interrelated and ever greater wholes?

The questions can be multiplied.

4. A fundamental change of premises in our understanding of knowing and in our sense of the world will require an unrelenting questioning of the unexamined presuppositions and assumptions about reality that pervade our classrooms, textbooks, and media. We will need to begin to make a clear distinction between science, a marvelous human instrument, and scientism, a spurious and quasi-religious worldview. We will need to question that temporal provincialism which holds that only the modern age counts and has the right opinions. We will need to attempt in the best comparative study to engage in open and meaningful dialogue with the beliefs and practices of other cultures. We can begin to appreciate the terror of many traditional cultures before the threat of "modern development," even as they are beguiled by it, and we will become sensitive to that traditional wisdom, essential to all humanity, which is in danger of being lost irrevocably.

5. An awareness of knowing as participatory and experiential reveals the importance of being and the quality of being in the teacher. The teacher must embody in his own being what it means to create, to question, to think, to reflect. Passion and emotions—focused, disciplined, attentive—are seen not to be a hindrance to rationality, but part and parcel of the activity of Insight. The education of the emotions and the emotions as educational come together in a curriculum that recognizes the quality of being as paramount. Such an education will not avoid the great issues of being human—death, tragedy, peace, conflict, love and hate.

Peter Abbs wrote in reflecting on the symposium: "As we are ultimately responsible for our own being, so we are responsible to that knowledge which derives from our being. The implications of this insight for the curriculum are indeed momentous. They invite us to join together all that we have split asunder; to join together, for example, values and technologies, conscience and science, poetry and existence. If within knowledge there is an ethical burden, then we can also say that our schools have been responsible for conveying a terrible misconception about pure objectivity, a misconception that may well account for many of the moral and ecological crises which now press so relentlessly upon us."

The process of education also assumes crucial importance, not as a matter of method and manipulation, but as an expression of authentic being. What is done, known, taught cannot be separated from the how and why of doing, knowing, teaching.

6. A radical change of premises and a total transformation in our ways of knowing may give to education an unsuspected and profound social dimension. In the first place it will foster an appreciation of a diversity of excellences, a diversity of gifts—logical, mathematical, technological, musical, linguistic, artistic, personal excellences—each deserving reverence and capable of revealing dimensions of reality. Perhaps what will then be required will be a diversity of institutional supports for a diversity of excellences, rather than the too-common sentimental demands for abandonment of all excellence in the face of a single-track reward system geared only to academic excellence narrowly defined. But recognizing such diversity may link education most directly with a concern for a just global society, for it demands a world in which diversity in wholeness is cherished. A holistic education demands a just and caring society.

Second, a recovery of the objective aspect of qualities, as Barfield put it, relates education directly to the quality of the environment, the economy, the social structure. It jars to lecture authentically on aesthetics in barren classrooms and ugly neighborhoods. And it would jar to continue to treat the earth as a machine or a dead slag heap while increasingly cognizing it as a living being.

Third, a transformation of knowing could induce a renewed sense of civic pedagogy and the formation of an enlightened and committed public. Recognizing the connections between knowledge and values demands sustained public dialogue about the kind of society and culture desired. Events such as the symposium become public educational occasions in which the kinds of public issues that make "a vital difference," as Hubert Dreyfus put it, are explored. The educational responsibilities of the media, the family, churches, political groups, business, and a variety of other institutions and agencies become manifest.

As the transformation of knowing that is upon us deepens and grows, its full and detailed educational implications will become even clearer. The potential of this transformation, and what the symposium was about, was well expressed by Peter Abbs in his reflections, cited earlier:

> It would seem that in the Western World we have reached a historic moment of transition from an exhausted paradigm to a new broader paradigm now in the making, with all the confusion and uncertainty and turmoil that attends such making. The new paradigm is, in part, a creative response to all the ethical, existential and ecological dilemmas which have accumulated largely because of the defensive narrowness of the traditional epistemology. We have arrived at that volatile moment when the significant intellectual minority (both in the West and in the Soviet Union—in Sakharov and Solzhenitsyn) cannot only see through limitations of the post-Renaissance world-picture, but can also begin to formulate and defend

what has been for so long excluded. What we see, in fact, is not a denial of the previous intellectual commitments (for, yes, we need both inductive and deductive methods) but rather a remarkable expansion of our understanding of the kinds of knowledge open to human beings; an expansion which gives due appreciation to deeper forms of knowing—ethical knowing, aesthetic knowing, personal knowing, imaginal knowing. This sudden reclaiming of lost forms of knowing is on such a momentous scale that it does not merely modify the traditional paradigm, it transforms it. We are taken into new philosophical ground—and the ground is so rich and so prolific it will take decades to harvest the fruit or, to put it conceptually, to explicate for education and society, and not least, our own personal lives, the innumerable implications.

The symposium was a beginning effort to chart the possibilities of a transformation in our ways of knowing and "the innumerable implications" for our earth, our culture, our education.

Insight, Knowledge, Science, and Human Values

DAVID BOHM
Birkbeck College, University of London

INTRODUCTION

The title of this symposium is "Knowledge, Education, and Human Values."[1] One of the main reasons why such a symposium is felt to be necessary is that knowledge and values have been largely separated in modern times, and that this separation has introduced a certain deep confusion in what is felt to be the meaning and purpose of education. Such a division between knowledge and values is indeed most pronounced in science, which is now commonly supposed to yield knowledge that is free of all values (except for the value of objective truth itself). This has helped to lead not only to a dangerously irresponsible use of knowledge, especially scientific, but even more to a general loss of meaning in life as a whole. Thus, the universe is now pictured, according to modern science, as a vast space full of dead matter moving mechanically, while man is a tiny creature living on a mere speck of dust in this space, trying desperately to make his life seem worthwhile by projecting his own arbitrary and inevitably petty ends and goals.

Of course, it is important to emphasize here that science itself does not necessarily produce this state of affairs. Rather, what has gone wrong is the development of a general attitude toward knowledge that is one of thorough-going fragmentation, and the present approach in science is only a special case of this. Seeing the intrinsically destructive nature of such an attitude, and the many kinds of disaster to which it now seems to be leading, we must then inevitably raise the question: How are we to change all this?

KNOWLEDGE AS AN UNDIVIDED PROCESS
IN FLOWING MOVEMENT

As a first step in our inquiry into the above question, it seems natural to ask: What *is* knowledge? Of course we are all familiar with *abstract knowledge*, which is stored up in memory, in books, records, computers, and so forth, and which is waiting passively, so to speak, constantly ready to be used for our convenience. But knowledge goes much further than this, in the sense that it is active as well as passive. Thus, it includes all sorts of skills, which are integral parts of our knowledge and without which the latter would indeed have no application and therefore no significance. This has been called *tacit knowl-*

edge by Polanyi,[2] who gives bicycle riding as an example. What this sort of knowledge is cannot be stated in words, and yet it is a definite content that is somehow stored up in the brain, nerves, muscles.

A further important part of active knowledge is our set of beliefs, which motivate us, often to extremes of passion in which we are ready for their sake to sacrifice everything. Such beliefs are based on *presuppositions*, which constitute a kind of knowledge of which we are not generally aware. One can give here the simple example of walking on what one presupposes to be a level road. Once made, the presupposition ceases to be conscious, but simply functions through an overall *disposition* or general "set" of the body, which is suitable for such a road. If, however, one encounters a pothole, this disposition is no longer suitable, so that one cannot properly walk on such a road without dropping the presupposition that it is level. Our whole approach to life is evidently full of presuppositions, which deeply affect not only our actions, but also our thoughts, feelings, urges, desires, motivations, the content of the will, and, indeed, our general way of experiencing almost everything. Thus, for example, through presuppositions of the inferiority of certain kinds of people, we are very likely actively to perceive and experience them as inferior, and so we will feel the urge to treat such people accordingly. (This is evidently the basis of prejudice, i.e., prejudgment.)

At this point, I feel that it will be useful to call attention to the distinction between abstract knowledge and concrete knowledge. In English, these are both covered by the same word, but in the Latin languages, there are two words. Thus in French, the word *savoir* means "to know abstractly" while *connaitre* means "to know concretely." In English, the verb "to recognize" is based on the same root as *connaitre,* and it means literally "to know again, in a concrete sense." Clearly, concrete and abstract knowledge cannot be separated in any permanent way. Rather, there is a constant interplay of both, in which any particular content passes from one to the other and back. It is this interplay that gives effect to knowledge, and in it knowledge has its concrete existence as an actual living process. The two sides are thus fused and interwoven, and only in abstraction is it proper to take them as separate. In its actual concrete existence, knowledge is an *undivided whole* in *flowing movement,* an ongoing process, an inseparable part of our overall reality.

In emphasizing this notion of knowledge, I realize that I am going against the generally accepted view, which not only fails to give adequate consideration to skills, beliefs, presuppositions, and so forth, as integral constituents of knowledge, but which also tends even in the abstract sense it attributes to the word to include only *correct knowledge,* and to regard what is incorrect as no knowledge, a mere figment, or perhaps delusion. But I wish to emphasize that at any moment knowledge is necessarily a mixture of what is correct and what is incorrect. Until a given item of knowledge is actually found to be incorrect, there is no way to distinguish it from correct knowledge. *Both* will contribute in similar ways to our actions, beliefs, attitudes, modes of experiencing. That is to say, the two are merged and fused in their functioning. So to consider knowledge properly as an undivided and active whole, we have to say that whatever anyone feels that he knows, at a given moment, is knowledge for him, at that moment. Likewise, whatever a society regards as known at a given moment is part of the knowledge of that society, at that moment. For both individual and society, knowledge, whether correct or incorrect, contributes in a basic and inseparable way to what the individual or society *is*.

All this implies, of course, that knowledge is not fixed in its total content. Parts of it are constantly dropping out as we get to "know better," in the act of *learning* and knowing. Also, we are constantly obtaining new knowledge. We do this not merely with the aid of the stored reservoir of human knowledge (e.g., by reading books or listening to lectures), but also by direct perception of actual fact, leading to new content. Experience is thus, in general, a fusion of perception and knowledge. To understand the whole, which is in a process of unceasing flux and change, it is essential not to try to divide it up into fixed fragments, for example by regarding perception, experiences, and knowledge as being in separate compartments, and by regarding knowledge as a purely abstract sort of thing that has to be "applied" to a separately existent concrete experience. Rather, we can see that the concrete experience, containing its associated images, motivations, intentions, and desires, arises in the one process, in which particular aspects of knowledge are constantly created, sustained, and dropped. And I suggest that only by starting from this whole process can we understand how knowledge, education, and values are related.

INSIGHT AND THE CURRENT CRISIS IN HUMAN VALUES

In most experience, the contribution of perception is limited to what fits into the overall general framework or context provided by past knowledge, both concrete and abstract. From time to time, however, challenges arise that require a creative and original response, going beyond the whole field of what can be handled by assimilation within known general frameworks. What is then needed is *insight*. As the word indicates, this is primarily an inward perception (i.e., through the mind). And as will be brought out in this paper, it is inward, not only in the sense of *looking into* the very essence of the content that is to be known and understood, but also in the sense of looking into the mind that is engaged in the act of knowing. The two must happen together. Such perception may then make possible the creation of new forms of response that are able to meet the challenge of new conditions.

Now it has been fairly commonly agreed that we are at present faced with the challenge of a breakdown in human values that threatens the stability of society throughout the whole world. I suggest that existing knowledge cannot meet this challenge, and that only insight can give rise to the sort of overall new approach that might meet it. This means that in discussing the questions raised by the symposium, it will be important to keep insight in mind, as a key factor.

INSIGHT IN SCIENCE

Although science has been, at least in part, responsible for the present crisis in values, I would like to propose that by studying certain features of the actual development of science we can be helped to understand the meaning of insight, and that this understanding (or insight into insight) may bring about the possibility of yet further insight into knowledge, education, and values.

Now, in the field of science, one of the best ways of seeing what insight means is to look at those scientific theories that aim to provide *universal* laws that would be of *fundamental* significance for the *totality* of matter, independently of conditions of time and space. As far as we know, the notion that theories of this kind could be proposed and discussed freely began with the ancient Greeks. (Before that such theories had generally been incorporated into systems of religious beliefs, so that there were strong psychological and social pressures that interfered with this freedom.) Greek philosophers proposed and discussed with great passion a wide range of fundamental theories including, for example, the notion that all is fire, all is water, all is air in various degrees of condensation, and so forth.

In these discussions, there emerged a certain basic notion of *universal order*, which was later carried forward into Medieval Europe. This was that between earth and the heavens, there is an order of increasing perfection. The extreme imperfection of earthly matter was expressed in complicated ugly movements that are generally found on the surface of the earth, while the perfection of celestial matter was expressed in the most perfect and beautiful of orbits, which was considered to be a circle.

Actual observations soon showed, however, that the planets are not in fact moving in circles. But these observations did not lead the Greeks to question the notion of a universal order of increasing perfection from earth to heaven. Rather the observed facts were accommodated by saying that the orbits are composed of epicycles (i.e., circles superimposed on circles). This description turned out to be quite useful, both for navigational and for astrological calculations. Nevertheless, in a deeper sense, it is clear that it served mainly as a means of evading a challenge to existing notions of order, since almost everything that might be found in astronomical observations could be made to fit by introducing a sufficiently complicated set of epicycles.

One reason these observations did not lead Greek philosophers to seriously question the order of increasing perfection was that they generally took reason as the highest value, while they regarded the senses as tending to be unreliable and deceptive. But what is even more important here is that, as indicated earlier in this paper, knowledge is an *active process*, which is present not only in abstract thought, but which enters pervasively into desire, will, action, and indeed into the whole of life. Notions of *universal* order are particularly powerful in such activity, since on the one side they generate strong feelings of attraction, while on the other side any doubts about their validity tend to be sensed as threats to the order of the whole of existence. The resulting reluctance to question such notions of order readily leads to the uncritical acceptance of various adaptations (such as the use of epicycles) that fit what is known without "upsetting the applecart."

Toward the end of the Middle Ages, there arose a revolutionary new approach, first indicated by Roger Bacon, who suggested that observation and experience (later extended to experiment) have to be given a value at least as high as that of the faculty of reason. This was, of course, the germ of the modern *scientific approach*, in which what is actually observed or perceived may be taken as a fundamental challenge to ideas that have thus far appeared to be reasonable. By thus correcting the Greek bias toward reason and away from the senses, Roger Bacon's suggestion opened the way to give due weight to the observed fact, and so to limit the extremely great power of knowledge, especially that which had belief in certain forms of universal order as its content.

As this new approach began to take hold, observation and experience accumulated implying that celestial matter is not fundamentally different from earthly matter. Thus, experience indicated that one could fit the facts in a simpler way by supposing that the sun, and not the earth, was the center of the planetary system. Kepler showed that the actual orbits were ellipses, for which the notion of the perfection of the circle had no significance. Later observations with telescopes showed that the moon had highly irregular mountains, as "imperfect" as any to be found on the earth. These facts, along with a great deal of further evidence that we shall not discuss here, implied that all matter is basically the same in nature independent of its position relative to the earth.

By the time of Newton, such knowledge coming from observation and experience was available to the scientific community and was present as a sort of background that was perhaps hardly noticed. People were, however, generally not fully aware of how this knowledge constituted a fundamental challenge to the prevailing ideas about the nature of matter. It was Newton who sensed this question and first faced this challenge fully. How it happened is that he saw the apple falling, and by implication asked himself, "Why doesn't the moon fall?" His answer was that the moon *is* falling, and indeed, because all matter is basically of the same nature, every such free body is falling toward every other, thus implying a universal force of gravitational attraction, similar to that experienced on the surface of the earth. Then he had to ask himself a second question. "Why doesn't the moon ever reach the ground?" He explained this by the fact that it was in motion in an orbit, which tended to keep it moving away as it fell.

Of course, he then had to supplement the above with a *hypothesis* as to how the force of gravity was related to the distance from the earth. He had the good fortune to hit quickly on a correct hypothesis (the inverse square law). But if this choice had not been a good one, he could have tried another and another, until he found one that worked. That is to say, the basic idea of universal gravitation was not dependent on such hypotheses. Newton's discovery was, for him at that time, not a hypothesis, but a flash of perception, an insight. What he perceived was that if all matter is basically the same, and if there is gravitation on the earth, there must be universal gravitation.

This may seem fairly obvious *now*, but in the context of the times, Newton's ability to have perception of this kind was an indication of a certain quality of genius that is not at all common. This quality involved in an essential way an intense interest in questioning what is commonly accepted, which amounts to true passion. When this sort of passion is absent, the mind is in a state of low energy, in which it cannot go beyond certain habitual frameworks of thought, in which it feels comfortable, safe, secure, respectable. It therefore cannot properly face the challenge of questioning basic notions, of which it is at best only dimly conscious.

Thus, in Newton's time, it was commonly known by scientists that there was a great deal of evidence that celestial matter is basically similar to earthly matter. However, this thought was put in one compartment, which was not allowed to disturb another compartment. In this other compartment was the idea that there is really no problem at all. The moon does not fall because, of course, its celestial nature makes it stay in the sky where it belongs.

Now the key question is, "How could people maintain such compartments, which allowed two ideas that contradicted each other to exist comfortably side by side?" The reason is the same as the one already indicated in connection with the question of how the Greeks were able to go on comfortably, in spite of observations suggesting the contrary, with their assumptions of a universal order of increasing perfection from earth to heavens. As stated earlier, knowledge is not just an accumulation of information waiting passively in the library or elsewhere to be consulted at will. Rather, it is an active and indeed often dominant process, creating for example the desire to believe in certain familiar notions of universal order and containing presuppositions that largely control the general operation of the mind, without our being conscious of their existence. It takes a high level of mental energy to be aware of this activity of what may be called the *knowledge process*.

What is being proposed here is that the essence of insight is such mental energy, which in effect perceives and dissolves the subtle and yet powerful forces in knowledge—emotional, social, and still others that are beyond description—that hold us in rigid compartmentalization of functions and ideas, and make us extremely reluctant to give up our beliefs in certain universal notions of order.

If we use the term *insight* to refer to the action of a general mental energy as indicated above, then we may say that after the mind is thus freed of certain blocks that are inherent in its accumulated knowledge, it is able to operate in new ways. We will then say that *particular insights* are what flow out of such new modes of operation. But it is important to emphasize here that what is essential is the *general action* of insight in dissolving blocks and barriers, which allows the ordinary faculties of the mind to give rise to suitable new particular responses (e.g., in science, the faculty of reason is mainly what is able to produce fresh and original concepts and theories in this way).

The theoretical ideas deriving from Newton's many insights (of which the notion of gravitation was only one) continued to dominate physics until the early twentieth century. Einstein brought about the first set of fundamental challenges to these ideas. Even when he was only fifteen years old, he was already asking himself the question "What would happen if an observer were to move at the speed of light and look into a mirror in front of him?" It is clear that the light would never leave his face, so that he would see nothing.

The paradox implicit in this question shows that Einstein had already had an insight into certain deep questions in physics. One can bring out what this was by noting that in terms of the Newtonian conceptions prevailing at that time, it is always possible for any speed to be reached and overtaken. For example, the speed of sound can be reached and overtaken by an airplane. But Einstein's question shows that he felt that there was an essential difference between the speed of light and other speeds (which later analysis shows was grounded in his appreciation of the fact that through its electromagnetic nature light is related to the deep structure of matter in a way in which other waves, such as sound, are not). He thus sensed that there was something wrong with the notion that the speed of light can be reached and overtaken. The energy of insight is revealed in his ability to question presuppositions of common scientific knowledge that had hitherto been so much a part of the unconscious general background that they were, in effect, taken to be truths, rather than presuppositions.

As Newton answered his question "Why doesn't the moon fall?" in a surprising way by saying that it *is* falling, so Einstein answered his question "What would happen to an observer at the speed of light?" in an equally surprising way by saying that no material object can ever reach or exceed the speed of light. For Newton it was possible quickly to come on a detailed hypothesis that gave his insight a definite mathematical form, but for Einstein, this required ten years of hard work. Nevertheless, it is clear that the germ of what he did was in the original insight that he had at the age of fifteen.

Those who knew Einstein will agree that his work was permeated with great passion. It was perception growing out of such passion that made possible the dissolution of mental barriers, contained in the previously existent state of knowledge. In the case of special relativity, one of the principle barriers was the notion that because it had worked so well for several centuries, the entire structure of Newton's thought on the subject constituted an absolute truth. This implied that one had to accept *en bloc* all of Newton's basic presuppositions, including, of course, the one that any velocity can be reached and overtaken.

Few scientists had the energy of mind needed to question ideas with such great prestige, and yet Einstein did not mean to disparage Newton in doing so. Rather, he said that if he saw further than Newton, it was because he stood on

Newton's shoulders. Newton himself revealed a similar humility when he said that he felt like one walking on the shores of a vast ocean of truth, who had picked up a few pebbles that seemed particularly interesting. However, those who followed him generally treated these "pebbles" as absolute truths. The essential point here is that with a long period of successful application, the common scientific knowledge of a particular period tends to acquire a certain pride or hubris, which is an inseparable consequence of the development of the presupposition that it is an absolute truth. Like all other presuppositions, this one operates largely unconsciously. What this presupposition does is to dispose people who hold it to behave with what is in essence a kind of arrogance. But, of course, to those who are caught up in this process, what they are doing seems to be not arrogance, but merely the assertion of the absolute truth of their ideas with that firmness which is properly due to such absolute truth. The immense energy in insight is what is able to dissolve such hubris (which constitutes one of the greatest possible mental barriers) and to bring about that true humility which is needed for genuine rationality.

From all that has been said about the role of insight in science, it should now be clear that although Roger Bacon's suggestion of experience and experiment as a means of criticizing ideas that appear to be reasonable was an important contribution to making modern science possible, it was not enough to prevent the blocks inherent in the active functioning of common knowledge from imprisoning us in fixed beliefs and false presuppositions. These are generally unyielding, even in the face of a great deal of experimental evidence that should reasonably lead them to be questioned. What is needed further is the energy of insight, which dissolves such blocks. This has to be emphasized very strongly, as there is now little realization of the ultimate inability of the scientific approach to avoid the tendency to self-deception inherent in the active functioning of knowledge, if this is not penetrated by insight.

INSIGHT, IMAGINATION, AND REASON

To sum up what has been said thus far, insight is an act of perception, permeated with intense energy and passion, that brings about great clarity. This makes possible the dissolution of strong but subtle emotional, linguistic, intellectual, social, and other pressures that tend to hold the mind in rigid grooves and fixed compartments, and so to cause it to avoid fundamental challenges. From this germ can unfold a further perception not contained in the entire previously existent field of the known, within the structure of which such grooves and compartments had been an inseparable constitutent for all those who had been working in the field. This perception includes new forms of *imagination* and new orders of *reason*.

As the word indicates, imagination consists of mental images. Any image is some kind of *imitation* of how something looks, feels, sounds, acts, but in the process of imagination these images are produced primarily in the activity of the brain and nervous system rather than in some external medium, such as paint and canvas, photographs, imitative sounds and gestures, and so forth. Such an image brings about a *conscious experience*, containing sensations, forms, and movements similar to those arising in sense perception but different in that their origin is internal rather than external.

Of course, the major part of our mental images is based on memory, and so these are in effect an expression of knowledge. Generally speaking, the forms in such images arise either in a "replay" of what is already known, or else in a process of combining a set of known images, with at most a mechanical kind of novelty (equivalent to that of the forms arising in a kaleidoscope). The continual and generally associative movement of this sort of imagery is what is meant by fancy (or fantasy). As happens with other forms of knowledge, such imaginative fancy is not a mere passive display of information but an active response, in the sense that it contains urges, motivations, desires, fears, and so forth that may affect the whole of a person's perceptions and general behavior. If this response is not so intense as to "carry us away," imaginative fancy may be useful (e.g., we can arrange, plan, and design things in the mind first, before we carry them out in actuality). But when such fancy arises in thought having to do with what is felt to be universal, absolutely necessary, and supremely important, the resulting active responses can be so intense that they provide sustained mental blocks and barriers in all areas of life. (E.g., fantasies of great danger in young children can give rise to "imaginary" fears that remain with them as long as they live.) These blocks and barriers are indeed basically similar to those that have been described in connection with scientific thought, the main difference being that the blocks in imaginative fancy tend to have a strong component of "private" thoughts peculiar to the particular individual involved, while scientific blocks tend to be based mainly on public thought, that is, common knowledge.

It is in thought used in the arts that imagination tends to play a primary role (though, of course, reason is still important for such thought). Without insight, imaginative thought is confined within the barriers inherent in fancy, and in art the result will, of course, generally be mediocre. As in scientific work, what is needed to be free of these barriers is the intense energy of insight. Imagination that moves freely without barriers may then give rise to particular *imaginative insights*. Thus in poetry, for example, a fresh metaphor, which clearly can in general emerge only from a state of great mental energy, may lead creatively to new forms of imagination that are not merely imaginative fancy.[3] But as we have seen earlier in connection with science, what is of key importance here is not the particular new forms that may emerge in this act. Rather, it is the general energy and passion of insight, whose nature is basically undirected, the same for the arts as for the sciences, and indeed for every area of life.

In science, thought is, of course, primarily concerned with reason (though imagination still plays an important part, as shown for example by Einstein's image of himself moving at the speed of light and unable to see himself in a mirror). The particular fresh and original perception that may arise in this area when mental barriers dissolve away can then be called *rational insights* (to parallel the mainly imaginative insights in the thoughts of the artist).

Let us now go on to consider what is essential to the unfoldment of insight through reason. It is useful first to go into the roots of words, which may show deeper and more universal meaning that is still implicit, though it has been covered up in the routine usage developed out of tradition and habit. The word "reason" is based on the Latin *ratio*, which in turn comes from *ratus*, the past participle of *reri*, meaning "to think." This has further been traced back, though somewhat speculatively, to the Latin, Greek, and Indo-European meaning "to fit in a harmonious way." With all these meanings in mind, let us consider the word "ratio." Of course, we may have a simple numerical ratio as proportion. It is well known that in ancient times it was quite common to relate harmony, order, and beauty to such ratios (e.g., in music and art). But ratio actually has a much more general qualitative meaning, which can be put as: As *A* is related to *B*, so *C* is related to *D*.

It takes only a little reflection to see that such qualitative ratio permeates the whole of our thinking. Thus, the similarity of forms of two different people involves a vast number of such ratios, a typical example of which is: As the right eye is related to the left eye in any one person, so the corresponding eyes are related in any other person. Or else, in a house, one may begin with a row of bricks, which are related to form a wall. If we let *R* represent the relationship of the bricks in one wall, we can denote the relationships of bricks in a second wall perpendicular to the first by R_2. But now we can consider a series of similar houses. As the ratios R_1 and R_2 are related in a given house, so they are related in any house in the series. Evidently this constitutes a *relationship of relationships*, or a *ratio of ratios*.

Such a notion of a ratio of ratios is capable of indefinite development, to give rise to a vast and ever-growing totality of relationships, aspects of which may be found in mathematics, in science, and in every area of life. This totality is not restricted to thought and language, but evidently can be directly perceived by the senses (for example, in rows of objects, such as houses and trees). So ratio is a content that may pass freely from reason to the senses and back again. Indeed, ratio is perceived also in the emotions. Thus, we may say that a certain emotional response is, or is not, in proportion to the actual occasion that provoked it. It is therefore clear that ratio in its totality (i.e., reason) may be universal, not merely in the area of thought and language, but more generally, in that it permeates every phase of experience. In fact, it is just through this universality of reason that thought and its object may be related and this may be expressed in the ratio: As any set of elements is related in a correct idea, so the corresponding set is related in the object.

As an example of how universal ratio has developed in the field of science, let us consider once again Newton's discovery of gravitation. The ancient Greek notion of the cosmos implied that the fundamental ratio was that between different degrees of perfection. Newton, however, perceived that the fundamental ratio was in the sequence of positions covered by a material body in successive moments of its motion, and in the strengths of the forces suffered by this body as it underwent these movements. This was stated as a *law of motion*. Such a law is an expression of ratio, which is considered to be both *universal* and *necessary* in the sense that anything other than this form of ratio was not thought to be possible.

However, the further development of physics has constantly shown that each form of necessity is limited and not absolute. Thus, as indicated earlier, Einstein (and later still others) showed that some of Newton's ideas were only approximations, and that new laws were needed, containing those of Newton as simplifications, as special and limiting cases. For example, whereas Newton considered space and time to be absolutely separate and independent of each other, Einstein introduced the notion of a fundamental ratio or relationship between space and time.

What is indicated by this kind of development (which has in fact occurred in all sciences) is that there is no fixed and final form to the totality of ratio, but that it is capable of indefinite unfoldment. It is important to emphasize, however, that the germ of such unfoldment is insight. As has already been brought out, this is an energy that penetrates very deeply, removing barriers that are inherent in the activity of existent knowledge and freeing the mind to operate in new ways in various areas. It may further be said that reason is, in essence, a perception of new orders of relationship or ratio in the particular medium of abstract thought. But, as we have pointed out, though its conditions are determined by the medium of such thought its implications go through all other areas of experience including the imagination, emotion, and sensory experience.

Reason is thus seen to be an undivided flowing movement, in which no definable feature can safely be assumed to be fixed forever. We can, however, *abstract* a certain limited content from this flow of reason, and for the sake of convenience we may regard it as an unchanging framework. When we do this we have reduced reason to *formal logic*. Formal logic is always based on the complete fixing of a set of assumptions, hypotheses, axioms, and so forth, that provide what is generally regarded as "solid ground" for what may be termed the *universe of discourse*. The logical form of the movement from premises to conclusion (equivalent to the operation of a machine) may then be compared to a sort of game, played within this "make believe" abstraction of a universe. Formal logic is thus actually the intellectual counterpart of the rearrangement of known images that takes place in imaginative fancy.

Formal logic may (like imaginative fancy) often be both useful and necessary. However, if we go on to assume that its fixed framework is *always* valid and therefore an *absolute truth*, then this will become a presupposition of all that we do from that moment on. Such a presupposition acts to determine the general disposition of the mind, producing urges, motivations, and desires that have an unchangeable quality corresponding to the supposed absoluteness of the truth of our assumptions. And as described earlier, out of this grow the kind of blocks and barriers to new perceptions that we have been discussing; clearly, these are essentially the same for reason as for imagination, and in both cases their dissolution depends on penetration of the mind as a whole by insight.

INSIGHT IN LIFE AS A WHOLE

At this point, I would like very strongly to emphasize that insight is not restricted to great scientific discoveries or to artistic creations, but rather that it is of crucial significance in everything we do, especially in the ordinary affairs of life.

I shall begin to discuss this point by describing an experience that I had when I was eleven or twelve years old. As I recall, at that time I had developed a habit of always wanting to be able to map out my actions beforehand, to know exactly what I could expect so that I would feel quite secure before I actually did anything. I remember once when I was with some other boys and we had to cross a stream by leaping from rock to rock. I could not map this out, but started to follow the others with great trepidation. Suddenly in the middle of the stream I had a flash of insight that what I *am* is to be in a state of movement from one rock to the next, and that as long as I do not try to map out what I will do, I can cross safely, but that if I try to proceed from such a map, I will fall. Just in that very moment of being on the rock, there was a sudden change in the whole attitude of my body, along with all my thinking and feeling on the subject, which not only immediately removed difficulties with crossing the streams on rocks, but also affected my whole life thereafter, in many other ways. For example, since then, a great deal of my work has been directed toward the understanding of movement, with the aid of this particular insight, that is, that undivided flowing movement is what is primary, while its "map" in thought is merely an abstraction of distinct "markers" that indicate certain salient features of the movement (as musical ratio is similarly a set of markers indicating certain salient features of the movement of the music).

It is clear that insight affects all the different functions of the mind—physical, emotional, intellectual, and so forth—in one undivided act that does not involve time in any essential way. Thus, not only does it take place in a flash with no sensible duration but also its essence cannot be captured in thought. There is thus no meaning to choosing to have insight, and then trying to discover some *means* to produce the desired result as an end. Rather, the action of insight is total and immediate.

As has already been brought out, insight operates in two ways, negatively and positively. The negative operation is the removal of blocks or barriers and the positive operation is the new perception that this negative action makes possible. For example the block I had was evidently that I *always* had to have everything mapped out before I did anything. The crucial element in such a block is the "alwaysness" of this sort of requirement. Evidently, it is *sometimes* appropriate to proceed from such a map, and thus it would make no sense to say that one should never map out anything beforehand (indeed, *never* means "always not," so that it is just another form of alwaysness). What the flash of insight did was to remove the sense of alwaysness and thus to free the mind to map out or not to map out, as each occasion demanded.

This is very subtle, because the block is not just in words such as "always" and "never." Rather, it is in the entire associated content, especially in the sense of absolute necessity implicit in the whole meaning of such words. This sense of absolute necessity will penetrate every movement and thought, and everything that one does.[4]

The key point here is then that intention, will, and desire depend on what one *knows* (whether this be correct or incorrect). If one knows that something is absolutely necessary, he will have a correspondingly powerful intention to carry it out, however wrong that knowledge may be. Intention gives rise to *will*, which is, according to the dictionary, simply the determination and direction of activity, both physical and mental. The particular content of will is evidently strongly dependent on the totality of stored-up information, the general disposition of the mind that is implicit in one's stored-up presuppositions, and so on. All these act to incite the will and arouse desire toward certain ends or goals. And if the necessity in this content is presupposed to be absolute, then the resulting will is unyielding and desire irresistible.

Thus, a self-closing circular action is set up, which constitutes a trap. For such knowledge will include not only the notion of the absolute necessity of the content, which determines the direction of will and desire, but also the absolute necessity of maintaining this content, no matter what further information may become available later.

This kind of trap is very difficult indeed to get out of. For the presupposition of absolute necessity operates before one can think reflectively. By the time one can think in this way that he must get out of the trap, he has been carried very far into it by the operation of the stored-up presuppositions. It is generally already too late, because by then one has begun to relieve his sense of uneasiness about what he is doing by means of various forms of self-deception. For example, one may invent false reasons (or rationalizations) that seem to justify not eliminating contradictions in his overall behavior, and he does this because the sense of necessity is so absolute that it will yield to nothing, while everything else, including truth and observation of fact, must give way to it.

Thus, consider a person who believes absolutely in a certain religion, and who will constantly find reasons to support this belief even when the absurdity of these reasons is evident to those who are not caught in his particular belief. Similarly, beliefs in the absolute truth of certain political ideas, such as communism, will lead a person to justify whatever happens with reasons that also turn out to be false when looked at carefully. We find this sort of behavior in every phase of life, individual as well as collective. Such self-deception seems to be an inescapable function of knowledge that has absolute necessity as its content (e.g., recall the self-deceptive arrogance that tended to flow out of the notion of the absolute truth of certain ideas in physics).

A number of years ago Jacob Bronowski made a very interesting television program on the ascent of man through knowledge. However, I think that, to present a balanced view, he should also have made a complementary program on the descent of man through knowledge. Indeed, our troubles originate, for the most part, in knowledge that is, as we recall, a total activity containing what is implicit as well as what is explicit, what is concrete as well as what is abstract. It includes knowledge of one's fears, one's hopes, what sort of person one is, and so on. And this sort of knowledge is generally entrapped in notions of absolute necessity and alwaysness that we do not seem to be able to break out of.

In this connection, I remember reading a science fiction story a long time ago in which a scientist invented a ray that caused everybody to lose his memory. What happened was that Hitler was talking, and in the middle of this he suddenly ceased to know that he was Hitler, while the people who were listening to him no longer knew that they were Nazis. Similarly, a banker suddenly ceased to know about his insoluble financial problems. All over the world, there followed an initial period of serious disorientation. But people, now being freed of the absolute necessity of a wide range of absurdities in the general framework of past knowledge, were able to face the real problem, which was how to live harmoniously together. And so they could start out afresh to create a new world.

It is clear, however, that no "ray" of the kind described above is needed to free the mind of its many kinds of absolute commitments that give rise to contradiction, conflict, and general disorder in its functioning. What is actually needed is just insight, which, without interfering with necessary and useful memories, is able to dissolve the mind's attachments to absurdities that hold it a prisoner to its past. When this takes place, a human being is able to act in new ways, not only in abstract thought and in imagination, but also in sense perceptions, in emotional responses, in the movement of the body, in relationships between people, and in all other areas of life.

INSIGHT AND VALUES

The word "necessary" comes from the Latin *ne cesse*, meaning "not yielding." This is to say, if something is necessary it does not give way. It is clear then that a presupposition of *absolute* necessity implies something must *never* yield. The difficulty with such presuppositions is that they interfere with the proper operation of the entire notion of necessity in an extremely thoroughgoing way.

Thus, many things are necessary, but some of these conflict with each other, and for this reason there have to be priorities as to which necessities are to prevail under various conditions. If there are no priorities, then (as in a traffic intersection) there will be destructive "collisions" of necessities. But if a given necessity is absolute, it has total priority and, as has already been pointed out, it cannot yield to anything at all. It is clear, however, that any form of knowledge has to be able to yield to fresh perceptions or else rational thought and action become impossible. But as the knowledge of absolute necessity cannot yield to any kind of perception, it will simply distort, rationalize, and push aside undesired facts so that ultimately nothing is perceived that could disturb the general framework of absolute necessity in knowledge. Not only does this mean that consciousness is caught in self-deception but also that no orderly system of priorities is then possible.

This brings us to the question of values. The word "values" comes from the Latin *valere* meaning "to be strong and vigorous" (the words "valiant" and "valor" have the same root). Value is thus a kind of virtue, that is, a certain power to do something that makes what has value desirable or useful, or dear to us. Clearly, we have to establish priorities according to our sense of value, and that which is felt as having higher value will take priority over that which has lower value. So our values are equivalent to a set of priorities. We need such priorities to give order to our lives, not only in intellectual contexts, but also physically, emotionally, socially, and in every phase of our existence.

Knowledge evidently makes an essential contribution to the determination of our sense of values, for it helps us to ascertain what is the actual power or virtue of each thing, so that we need not, for example, be restricted to evaluating everything by our arbitrary and generally irrelevant subjective whims and desires. Vice versa, the sort of knowledge that we will want to pursue and, indeed, even the pursuit of any kind of knowledge at all will depend on our realization of the possible value (i.e., virtue) in such knowledge. So the separation of knowledge from values has no meaning except as a momentary abstraction made for convenience of discussion. The two are inseparably interwoven in a single undivided process, in which it is impossible to have one without the other. When someone tries to achieve what he regards as knowledge that is free of values, this generally means that he has uncritically accepted either the tacit values that may happen to be current in the community in which he lives and works or those values that are implicit in his subjective fancies.

Just because knowledge and values condition each other in the way described above, that knowledge whose content is absolute necessity will make it impossible, as has already been pointed out, to determine in a natural and orderly way which values have priority in any given context. *So no sense can be made of the whole question of values without clearing up what is to be done with the presuppositions of absolute necessity that generally go through the whole of our lives.*

As an example, we may consider the notion of national sovereignty, which means that each nation has ultimately to put its own interests first, as the highest priority, and that everything else takes a lower place, including not only morality and ethics but even the life of the individual, and if necessary the very existence of mankind. This leads to unending chaos and conflict, especially in the modern world in which all clearly depend on each other. To maintain this thought of absolute sovereignty against the plain fact of mutual interdependence, there has to be distortion and self-deception (for example, that brought about through censorship and propaganda). On the other side, individuals do essentially the same sort of thing. Each one puts his own self-interest as the highest priority, or else that of the group with which he is identified, his family, his tribe, his race, his religion. And he tends to defend such self-interest with the same sort of dishonesty and self-deception that is generally used to defend national sovereignty.

It is evident that this way of determining priorities is full of contradiction. Of course this contradictory state of affairs has been developing over thousands of years, if not more. Man has, probably mostly by imperceptible stages, slipped into his present condition, in which his life is pervaded by what is in essence a vast structure of meaningless nonsense that ultimately dominates almost the whole of the activity of human knowledge. It is therefore clear that no one in particular can be blamed for what has happened. Indeed, if one looks into himself, he will find that he too is caught in much the same sort of absurdities that others are caught in.

The real meaning of all this is that knowledge does not know what it is doing in all of its activity. In a way, knowledge can be said to be in the dark about itself, and that this darkness is largely self-created. That is, the knowledge of what is "always so" and "absolutely necessary" creates pressures for the mind to distort by covering things up and this gives rise to what we have called darkness. In this darkness, the mind falls again and again into the trap of alwaysness and absolute necessity, and tries through self-deception to obtain relief from the discomfort and disturbances flowing out of the mind's own self-contradictory mode of operation.

All this helps to create and sustain the general attitude of fragmentation to which I referred at the beginning. This attitude ignores the fact that actually all things flow into each other. It may be consistent to abstract them as separate and unchanging, for a certain period of time, but this cannot hold indefinitely. Consider a tree, for example. At first sight it appears to stand fixed and independent. But in fact it grows from a seed, in a process in which almost all the materials and the energy needed to make it grow come from the surrounding earth, air, water, and sunlight. They all work together to make a tree and sustain its existence, and in time they dissolve it back into something similar to its original constituents. So, if one is considering any appreciable length of time, it has no meaning to think of a tree as fixed. And insofar as one thinks of it as fixed, he has to regard it also as separate. It is only when one thinks of the process in which it is constantly created, sustained, and dissolved that one sees that it cannot correctly be regarded as separate.

Evidently, the same sort of thing holds for people, both physically and mentally, as well as for nations. A closer study shows that inanimate matter has to be understood in a similar way.[5] This sort of universality of flow and mutual interdependence is indeed so evident, after a little observation and reflection, that one might readily wonder why mankind has generally had very little awareness of it, at least throughout the period of recorded history. Of course, it is clear that in the development of practical technical work, as well as in the ordering of social relationships, it was necessary for mankind to deal with an ever-growing mass of particulars, which for the sake of convenience had to be treated as more or less separate and fixed. As civilization grew more complex and ramified it seems clear also that these particulars would demand more and more time and energy. Thus, sooner or later, mankind would approach its present general state, in which the total set of such details seems almost entirely to fill the immediate experience of reality in consciousness, leaving little room for awareness of an overall process in which all these particulars are constantly being created, sustained, and dissolved.

At this stage, the concentration on particulars has evidently been carried too far, and begins to lead to the state of contradiction and confusion in the general activity of human knowledge that has been described earlier. One of the key factors in all this contradiction and confusion is that each human being comes to experience *himself* and *his fellow human beings* as essentially fixed and separate from one another, not only physically, but also psychologically.[6] It then seems that to be a fixed and separate entity of this kind constitutes the very ground of the existence of each person. And so, every aspect of knowledge is assimilated in terms of a basically fragmentary structure, implying a commitment to the separate individual or group as the supreme value for the whole of life. The active response of this general self-centeredness in the content of knowledge then creates blocks and barriers that, in effect, cause evidence of the incorrectness of such knowledge to be distorted, covered up, devalued, ignored, to the point where it rarely enters the consciousness of the vast majority of mankind.

What is needed to dissolve these blocks and barriers is insight. But here we must have in mind not just insights into particular areas. Thus Newton had an insight into gravitation. Such an insight brings light into the limited field of physics. This light has its value, but the key point is that, as Krishnamurti brought out with great clarity and force, something of much greater value is needed, which is insight into the whole activity of knowledge.[7] For, as we have seen, this activity is pervaded with a content of absolute necessity, which generates a kind of darkness that goes through every area of life (rather as if it were spreading dense black clouds through the mind). An extremely intense insight is needed to penetrate this darkness so that the mind can see what it is actually doing when it inquires into the thought of absolute necessity, and thus be enabled to cease its absurd activity of generating darkness (which it cannot do while it is enveloped in the darkness that it has created). Such insight would evidently be much more significant than insight into particular areas such as physics, biology, or something else of that nature.

Or, to put it differently, one can say that people are generally seeking enlightenment through knowledge, without realizing that the latter has the possibility of creating "endarkenment." This can be dispelled only through insight, which is able to end the commitment to absolute necessity in all knowledge, including that knowledge which is involved in forming values. These will then be open to fresh perception, which can from moment to moment reveal what is the proper order of priorities that would be right for each occasion. And so the general question of values can be dealt with in a consistent way.

EDUCATION, AND THE VALUE OF INSIGHT

I shall first say a few words here about education, though this subject is not the main point of my paper.

Evidently education will have to take account of this whole question of insight. This is not the place to discuss in detail how this might be done. However, I can say that in my view the key point in this connection is that any human being has to be able constantly to question, with great energy and passion (as for example Newton did), whatever is not clear and whatever one suspects may not make sense. And it is not enough to ask such questions. One has further to question the questions. For in the beginning these usually contain the very presuppositions that are behind the unclarity and contradiction that led one to question in the first place. One has to do this not once or twice or three times, but, rather, it is necessary to sustain such questioning indefinitely, in spite of whatever difficulties and obstacles that one may encounter. This approach or attitude is what has to be communicated in education, that is, to be able to question ceaselessly, without any aggressive wish to demolish things but just simply because one sees that these things have to be questioned.

Such questioning is however, not an end in itself, nor is its main purpose to give rise to answers. Rather, what is essential here is the whole flowing movement of life, which can be harmonious only when there is ceaseless questioning, through which one can be freed of the common tendency to hold indefinitely to contradictory and confused knowledge that responds actively, to give rise to general disorder in the functioning of the mind.

This kind of approach is required not merely in the area of the particular *content* of knowledge; it has also to extend to one's own whole way of thinking, feeling, behaving. For example, something may happen at the personal level that makes one irritated or angry, and this will generally lead to distortion and self-deception (e.g., either one rationalizes to justify his anger or refuses to acknowledge that he is angry, saying, "I am not angry"). One has to question his own inconsistencies without letup, and thus to be aware of the thought of absolute necessity (for example of keeping one's own self-image intact) that is generally the source of such absurdities. Or, in the context of what is public, a scientist has to be aware, for example, that his knowledge is not generally free of all values other than that of objective truth. Thus, he may be conditioned by the sense of supreme value that he is likely to have in connection with his personal security and status, and with his commitment to the general way of thinking shared by his scientific community. Clearly, pressures of this kind, which are inherent in belonging to an institution, are not compatible with the notion that objective truth is generally the supreme value for a scientist. For example, I can remember reading a newspaper report of a scientist working with a certain atomic energy establishment, who said that although there were actually serious dangers in what was being done, his colleagues were evaluating the tests in such a way as to come to the conclusion that the danger was not serious. Evidently then, as happens with people in general, a scientist can easily slip into allowing his values to be founded on self-deception, and in doing this he can further deceive himself by supposing that, at least in his scientific work, his only value is objective truth. It is thus clear that the presuppositions of absolute necessity that determine false values in any one field are likely to operate through the mind and spread into all other fields. As Krishnamurti has emphasized, to meet this challenge properly requires the ability to question oneself in *every* area of one's activity.[8]

With regard to one's own values, the main thing to question is whether or not these arise out of presuppositions of absolute necessity. Knowledge is, as has been emphasized throughout, dependent on values and values on knowledge, but the essential point is that knowledge and values have to be free of absolute necessity. Like any particular features of the content of knowledge, values can then have a *relative* constancy implying that they may be fixed until further notice, but not *for always*.

But actually to do this is an immense challenge, not only to our habit of wanting the important things in life to be secure for always, but also because certain very deep and subtle questions are involved here, which are not at all easy to put clearly.

Consider, for example, what this approach means for beliefs. How are we to have the energy and passion needed to question ceaselessly whatever may not make sense without some sort of belief in the ultimate value of doing this?

To see further what is implied in this question, it is useful to note that the word *belief* is based on the old English "lief," which means "love." So, in this sense, what is believed is what is beloved, cherished because of its extremely high value (for example as one may say that we believe in a certain person). If this were all that was involved in the notion of belief, then it would present no insuperable difficulties. Thus, one could say that a certain kind of work can be seen to have very high value, and that one naturally cherishes this work. One is therefore ready to hold fast to it even if serious problems arise, and to go to great lengths to solve such problems, even when the prospects seem very discouraging. So there can be great passion and energy behind such work (which may, for example, be that of ceaselessly questioning presuppositions of absolute necessity).

The difficulty arises, however, from the further meaning of the word belief, which is in effect to hold fast to that which one *desires* to be true. That this meaning is very common indeed can be seen by considering how people often believe in certain things because these give comfort, a sense of security, and relief from unpleasant and disruptive mental reactions, such as anxiety. This sort of belief amounts to a presupposition of the absolute necessity of the content that is believed. (Otherwise, it would not provide comfort and relief.) It is evident, however, that such a presupposition is in no way necessary to true energy and passion, but that on the contrary it contains just the sort of blocks and barriers that prevent creative and original responses that would be of great value.

It is thus clear that if to believe means to hold to an idea because one desires it to be true, then this must inevitably lead to self-deception, aimed at gratification and at relief from mental suffering. On the other hand, whatever arises out of genuine love will not distract perception in this way. Rather, being permeated with real care for what is cherished, it presents the latter in a true light with all its faults, as well as its good points. It is therefore clear that it is quite possible to be constantly ready seriously to question what one values very highly whenever this shows inconsistencies or other features that may not make sense. Indeed, to fail to do this is both absurd and dangerous.

If one questions in this way, then there may be the energy of insight, which is, as we have seen, crucial for dissolving blocks and barriers, ending self-deception, and opening up the mind to new perceptions that may be relevant on each occasion. For this insight actually to operate, what is primarily needed is that one clearly perceive the great value of insight. At present, it must be said that insight is not actually given great value, neither in society in general nor in education in particular. Rather, there is a very strong bias in favor of accumulating knowledge far beyond the point where to do this would make sense, while the spirit of ceaseless questioning that is necessary for insight is generally ignored, if not positively discouraged. To be sure there is currently a great deal of discussion of the need to foster creativity (e.g., in various kinds of courses), but when what is actually done in this regard is examined carefully, this usually turns out to be mainly an attempt to develop imaginative fancy. In such an attempt, there is little or no understanding of the need for insight, without which neither imagination nor reason nor any other faculty can be truly creative. And more generally, even when insight is given some value one finds that this is usually because it is thought to be useful for making new knowledge possible, rather than because it is felt in itself to be directly and immediately important for the overall quality of human life.

However, if we see that insight has in itself a very high value in the sense indicated above, then we will have a different attitude toward everything, including, of course, knowledge, education, and values. Indeed, these latter will now be seen to constitute a field in which there is no end to the possibility of fresh and original perception made possible through insight. And such insight need not be restricted to a special elite group. Rather, it is open to any human being who actually sees that in the long run insight is necessary for a life that is worth living.

A BRIEF ADDENDUM ON PLATO

As the symposium developed for several days after this talk was given, it became clear that many of the participants felt that Plato was, as it were, implicitly present, at the heart of most of what was done in the conference. I therefore thought it might be appropriate to add a few words as to the relationship between the ideas expressed in my talk and some of those of Plato.

I feel that the key point that is relevant here can be approached by asking whether what I have said about insight allows for any value that is absolute[9] (rather than just something that is to be held "until further notice"). For example, throughout the past, many (and especially Plato himself) have regarded it as meaningful to consider *the good* as an eternal and supreme value. What is meant by this is not any particular good, nor even the general good of mankind, but rather the very essence of goodness. This not only acts to sustain what is good, to propagate it and to make it flower, but it is in itself of the quality of perfect love, harmony, beauty, and wholeness (which was generally what was meant also by the divine).

I feel that it would have no meaning to deny totally the possibility of this sort of supreme goodness. However, it is important to point out that there are serious questions that have to be raised with regard to this notion.

First, if the idea of the absolute good has any definable content at all, it is implied that this content must be felt to be absolutely necessary and that this feeling of absolute necessity must give rise to the same sort of arrogance and self-deception to which any other notions ascribing a definable content to the absolute will lead. Thus, as is well known, both in religion and politics, it is just those who were convinced of the absolute goodness of what they were doing who often ultimately produced the greatest evil. So it seems that, at the very least, the notion of absolute goodness can be consistent only if it has absolutely no definable content (so that it evidently could not be held in any form of knowledge). What could be meant by such a notion?

In answer to this, one might suggest that what is required is not an intellectual understanding of the subject but rather an *act* of turning toward the ultimate good. But this suggestion raises a yet more serious question. For as has been brought out in this talk, mankind has generally been conditioned over the ages to the absolute necessity of giving supreme value to the self, or to that with which the self is identified. Is a human being actually free just to *will* to turn away from such self-centeredness, toward the highest good? This does not seem to be so. Indeed, as has been brought out, the will cannot possibly be free when the mind is pervaded, as it generally tends to be, with presuppositions of absolute necessity, with their attendant blocks and barriers that keep the content of the will fairly strictly within the limits of the ego and its interests. Indeed, considering just the narrower and easier context of science, it is evidently not possible even for a highly competent scientist, by means of choice or will, to make himself as free of ego-based blocks and barriers in his thoughts in his own subject as were, for example, Newton and Einstein. How much less likely will this be in the much more difficult context of freeing oneself from the blocks and barriers of egotism in general?

As indicated throughout this talk, the intense energy of insight is what can dissolve all kinds of blocks and barriers, including even those that are responsible for self-centeredness. When the mind is free of these, then it can meaningfully consider the question of whether there is absolute and supreme goodness. To jump into this question without the necessary insight will tend to continue and even to add to the present general confusion around this question.

I would add here that while a considerable part of the content of my talk may be similar to what can be found in Plato, there is a difference of emphasis, which I regard as very important. I feel that in Plato not enough importance is given to the question of what is *actually* required to make it possible for mankind to turn away from self-centeredness toward goodness. One can perhaps make this point more sharply by considering Plato's allegory of the men in a cave, seeing only shadows thrown on a wall, and never being aware of the light outside. What I wish to suggest is that the analogy could be made yet more accurate in a significant way by supposing that, in order to try to light up the cave, men were constantly maintaining fires (i.e., knowledge), which poured out dense clouds of smoke, through which the light from outside could not penetrate in a clear way. Thus, they would have not merely to turn to the light, but also they would have to have insight into how the smoke from the "torches of knowledge" was blocking this light. Without this insight, the attempt to perceive the light would have no meaning.

Footnotes

1   This paper is an extension and modification of an article appearing in Douglas Sloan, ed., *Education and Values* (New York and London: Teachers College Press, 1980). See also *Teachers College Record*, February 1979.

2   Michael Polanyi, *Personal Knowledge* (Chicago: University of Chicago Press, 1958).

3   Coleridge appears to be the first to have introduced a distinction between imaginative fancy

and creative imagination (which is, in essence, what we have been saying flows out of insight). See Owen Barfield, *What Coleridge Thought* (Middletown, Conn.: Wesleyan University Press, 1971). See also, David Bohm, in *Evolution of Consciousness*, ed. Shirley Sugarman (Middletown, Conn.: Wesleyan University Press, 1976).

4   The far-reaching effects of words such as "all," "always," etc. has been systematically explored by A. Korzybsk, *Science and Sanity* (Lakeville, Conn.: Non-Aristotelean Library Publishing Co., 1950).

5   See David Bohm, *Wholeness and the Implicate Order* (London: Routledge & Kegan Paul, 1980).

6   See ibid., Chap. 1, for more detailed discussion on this point.

7   See, for example, J. Krishnamurti, *Freedom from the Known* (London: Gollancz, 1969).

8   Ibid.

9   This question was raised, after the symposium, in a circular letter sent by Catherine Roberts to all the participants.

The Self-Conscious Mind and the Meaning and Mystery of Personal Existence

SIR JOHN C. ECCLES
Contra, Switzerland

CONSCIOUSNESS AND SELF-CONSCIOUSNESS

Following the procedure adopted by Popper and Eccles,[1] it is proposed to use the term *self-conscious mind* for the highest mental experiences. It implies knowing that one knows, which is of course initially a subjective or introspective criterion. However, by linguistic communication it can be authenticated that other human beings share in this experience of self-knowing. One has only to listen to ordinary conversation, which is largely devoted to recounting the conscious experiences of the speakers. At a lower level there can be consciousness or awareness as indicated by intelligent learned behavior and by emotional reactions. We can speak of an animal as conscious when it is capable of assessing the complexities of its present situation in the light of past experience and so is able to arrive at an appropriate course of action that is more than a stereotyped instinctive response. In this way it can exhibit an original behavior pattern that can be learned and that includes a wealth of emotional reactions. Reference should be made to the excellent accounts by Wilson, Thorpe, and Griffin.[2] It will be appreciated that there is no indubitable test for consciousness, but it is generally accepted that birds and mammals display conscious behavior when they act intelligently and emotionally and are able to learn appropriate reactions.

You may well ask: When does self-consciousness develop out of such a consciousness? A test for self can be identification in a mirror. Gallup[3] has found that a chimpanzee can learn with difficulty to recognize itself in a mirror, as shown by its use of the mirror image to remove a colored mark on its face. Monkeys never learn in this way and there are no reported examples with other mammals. So it would seem that anthropoid apes may have some primitive knowledge of self. Yet I have the impression that the initial high hopes of being able to communicate with apes at a human level have been disappointed, as can be recognized in an overview of a recent symposium.[4] Their use of sign or symbolic language was entirely related to the request for "desirables," that is, it was pragmatic. There was no mathetic linguistic usage in the effort to understand the world. No questions were asked. There was no evidence that they had any linguistic concept of self. They had no recognition of time, no sense for the future, and no knowledge of their future death. They had no recognition of number abstracted from collections of similar objects. In summary we can say that there is no evidence that apes "think" in a cognitive manner, so there is no evidence for self-consciousness. We can then ask: When did self-consciousness develop in the hominid evolution?

PHYLOGENY OF SELF-CONSCIOUSNESS

Archaeological evidence derived from detailed examination of Australo-pithicine sites of about two million years ago provides clear testimony that the food of the hunt was carried to the "living site" for communal consumption.[5] It was not eaten at the site of the catch. Thus these primitive hominids had already progressed from the selfish feeding habits not only of anthropoid apes, but of all their primate ancestors. Isaac suggests that this behavior of some two million years ago was probably linked with division of labor and the beginning of culture. It was probably associated with the beginning of a language that was more than animal calls and cries. Certainly it was at the beginning of the rapid increase in brain size, which seems most probably to be explained as due to the demands for increasing cerebral capacity to match the increasing linguistic performance. This process of cerebral development would be due to the natural selection very effectively given by the improved communication among members of the tribe.[6] But this result of biological evolution, a propensity to speak, is linked with the creation of linguistic communication, which is a World 3 phenomenon belonging to cultural evolution.[7] There is no way of obtaining information about the postulated linguistic development of hominids, but we can regard food sharing as indicative of an improved communication between members of a tribe. Possibly food sharing by hominids could be the first example of altruistic behavior in the history of our planet.

It is surprising how sparse is the evidence of altruistic behavior in hominids. However, with Neanderthals 80,000 years ago we have the first known examples of ceremonial burials, which certainly are altruistic acts. In human prehistory (60,000 years ago) the first evidence of compassionate behavior has been discovered by Solecki in the skeletons of two Neanderthal men that were incapacitated by severe injuries.[8] Yet the bones indicated that these incapacitated creatures had been kept alive for up to two years, which could have occurred only if they had been cared for by other individuals of the tribe. Compassionate feelings can also be inferred from the remarkable discovery that burials at that time in the Shanidar cave were associated with floral tributes, as disclosed by pollen analysis.[9] We may thus date the earliest known signs of altruism in human prehistory at 80,000 to 60,000 years ago. One could hope that it could be earlier because Neanderthal men with brains as large as ours existed at least 100,000 years ago.

In this account of the coming of altruism it is assumed that it was linked with the coming of self-consciousness, that is, with the recognition of oneself and others as conscious selves. From this recognition would flow the caring for others when alive and the caring for the dead by the ceremonial burial customs. The Neanderthal brain came at the end of an amazingly rapid development with a trebling of size over some three million years, which is an almost incredibly rapid evolutionary advance. Doubtless this cerebral capacity was required for linguistic performance, which would be of the greatest importance in welding a tribe together for hunting and warfare, as well as for social cohesion. However, the emergence of self-consciousness apparently came much later, after the brain had grown at about 100,000 years ago to a size matching ours. This emergence is referred to as a "transcendence" by Dobzhansky.[10] Then came the first clear evidence of altruism in the ceremonial burial customs, though possibly it could be much earlier in the food sharing of hominids as described above.

THE HUMAN PERSON

Each of us continually has the experience of being a person with a self-consciousness—not just conscious, but knowing that you know. In defining *person* I will quote two admirable statements by Immanuel Kant: "A person is a subject who is responsible for his actions"; and "A person is something that is conscious at different times of the numerical identity of its self." These statements are minimal and basic, and they could be enormously expanded. For example, Popper and I have recently published a 600-page book, *The Self and its Brain*.[11] On page 144 Popper refers to "that greatest of miracles: the human consciousness of self."

We are not able to go much further than Kant in defining the relations of the person to its brain. We are apt to regard the person as identical with the ensemble of face, body, limbs, and so forth, that constitute each of us. It is easy to show that this is a mistake. Amputation of limbs, loss of eyes, for example, though crippling, leave the human person with its essential identity. This is also the case with the removal of internal organs. Many can be excised in whole or in part. The human person survives unchanged after kidney transplants or even heart transplants. You may ask what happens with brain transplants. Mercifully this is not feasible surgically, but even now it would be possible successfully to accomplish a head transplant. Who can doubt that the person "owning" the transplanted head would now "own" the acquired body, and not vice versa? We can hope that with human persons this will remain a Gedanken experiment, but it has already been successfully done in mammals. We can recognize that all structures of the head extraneous to the brain are not involved in this transplanted ownership. For example eyes, nose, jaws, scalp, are no more concerned than are other parts of the body. So we can conclude that it is the brain and the brain alone that provides the material basis of our personhood.

But when we come to consider the brain as the seat of the conscious personhood, we can also recognize that large parts of the brain are not essential. For example, removal of the cerebellum gravely incapacitates movement, but the person is not otherwise affected. It is quite different with the main part of the brain, the cerebral hemispheres. They are very intimately related to the consciousness of the person, but not equally. In 95 percent of persons there is dominance of the left hemisphere, which is the speaking hemisphere (Fig. 1). Except in infants its removal results in a most severe destruction of the human person, but not annihilation. On the other hand, removal of the minor hemisphere (usually the right) is attended with loss of movement on the left side (hemiplegia) and blindness on the left side (hemianopia) but the person is otherwise not gravely disturbed. Damage to other parts of the brain can also greatly disturb the human personhood, possibly by the removal of the neural inputs that normally generate the necessary background activity of the cerebral hemispheres.

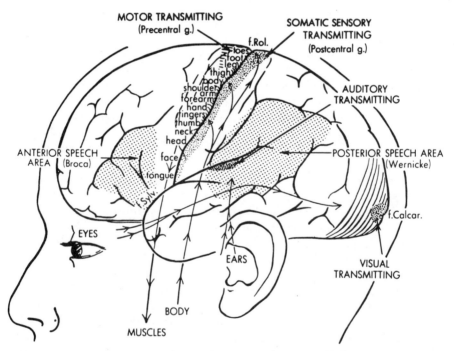

Fig. 1. The motor and sensory transmitting areas of the cerebral cortex. The approximate map of the motor transmitting areas is shown in the precentral gyrus, while the somatic sensory receiving areas are in a similar map in the postcentral gyrus. Actually the toes, foot, and leg should be represented over the top on the medial surface. Other primary sensory areas shown are the visual and auditory, but they are largely in areas screened from this lateral view. The frontal, parietal, occipital, and temporal lobes are indicated. Also shown are the speech areas of Broca and Wernicke.

Popper states

that there is not only the problem of the identity of the self (linked to that of the brain), but also the problem of the unity of the self. Our experiences are often complex, and sometimes even our attention is divided; yet each of us knows—obviously from introspective experience—that he or she is one. . . .

I have called this section "The Self and Its Brain," because I intend here to suggest that the brain is owned by the self, rather than the other way round. The self is almost always active. The activity of selves is, I suggest, the only genuine activity we know. The active, psycho-physical self is the active progammer to the brain (which is the computer), it is the executant whose instrument is the brain. The mind is, as Plato said, the pilot. It is not, as David Hume and William James suggested, the sum total, or the bundle, or the stream of its experiences; this suggests passivity. It is, I suppose a view that results from passively trying to observe oneself, instead of thinking back and reviewing one's past actions. . . .

Like a pilot, it (the self) observes and takes action at the same time. It is acting and suffering, recalling the past and planning and programming the future; expecting and disposing. It contains, in quick succession, or all at once, wishes, plans, hopes, decisions to act, and a vivid consciousness of being an acting self, a centre of action. And it owed this selfhood largely to interaction with other persons, other selves, and with World 3.[12]

So, to sum up the evidence, we can say that the human person is intimately associated with its brain, probably exclusively with the cerebral hemispheres, and is not at all directly associated with all the remainder of its body. The association that you experience of limbs, face, eyes, and so forth, is dependent on the communication by nerve pathways to the brain, where the experience is generated. We are on the threshold of brain-mind problems that will be fully considered in a later section. Our immediate concern is with the question "How does a human person come to exist?"

ONTOGENY OF THE HUMAN PERSON WITH SELF-CONSCIOUSNESS

Let us now briefly consider how a human embryo and baby becomes eventually a human person. It is a route that all of us have traversed, but much is unremembered. A baby is born with a brain that is very fully formed in all its detailed structure, but of course it has yet to grow to the full adult size of about 1.4 kg. The nerve cells, the unitary components of the brain, have almost all been made. All the major lines of communication from the periphery and from one part of the brain to another have been grown ready for use. Much earlier, the brain has been causing the movements sensed by the mother. And even before birth the child can respond to sounds. Its hearing system is already functioning well by birth, far earlier than vision. It is remarkable that by seven days after birth a baby has learned to distinguish its mother's voice from other voices, just as happens with lambs. Then follows a long period of learning to see and to move in a controlled manner.

As we all know, even in the first months of life a baby is continually practicing its vocal organs and so is beginning to learn this most complex of all motor coordinations. Movements of larynx, palate, tongue, lips, have to be coordinated and blended with respiratory movements. It is another variety of motor learning, but now the feedback is from hearing, not from vision. Vocal learning is guided by hearing and is at first imitative of sounds heard. This leads on to the simplest types of words like dada, papa, mama, that are produced at about one year. It is important to realize that speech is dependent on feedback from hearing the spoken words. The deaf are mute. In linguistic development recognition outstrips expression. The child has a veritable word hunger, asking for names and practicing incessantly even when alone. It dares to make mistakes devolving from its own rules, as for example with the irregular plural of nouns. Language does not come about by simple imitation. The child abstracts regularities and relations from what it hears and applies these principles in building up its linguistic expressions.

The investigations of Amsterdam[13] led him to give eighteen months for the transition from the conscious baby to the self-conscious child. He used the same technique as Gallup[14] did, but with the red mark on the face of the child. The children's reactions showed that they recognized the mirror image as their own.

To be able to speak given even minimal exposure to speech is part of our biological heritage. This endowment has a genetic foundation, but one cannot speak of genes for language. On the other hand the genes do provide the instructions for the building of the special areas of the cerebral cortex concerned with language (Fig. 1), as well as all the subsidiary structures concerned in vocalization.

The earliest stages of functional development may be almost entirely pragmatic, as the child uses its protolanguage to regulate those around it, to acquire desirables, and to invite interaction. Those protofunctions in which the child uses objects as foci for interaction develop into the more mature mathetic function, in which the child uses language to learn about the world—its cognitive aspect. But of course these two functions, the pragmatic and the mathetic, are inextricably mixed in the language that a child uses from moment to moment. I would suggest that the remarkable linguistic progress by the child in the first few years is accountable to the developing self-consciousness of the child in its struggle for self-realization and self-expression. Its mental development and its linguistic development are in reciprocal positive interaction.

The 3 World philosophy of Popper forms the basis of my further exploration by the way in which a human baby becomes a human person. All the material world including even human brains is in the matter-energy World 1. World 2 is the world of all conscious experiences (cf. Fig. 2) and World 3 is the world of culture, including especially language. At birth the human baby has a human brain, but its World 2 experiences are very rudimentary and World 3 is unknown to it. It, and even a human embryo, must be regarded as human beings, but not as human persons.

The emergence and development of self-consciousness (World 2) by continued interaction with World 3 is an utterly mysterious process. It can be likened to a double structure (Fig. 3) that ascends and grows by the effective cross-linkage. The vertical arrow shows the passage of time from the earliest experiences of the child up to the full human development. From each World 2 position an arrow leads through the World 3 at that level up to a higher, larger level that illustrates symbolically a growth in the culture of that individual. Reciprocally the World 3 resources of the self act back to give a higher, expanded level of consciousness of that self (World 2). And so each of us has developed progressively in self-creation. The greater the World 3 resources of the individual, the more does it gain in the self-consciousness of World 2. What we are is dependent on the World 3 that we have been immersed in and how effectively we have utilized our opportunities to make the most of our brain potentialities. The brain is necessary but not sufficient for World 2 existence and experience. This is indicated in Figure 5, which is a dualist-interactionalist diagram showing by arrows the flow of information across the interface between the brain in World 1 and the conscious self in World 2.

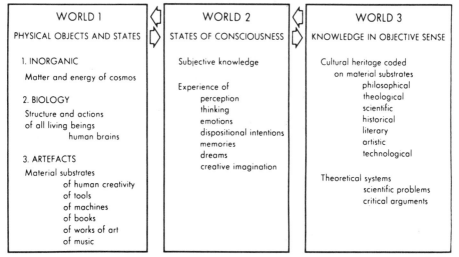

Fig. 2. Tabular representation of the three worlds that comprise all existents and all experiences, as defined by Popper.

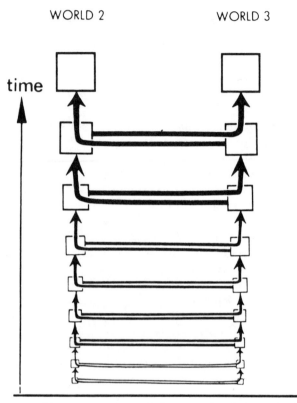

Fig. 3. Diagrammatic representation of the postulated interrelationship of the developments of self-consciousness (World 2) and of culture (World 3) in time as shown by the arrows.

There is a recent tragic case illustrative of Figure 3. A child, Genie, was deprived of all World 3 influence by her psychotic father. She was penned in isolation in a small room, never spoken to, and minimally serviced from the age of twenty months up to thirteen years and eight months. On release from this terrible deprivation she was of course a human being, but not a human person. She was at the bottom rung of the ladder in Figure 3. Since then, with the dedicated help of Dr. Susan Curtiss, she has been slowly climbing up that ladder of personhood for the last eight years.[15] The linguistic deprivation seriously damaged her left hemisphere, but the right hemisphere stands in for a much depleted language performance. Yet, despite this terrible delayed immersion in World 3, Genie has become a human person with self-consciousness, emotions, and excellent performance in manual dexterity and in visual recognition. We can recognize the necessity of World 3 for the development of the human person. The brain is built by genetic instructions (that is, nature), but development to human personhood is dependent on the

World 3 environment (that is, nurture). With Genie there was a gap of over thirteen years between nature and nurture.

It may seem that a complete explanation of the development of the human person can be given in terms of the human brain. It is built anatomically by genetic instructions and subsequently developed functionally by learning from the environmental influences. A purely materialist explanation would seem to suffice with the conscious experiences as derivatives from brain functioning. However, it is a mistake to think that the brain does everything and that our conscious experiences are simply a reflection of brain activities, which is a common philosophical view. If that were so, our conscious selves would be no more than passive spectators of the performances carried out by the neuronal machinery of the brain. Our beliefs that we can really make decisions and that we have some control over our actions would be nothing but illusions. There are of course all sorts of subtle cover-ups by philosophers from such a stark exposition, but they do not face up to the issue. In fact all people, even materialist philosophers, behave as if they had at least some responsibility for their own actions. It seems that their philosophy is for "the other people, not for themselves," as Schopenhauer wittily stated.

These considerations lead me to the alternative hypothesis of dualist-interactionism, which has been expanded at length in the recent book *The Self and its Brain*.[16] It is really the commonsense view, namely that we are a combination of two things or entities: our brains on the one hand, and our conscious selves on the other. The self is central to the totality of our conscious experiences as persons through our whole waking life. We link it in memory from our earliest conscious experiences. It lapses during sleep, except for dreams, and it recovers for the next day by the continuity of memory. But for memory we as experiencing persons would not exist. Thus we have the extraordinary problem that was first recognized by Descartes: How can the conscious mind and the brain interact?

HYPOTHESES RELATING TO THE BRAIN-MIND PROBLEM

It is not possible here to give a detailed appraisal of the immense philosophical literature on the brain-mind or body-mind problem. Fortunately this has recently been done in a masterly manner by Popper.[17] He has critically surveyed the historical development of the problem from the earliest records of Greek thought. I will begin by a simple description and diagram of the principal varieties of this extremely complex and subtle philosophy, concentrating specifically on the formulations that relate to the brain rather than the body, because clinical neurology and the neurosciences make it abundantly clear that the mind has no direct access to the body. All interactions with the body are mediated by the brain, and furthermore only by the higher levels of cerebral activity.

The dominant theories of the brain-mind relationship that are today held by philosophers and neuroscientists are purely materialistic in the sense that the brain is given complete mastery. The existence of mind or consciousness is not denied, but it is relegated to the passive role of mental experiences accompanying some types of brain action, as in psychoneural identity, but with absolutely no *effective* action on the brain. The complex neural machinery of the brain functions in its determined materialistic fashion regardless of any consciousness that may accompany it. The "commonsense" experiences that we can control our actions to some extent or that we can express our thoughts in language are alleged to be illusory. An effective causality is denied to the self-conscious mind per se.

In Figure 4, World 1 is divided into World 1_P and an infinitesimally small World 1_M. In general, materialist theories are those subscribing to the statement that mental events can have no effective action on the brain events in World 1—that World 1 is closed to any conceivable outside influence such as is postulated in dualist-interactionism. This closedness of World 1 is ensured in four different ways in the four varieties of materialism illustrated in Figure 4.

1. *Radical materialism.* It is asserted that all is World 1_P. There is a denial or repudiation of the existence of mental events. They are simply illusory. The brain-mind problem is a nonproblem.
2. *Panpsychism.* It is asserted that all matter has an inside mental or proto-psychical state. Since this state is an integral part of matter, it can have no action on it. The closedness of World 1 is safeguarded.

DIAGRAMMATIC REPRESENTATION OF BRAIN-MIND THEORIES

World 1 = All of material or physical world including brains
World 2 = All subjective or mental experiences
World 1_P is all the material world that is without mental states
World 1_M is that minute fraction of the material world with associated mental
     states

Radical Materialism:	World 1 = World 1_P; World 1_M = 0; World 2=0.
Panpsychism:	All is World 1-2, World 1 or 2 do not exist alone.
Epiphenomenalism:	World 1 = World 1_P + World 1_M
	World $1_M \rightarrow$ World 2
Identity theory:	World 1 = World 1_P + World 1_M
	World 1_M = World 2 (the identity)
Dualist-Interactionism:	World 1 = World 1_P + World 1_M
	World $1_M \rightleftarrows$ World 2; this interaction occurs in
	the liaison brain, LB = World 1_M.
	Thus World 1 = World 1_P + World 1_{LB}, and World
	$1_{LB} \rightleftarrows$ World 2

Fig. 4. Schematic representation of the various theories of brain and mind.

BRAIN⇌MIND INTERACTION

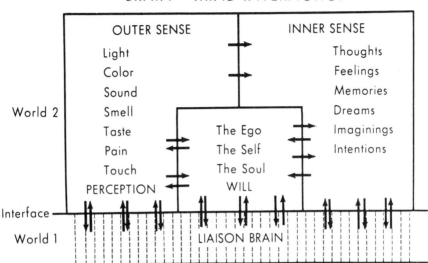

Fig. 5. Information flow-diagram for brain-mind interaction. The three components of World 2: outer sense, inner sense, and the ego or self are diagrammed with their communications shown by arrows. Also shown are the lines of communication across the interface between World 1 and World 2, that is, from the liaison brain to and from these World 2 components. The liaison brain has the columnar arrangement indicated by the *vertical broken lines*. It must be imagined that the area of the liaison brain is enormous, with open modules numbering over a million, not just the two score here depicted.

3. *Epiphenomenalism.* Mental states exist in relation to some material happenings, but causally are completely irrelevant. Again the closedness of World 1 is safeguarded.

4. *The identity or central state or psychoneural identity theory.* Mental states exist as an inner aspect of some material structures that in present formulations are restricted to brain structures such as nerve cells. This postulated "identity" may appear to give an effective action, just as the "identical" nerve cells have an effective action. However the result of the transaction is that the purely material events of neural action are themselves *sufficient* for all brain-mind responses, hence the closedness of World 1 is preserved. This has been very well argued by Beloff.[18]

In contrast to these materialist or parallelist theories are the *dualist-interaction* theories, as diagrammed at the bottom of Figure 4. The essential feature of these theories is that mind and brain are independent entities, the brain being in World 1 and the mind in World 2, and that they somehow interact, as illustrated by the arrows in Figure 5. Thus there is a frontier, as diagrammed in Figure 5, and across this frontier there is interaction in both directions, which can be conceived as a flow of information, not of energy. Thus we have the extraordinary doctrine that the world of matter-energy (World 1) is not completely sealed, which is a fundamental tenet of physics, but that there are small "apertures" in what is otherwise the completely closed World 1. On the contrary, as we have seen, closedness of World 1 has been safeguarded with great ingenuity in all materialist theories of the mind. Yet I shall now argue that this is not their strength, but instead their fatal weakness.[19]

CRITICAL EVALUATION OF BRAIN-MIND HYPOTHESES

Great display is made by all varieties of materialists that their brain-mind theory is in accord with natural law as it now stands. However, this claim is invalidated by two most weighty considerations.

First, nowhere in the laws of physics or in the laws of the derivative sciences, chemistry and biology, is there any reference to consciousness or mind. Shapere[20] makes this point in his strong criticisms of the panpsychist hypothesis of Rensch[21] and Birch[22] in which it was proposed that consciousness or protoconsciousness is a fundamental property of matter. Regardless of the complexity of electrical, chemical, or biological machinery there is no statement in the "natural laws" that there is an emergence of this strange nonmaterial entity, consciousness or mind. This is not to affirm that consciousness does not emerge in the evolutionary process, but merely to state that its emergence is not reconcilable with the natural laws as at present understood. For example, such laws do not allow any statement that consciousness emerges at a specified level of complexity of systems, which is gratuitously assumed by all materialists except panpsychists. Their belief that some primordial consciousness attaches to all matter, presumably even to atoms and subatomic particles,[23] finds no support whatsoever in physics. One can also recall the poignant questions by computer-lovers: At what stage of complexity and performance can we agree to endow them with consciousness? Mercifully this emotionally charged question need not be answered. You can do what you like to computers without qualms of being cruel!

Second, all materialist theories of the mind are in conflict with biological evolution. Since they all (panpsychism, epiphenomenalism, and the identity theory) assert the causal ineffectiveness of consciousness per se, they fail completely to account for the biological evolution of consciousness, which is an undeniable fact. There is first its emergence and then its progressive development with the growing complexity of the brain. In accord with evolutionary theory only those structures and processes that significantly aid in survival are developed in natural selection. If consciousness is causally impotent, its development cannot be accounted for by evolutionary theory. According to biological evolution, mental states and consciousness could have evolved and developed *only if they were causally effective* in bringing about changes in neural happenings in the brain with the consequent changes in behavior. That can occur only if the neural machinery of the brain is open to influences from the mental events of the world of conscious experiences, which is the basic postulate of dualist-interactionist theory. As Sherrington states:

> The influence of mind on the doings of life makes mind an effective contribution to life. We can seize then how it is that mind counts and has counted. That it has been evolved seems to assure us that it has counted. How it has counted would seem to be that the finite mind has influenced its individual's "doing."[24]

Finally, the most telling criticism of all materialist theories of the mind is against its key postulate that the happenings in the neural machinery of the brain provide *a necessary and sufficient explanation of the totality both of the performance and of the conscious experience of a human being.* For example, the willing of a voluntary movement is regarded as being *completely determined* by events in the neural machinery of the brain, as also are all other cognitive experiences. But as Popper states in his Compton Lecture:

> According to determinism, any such theory such as say determinism is held because of a certain physical structure of the holder—perhaps of his brain. Accordingly, we are deceiving ourselves and are physically so determined as to deceive ourselves whenever we believe that there are such things as arguments or reasons which make us accept determinism. In other words, physical determinism is a theory which, if it is true, is unarguable since it must explain all our reactions, including what appear to us as beliefs based on arguments, as due to purely physical conditions. Purely physical conditions, including our physical environment make us say or accept whatever we say or accept.[25]

This is an effective *reductio ad absurdum.* This stricture applies to all of the materialist theories. So perforce we turn to dualist-interactionist explanations of the brain-mind problem, despite the extraordinary requirement that there be effective communication in both directions across the frontier shown in Figure 5.

Necessarily, the dualist-interactionist theory is in conflict with present natural laws, and so is in the same "unlawful" position as the materialist theories of the mind. The differences are that this conflict has always been admitted and that the neural machinery of the brain is assumed to operate in strict accordance with natural laws except for its openness to World 2 influences.

Moreover, as stated by Popper, the interaction across the frontier in Figure 5 need not be in conflict with the first law of thermodynamics.[26] The flow of information into the modules could be effected by a balanced increase and decrease of energy at different but adjacent microsites, so that there is no net energy change in the brain. The first law at this level may be valid only statistically.

It is useful to think of the brain as an instrument, our computer, that has been our lifelong servant and companion. It provides us, as programmers, with the lines of communication from and to the material world (World 1), which comprises both our bodies and the external world (Fig. 6). It does this by receiving information by the immense sensory system of millions of nerve fibers that fire impulses into the brain where it is processed into the coded patterns of information that we read out from moment to moment in deriving all our experiences—our percepts, thoughts, ideas, memories. But we as experiencing persons do not slavishly accept all that is provided for us by our computer, the neuronal machine of our sensory system and of our brain. We select from all that is given according to interest and attention, and we modify the actions of the neuronal machinery of our computer, for example, to initiate some willed movement or in order to recall a memory or to concentrate our attention.

How then can we develop ideas with respect to the mode of operation of the brain? How can it provide the immense range of coded information that can be selected from by the mind in its activity of reading our conscious experiences? It is now possible to give much more informative answers because of very recent work on the essential mode of operation of the neocortex. By the use of radio-tracer techniques it has been shown that the great brain mantle, the neocortex, is built up of units or modules. The total human neocortex has an area of about 2,500cm² and is about 3 mm thick. It contains about ten thousand million nerve cells. These are arranged in small ensembles in the form of a column or module that runs through the whole 3 mm thickness of the cortex. It is a functional unit because of its selective communication with other modules of the neocortex (Fig. 7). The projection is seen to be in a completely overlapping manner and not diffuse.[27]

This modular organization has provided most valuable simplification of the enterprise of trying to understand how this tremendously complex structure works. The potential performance of ten thousand million individual units is beyond all comprehension. The arrangement in modules of about four thousand nerve cells reduces the number of functional units of the neocortex to between two and three million.

It can, however, be questioned if this number of modules of the neocortex is adequate to generate the spatio-temporal patterns that encode the total cognitive performance of the human brain—all the sensing, all memories, all linguistic expression, all creativities, all aesthetic experiences—and for our whole lifetime. The only answer I can give is to refer to the immense potentialities of the eighty-eight keys of a piano. Think of the creative performances of the great composers, Beethoven and Chopin for example. They could utilize only four parameters in their creation of piano music with the eighty-eight keys, each of which has an invariant pitch and tonal quality.

MODES OF INTERACTION BETWEEN HEMISPHERES

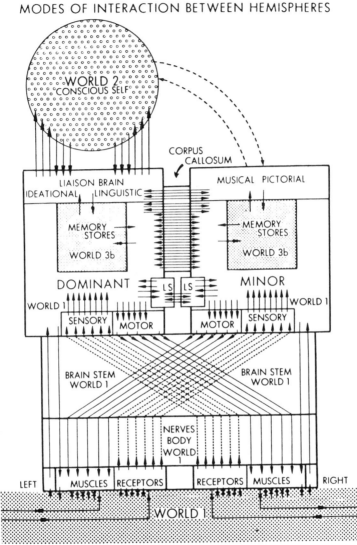

Fig. 6. Communications to and from the brain and within the brain. Diagram to show the principal lines of communication from peripheral receptors to the sensory cortices and so to the association areas of the cerebral hemispheres. Similarly, the diagram shows the output from the cerebral hemispheres via the motor cortex and so to muscles. Both these systems of pathways are largely crossed as illustrated, but minor uncrossed pathways are also shown by the vertical lines in the brain stem. The dominant left hemisphere and minor right hemisphere are labeled, together with some of the properties of these hemispheres that are described in the text. The corpus callosum is shown as a powerful cross-linking of the two hemispheres, and, in addition, the diagram displays the modes of interaction between Worlds 1 and 2, as described in the text, and also illustrated in Fig. 5. Note the blocks marked LS, which represent the limbic system with the ipsilateral and commissural connectivities.

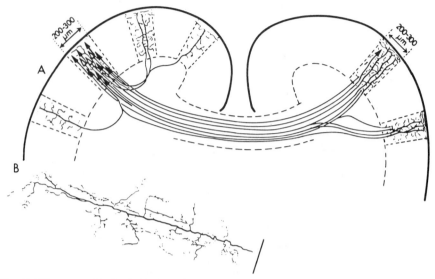

Fig. 7. The general principle of cortico-cortical connectivity shown diagrammatically in a nonconvoluted brain. The connections are established in highly specific patterns between vertical columns of 200-300 μm diameter in both hemispheres. Ipsilateral connections are derived mainly from cells located in layer III (cells shown at left in *outlines*), while contralateral connections (cells shown in *full black*) derive from all layers II–VI. The diagram does not try to show the convergence from afferents originating from different parts of the cortex to the same columns. B Golgi stained branching of a single cortico-cortical afferent, oriented in relationship to the module with a single afferent in A, but at several times higher magnification. It illustrates the profuse branching in all laminae. Bar = 100 μm.

I think it will be recognized that the enormous generation of musical patterns using the eighty-eight keys of a piano points to a virtually infinite capacity of the two to three million modules to generate unique spatio-temporal patterns. Moreover, it must be realized that these patterns giving the conscious experiences are dependent on the same four parameters as those for the piano keys. We can imagine that the intensities of activation are signaled symbolically by the momentary lighting up of modules. So if we could see the surface of the neocortex, it would present an illuminated pattern of 50 cm by 50 cm composed at any moment of modules 0.4 mm across that have all ranges from dark to dim to lighter to brilliant (Fig. 8). And this pattern would be changing in a scintillating manner from moment to moment, giving a sparkling spatio-temporal pattern of the millions of modules, appearing exactly as on a television screen. This symbolism gives some idea of the immense task confronting the mind in generating conscious experiences. The dark or dim modules would be neglected. Moreover, it is an important feature of the hypothesis of mind-brain interaction that neither the mind nor the brain is passive in the transaction. There must be an active interchange of information across the frontier (Fig. 5) between the material brain and the nonmaterial mind. The mind is not in the matter-energy world, so there can be no energy exchange in the transaction, merely a flow of information. Yet the mind must be able to change the pattern of energy operations in the modules of the brain, else it would be forever impotent.

It is difficult to understand how the self-conscious mind can relate to such an enormous complexity of spatio-temporal modular patterns. This difficulty is mitigated by three considerations. First, we must realize that our self-conscious mind has been learning to accomplish such tasks from babyhood onward, a process that is colloquially called "learning to use one's brain." Second, by the process of attention the self-conscious mind selects from the total ensemble of modular patterns those features that are in accord with its present interests. Third, the self-conscious mind is engaged in extracting "meaning" from all that it reads out. This is well illustrated by many ambiguous figures, for example, a drawing that can be seen as either a staircase or an overhanging cornice (Fig. 9). The switch from one interpretation to the other is instantaneous and holistic. There is never any transitional phase in the reading out by the mind of the modular pattern in the brain.

A key component of the hypothesis of brain-mind interaction is that the unity of conscious experience is provided by the self-conscious mind and not

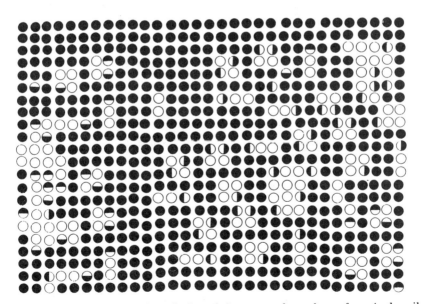

Fig. 8. Diagrammatic plan of cortical modules as seen from the surface. As described in the text the modules are shown as circles of three kinds, *open, closed (solid black)*, and *half open*. Further description in the text.

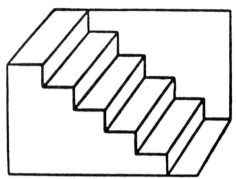

Fig. 9. The staircase-cornice ambiguous figure. There is a reversal of near and far faces.

by the neuronal machinery of the neocortex. Hitherto it has been impossible to develop any theory of brain function that would explain how the immense diversity of brain events comes to be synthesized so that there is a unity of conscious experience. The brain events remain disparate, being essentially the individual actions of countless modules.

UNIQUENESS OF THE PSYCHE

It is not in doubt that each human person recognizes its own uniqueness, and this is accepted as the basis of social life and of law. When we enquire into the grounds for this belief, the evidence just presented eliminates an explanation in terms of the body. There are two acceptable alternatives: the brain or the psyche. Materialists must subscribe to the former, but dualist-interactionists have to regard the psyche or World 2 (cf. Fig. 5) as being the vehicle for the uniqueness of the experienced self. This of course is not to deny that each brain is also unique. A structure of such complexity can *never* be duplicated down to the most minute detail, and it is the minute detail that counts. This is true even when there is the genetic identity of uniovular twins. But our inquiry concerns the experienced uniqueness, and this can be preserved even when there are profound changes in the brain in surgery, cerebral injuries, and degenerations.

As a dualist-interactionist, I believe that my experienced uniqueness lies not in the uniqueness of my brain, but in my psyche. It is built up from the tissue of memories of the most intimate kind from my earliest recollection (at just before 1 year) onward to the present. I found myself as an experiencing being in Southern Australia (Victoria) in the early years of this century. I can ask: why there? and why then? These are the questions asked by Pascal. His answer was that it was God's will.

It is important to disclaim a solipsistic solution of the uniqueness of the self. Our direct experiences are of course subjective, being derived solely from our brain and self. The existences of other selves *are established* by intersubjective communication. The obvious explanation of my experienced uniqueness is that it results from my unique genetic endowment and that this is a necessary and sufficient condition. But I shall show that this solution is untenable because of its unimaginable improbability.

A provisional statistical evaluation relating to my inherited material uniqueness is derived from the process of generation of spermatozoa and ova. Each spermatozoon would have carried a genetic endowment in its twenty-three chromosomes that is a unique sample of the paternal twenty-three pairs of chromosomes. Due to the selection of twenty-three from the original forty-six with the crossing over and recombination within each chromosome pair, there is a shuffling of the paternal genes so that each of the 400 million or so spermatozoa in an emission has a unique gene composition. The same is also true for the meiotic process in the maternal production of ova, each again having a unique genetic composition. The fertilized ovum that developed into one's body and brain was the material product of a chance fertilization of an ovum by one of the hundreds of millions of spermatozoa ejaculated in one sex act.

So, even in that fragment of the genetic lottery, it was an incredibly chanceful fertilization that gave me my genetic uniqueness. This simple and limited description illustrates the improbability attending success in the genetic lottery. But on top of that improbability there is piled improbability on improbability. Long ago the great biologist H. S. Jennings[28] expressed this well, as I pointed out many years ago,[29] and Thorpe has also quoted Jennings with approval:

> If the existence of *me* is thus tied to the formation of a particular combination of genes, one may enter upon calculations as to the chances that I should ever have existed. What are the chances that the combination which produced me should ever have been made? If we depend on the occurrence of the exact combination of genes that as a matter of fact produced us, the odds are practically infinite against your existence or my existence.[30]

And of course to go further backward in our genetical tree makes the problem even more preposterously fantastic. Hence I must reject this materialistic doctrine. What then determines the uniqueness of my psyche?

I have found that a frequent and superficially plausible answer to this question is the statement that the determining factor is the uniqueness of the accumulated experiences of a self throughout its lifetime. And this factor is also invoked to account for the distinctiveness of uniovular twins despite their genetic identity. It is readily agreed that my behavior, my character, my memories, and in fact the whole content of my inner conscious life are dependent on the accumulated experiences of my life; but no matter how extreme the change that can be produced by the exigencies of circumstance, I would still be the same self able to trace back my continuity in memory to my earliest remembrances at the age of one year or so, the same self in quite another guise. Thus the accumulated experiences of a lifetime cannot be invoked as the determining or generating factor of the unique self, though naturally they will enormously modify all the qualities and features of that self.

Jennings must have appreciated the fallacy of attempting to derive the uniqueness of self from the experiential history of an individual, for in searching for an explanation he develops the following remarkable speculations:

> To work this out in detail, one would apparently have to hold that the human self is an entity existing independently of genes and gene combinations, and that it merely enters at times into relations with one of the knots formed by the living web. If one particular combination or knot should not occur, it would enter into another. Then each of us might have existed with quite different characteristics from those we have—as our characteristics would indeed be different if we had lived under different environments. It could be held that there is a limited store of selves ready to play their part, that the mere occurrence of two particular cells which may or may not unite has no determining value for the existence of these selves, but merely furnishes a substratum to which for reasons unknown they may become temporarily attached. . . . And what interesting corollaries might be drawn from such a doctrine, as to the further independent existence of the selves after the dispersal of the gene combinations to which they had been attached.[31]

Jennings is here proposing, apparently unknowingly, the creationist doctrine that each soul is a divine creation, which is attached *to the growing fetus at some time between conception and birth.* It is the existence of my inner core of unique individuality that *necessitates* the "divine creation." I submit that no other explanation is tenable, neither the genetic uniqueness with its impossible lottery nor the environmental differentiations, which do not *determine* one's uniqueness but merely modify it. The genetic makeup actualized in the newly created life is random from an almost infinite number of possibilities. *The unique individuality comes from the infused soul.*

It is appropriate now to refer to the analogy quoted above from Popper. The human brain (and body) is the computer and the conscious self, psyche, or soul is the programmer. The computer is built by genetic instructions and thus is a creation of biological evolution, being in World 1. The programmer is not in the biological world, but is in World 2 (cf. Fig. 5). It is proposed that the programmer is a divine creation. Each of us is created as a unique psyche or programmer, and is given for life a unique computer, our brain, that is our sole means of receiving from and giving to the World in which we are immersed. This World comprises the three major constituents: Worlds 1, 2, and 3 (Fig. 2).

There is a tendency in religious thinking to talk about persons or people, body plus soul, as the subjects of religious concern. However, I want to refer to the dualist-interactionist diagrams of Figures 5 and 6 in insisting that World 2 (the soul or psyche) must *not* be blended in with the brain and body of World 1. There *is* an interface or frontier.

A very special problem is raised by identical twins that are completely distinct in their self-conscious experiences, alike as they appear to be to external observers. The same genetic endowments must therefore be compatible with different experiencing selves. *Evidently genetic constitution is not the necessary and sufficient condition for experienced uniqueness.* With the identical twins there would be a difference in the infused souls, just as with any other fetuses, fraternal twins for example.

Though the hypothesis of the infusion of the soul into the fetus at some time between fertilization and birth accounts for the uniqueness of the experiencing self as it develops self-consciousness and human personhood, there are many perplexing problems that are not usually formulated. For example: At what stage in their evolution did hominids acquire souls? What is the fate of the soul when death occurs before it can achieve expression in self-consciousness and personhood? At what stage in the developing embryo does it acquire a soul? What happens when the fetus develops with a gross abnormality of the brain as in an encephalic idiocy or in a double-headed monster? I prefer not to speculate in such obscure fields except to state that the infusion may be gradual, and that it cannot be immediately after fertilization else we would be in trouble with the duality of the souls of uniovular twins.

DEATH AND IMMORTALITY?

In all materialist theories of the mind there can be no consciousness of any kind after brain death. Immortality is a nonproblem. But with dualist-interactionism it can be recognized from the standard diagram (Fig. 5) that death of the brain need not result in the destruction of the central component of World 2. All that can be inferred is that World 2 (the programmer) ceases to have any relationship with the brain (the computer) and hence will lack all sensory information and all motor expression. There is no question of a continued shadowy or ghostlike existence in some relationship with the material world, as is claimed in some spiritualist beliefs. What then can we say?

Belief in some life after death came very early to mankind, as is indicated by the ceremonial burial customs of Neanderthal man. However, in our earliest records of beliefs about life after death it was most unpleasant. This can be seen in the Epic of Gilgamesh or in the Homeric poems, or in the Hebrew belief about Sheol. Hick points out that the misery and unhappiness believed to attend the life hereafter very effectively dispose of the explanation that such beliefs arose from wish-fulfillment![32]

The idea of a more attractive afterlife is a special feature of the Socratic dialogues, being derived from the Orphic mysteries. There was a particularly clear affirmation of immortality by Socrates in the *Phaedo* just before his death.

After the poignant simplicity of Socrates' messages before death, it is quite an experience to contemplate the many kinds of immortality that have been the subject of speculation. The idea of immortality has been sullied and even made repugnant by the many attempts from the earliest religions to give an account that was based on the ideologies of the time. Thus today intellectuals are put off by these archaic attempts to describe and depict life after bodily death. I am put off by them too. I would suggest that it is not valuable to speculate on this "body"-soul problem after death. It is perplexing enough during life! Self-recognition and communication may be possible for the psyche in ways beyond our imagination.

We normally have the body and the brain to assure us of our identity, but, with departure of the psyche from the body and brain in death, none of these landmarks is available to it. All of the detailed memory must be lost. If we refer again to Figure 5, memory is also shown located in World 2. I would suggest that this is a more general memory related to our self-identity, our emotional life, our personal life, and to our ideals as enshrined in the values—in fact the whole identity of the programmer. All of this should be sufficient for self-identity. Reference should be made to the discussion on the creation of the psyche by infusion into the developing embryo. *This divinely created psyche should be central to all considerations of immortality and of self-recognition.*[33] With the disintegration of our computer at brain death, we have lost this wonderful instrument, the most intimate companion of a lifetime. Is there no further existence for the programmer?

THE QUEST FOR MEANING

The theme of my first Gifford lectures was "The Human Mystery." Our life here on this earth and cosmos is beyond our understanding in respect to the Great Questions. We have to be open to some deep dramatic significance in this earthly life of ours that may be revealed after the transformation of death. We can ask: What does this life mean? We find ourselves here in this wonderfully rich and vivid conscious experience and it goes on through life, but is that the end? This self-conscious mind of ours has this mysterious relationship with the brain and as a consequence achieves experiences of human love and friendship, of the wonderful natural beauties, and of the intellectual excitement and joy given by appreciation and understanding of our cultural heritages. Is this present life all to finish in death, or can we have hope that there is further meaning to be discovered?

Man has lost his way ideologically in this age. It is what has been called the predicament of mankind. I think that science has gone too far in breaking down man's belief in his spiritual greatness, as exemplified in the magnificent achievements in World 3, and has given him the belief that he is merely an insignificant animal that has arisen by chance and necessity in an insignificant planet lost in the great cosmic immensity. This is the message given to us by Monod in *Chance and Necessity*. I think the principal trouble with mankind today is that the intellectual leaders are too arrogant in their self-sufficiency. We must realize the great unknowns in the material makeup and operation of our brains, in the relationship of brain to mind, in our creative imagination, and in the uniqueness of the psyche. When we think of these unknowns as well as the unknown of how we come to be in the first place, we should be much more humble. The unimaginable future that could be ours would be the fulfillment of this our present life, and we should be prepared to accept its possibility as the greatest gift. In the acceptance of this wonderful gift of life and of death, we have to be prepared not for the inevitability of some other existence, but we can hope for the possibility of it.

This is the message we would get from what Penfield[34] and Thorpe[35] have written; and I myself have also the strong belief that we have to be open to the future. This whole cosmos is not just running on and running down for no meaning. In the context of Natural Theology, I come to the belief that we are creatures with some supernatural meaning that is as yet ill defined. We cannot think more than that we are all part of some great design, which was the theme of my first Gifford series.[36] Each of us can have the belief of acting in some unimaginable supernatural drama. We should give all we can in order to play our part. Then we wait with serenity and joy for the future revelations of whatever is in store after bodily death.

Footnotes

1   K. R. Popper and J. C. Eccles, *The Self and its Brain* (Berlin, Heidelberg, and New York: Springer-International, 1977).

2   E. O. Wilson, *Sociobiology: The New Synthesis* (Cambridge: Harvard University Press, 1975); W. H. Thorpe, *Animal Nature and Human Nature* (London: Methuen, 1974); and D. R. Griffin, *The Question of Animal Awareness* (New York: Rockefeller University Press, 1976).

3   G. G. Gallup, "Self-recognition in Primates," *American Psychologist* 32 (1977): 329–38.

4   T. A. Sebeok and D. J. Umiker-Sebeok, *Speaking of Apes* (New York: Plenum Press, 1980).

5   G. Isaac, "The Food-sharing Behaviour of Protohuman Hominids," *Scientific American*, 238, no. 4 (1978): 9–108.

6.   J. C. Eccles, *The Human Mystery* (Berlin, Heidelberg, and New York: Springer-International, 1979), Lecture 5.

7   Popper and Eccles, *The Self and its Brain*.

8   R. S. Solecki, *Shanidar* (New York: Alfred Knopf, 1971).

9   R. S. Solecki, "The Implications of the Shanidar Cave: Neanderthal Flower Burial," *Annals of the New York Academy of Science* 293 (1977): 114–24.

10   T. Dobzhansky, *The Biology of Ultimate Concern* (New York: The New American Library, 1967).

11   Popper and Eccles, *The Self and its Brain*.

12   Ibid., p. 120.

13   B. Amsterdam, "Mirror Self-image Reactions before the Age of Two," *Developmental Psychobiology* 5 (1972): 297–305.

14   Gallup, "Self-recognition in Primates."

15   S. Curtiss, *Genie: A Psycholinguistic Study of a Modern-day "Wild Child"* (New York: Academic Press, 1977).

16   Popper and Eccles, *The Self and its Brain.*

17   Ibid., Chaps. P1, P3, P4, and P5.

18   J. Beloff, "Mind-body Interactionism in the Light of the Parapsychological Evidence," *Theoria to Theory* 10 (1976): 125-37.

19   Popper and Eccles, *The Self and its Brain.*

20   D. Shapere, "Discussion of Rensch," in *Studies in the Philosophy of Biology,* ed. F. J. Ayala and T. Dobzhansky (London: Macmillan, 1974).

21   B. Rensch, "Polynomistic Determination of Biological Processes," in ibid.

22   C. Birch, "Chance, Necessity and Purpose," in ibid.

23   B. Rensch, *Biophilosophy* (New York: Columbia University Press, 1971).

24   C. S. Sherrington, *Man and His Nature* (London: Cambridge University Press, 1940).

25   K. R. Popper, *Objective Knowledge* (Oxford: Clarendon Press, 1972), Chap. 6.

26   Popper and Eccles, *The Self and its Brain,* Dialogue XII.

27   J. Szentagothai, "The Neuron Network of the Cerebral Cortex: A Functional Interpretation," *Proceedings of the Royal Society London* B 201 (1978): 219-48.

28   H. S. Jennings, *The Biological Basis of Human Nature* (New York: W. W. Norton, 1930).

29   J. C. Eccles, *The Brain and the Unity of Conscious Experience* (Eddington Lecture) (London: Cambridge University Press, 1965); and J. C. Eccles, *Facing Reality* (Heidelberg, Berlin, and New York: Springer-Verlag, 1970).

30   Thorpe, *Animal Nature and Human Nature.*

31   Jennings, *The Biological Basis of Human Nature.*

32   J. Hick, *Death and Eternal Life* (London: Collins, 1976).

33   H. D. Lewis, *Persons and Life after Death* (London: Macmillan, 1978).

34   W. Penfield, *The Mystery of the Mind* (Princeton, N.J.: Princeton University Press, 1975).

35   W. H. Thorpe, *Biology and the Nature of Man* (London: Oxford University Press, 1962).

36   Eccles, *The Human Mystery.*

Language, Evolution of Consciousness, and the Recovery of Human Meaning

OWEN BARFIELD

Dartford, Kent, England

I want to start with some observations of David Bohm in his article "Insight, Knowledge, Science, and Human Values" in this volume. He distinguishes the new knowledge that can be obtained by energetic insight from the kind of knowledge that amounts only to a rearrangement of things already known, or falsely assumed to be known. The former kind of knowledge, he says, requires an uncommon degree of energy; in fact it requires something like genius, because our minds are hedged in by all manner of presuppositions and, unless we are able and willing to take the bold step of questioning these presuppositions, we cannot (as he puts it) "get beyond the field of all that happens to be known at the present moment." I believe it was Hilaire Belloc who pronounced the maxim:

> Oh, let us never never doubt
> What nobody is sure about!

Insight, for the man who has it, does what mischief did for Belloc when he neatly substituted "nobody" for "everyone" in the second line. I imagine almost any enlightened educator would agree that a worthy, if not an essential, aim of education is to remove the burden of at least some of these presuppositions, so as to make the former kind of knowledge, the new knowledge, accessible not only to a few geniuses here and there but to a much wider section of the population.

But then Professor Bohm goes on to say that these presuppositions, which only insight can dislodge, are particularly difficult to dislodge, because many of them have become inseparable from value judgments; and in that connection he goes at some length, with the help of etymology, into the true meaning of the word *value*. It is here that I should like to add my corollary: namely, that one of the most immovable of all our contemporary presuppositions is a subconscious one about the meaning of the word *value* itself.

Many years ago, in 1912 to be exact, the English writer Logan Pearsall Smith produced a modest little book called *The English Language,* in the final chapter of which, entitled "Language and Thought," he made an important observation, and one which I have no doubt is no less applicable to other European languages than it is to English. He pointed to a group of words that appeared for the first time in the eighteenth century: He called them "a curious class of verbs and adjectives which describe not so much the objective qualities and activities of things, as the effects they produce on us, on our own feelings and sensations." He cited among others the adjectives *entertaining, exhilarating, perplexing, refreshing*—and of course *interesting*, which, as he said, "is put to so many uses that we can hardly imagine how life or conversation could be carried on without it." After adding that *interesting* appeared in the language at about the same time as the verb *to bore*, he comments as follows:

> If we wish to enter into the state of mind of past ages, [we must] try to imagine a time when people thought more of objects than of their own emotions, and when, if they were bored or interested, they would not name their feeling, but mention the quality or object that produced it.

Here I think the author was drawing attention to a very important shift in the focus of consciousness, more important than he himself realized. And it is significant that it is through the historical contemplation of language that it becomes most readily apparent. It is so clearly reflected there; sometimes in the appearance of new words, more often—and, I would say, more significantly—in the change or displacement of the meaning of an old one. We watch the word *charming*, for instance, ceasing (unless you happen to be talking of snakes) to be a present participle active, betokening influence originating from without, and turning into an adjective signifying only a state of mind resulting within.

If now, in the light of such considerations as these, we turn our attention to such words as the semi-obsolete *valor*, to *value* and *values* as they are used today, and to *valuable*, it seems to me that any reflective mind is forced to ask itself some such question as "Do we value a thing because it has value, or is it valuable because we value it?" We know that the second alternative applies in the case of things like rare postage stamps. But does it apply to everything? One of the things I have particularly noticed in the course of my life is the ever-increasing vogue of that word *value*, and especially its plural, *values*, as well as of relatively modern concepts like *value judgments* and *value free*, in philosophy, psychology, sociology, journalism, and elsewhere. One of the questions I want to ask is: Why should this have come about? I feel we are in a better position to answer questions like that today than we were in 1912, and I suggest that it is best answered by looking, to begin with, at another word altogether, namely, *quality*. Look closely and you will find that there is today a widespread presupposition, subconscious for the most part, but raised to the level of consciousness in the philosophy of a value-free science, that there is really no such thing as quality. There is the useful and the useless, the desirable and the undesirable, and that is all.

There are welcome signs that an increasing number of people are beginning to feel dissatisfied with the results that flow from such a metaphysic, express or implied. And this has led some of them to compare it with older ways of thinking and feeling—and not infrequently to the realization that the whole relation between the human psyche and the natural world was a strikingly different one before the scientific revolution from what it has become today. I believe however that, for the kind of insight that is needed to unfix the presupposition implicit in our distrust of objective qualities and our habitual, and sometimes rather slick, resort to that word "values," we need to examine the origin of that distrust a little more closely. It is not enough just to say: "They thought and felt otherwise in those days."

The philosophy of science, as we have it, began with the rigorous elimination from its legitimate field of all so-called occult qualities. The term *occult quality* was used to denote any immaterial, and therefore imperceptible, force, or process, or substance, or being. These, if indeed they existed, were henceforth to be treated as (1) unknowable and (2) without causal significance for the phenomenal world. At the same time all other qualities were, at first, divided into so-called primary and secondary qualities, according to whether they were presumed to inhere in the natural world itself or to be bestowed on it by the perceiving mind of man. But that distinction did not last very long. It is a fairly familiar story nowadays how, with the further entrenchment of the empirical method, the increasing emphasis on mensuration, and the further discoveries and hypotheses elicited and determined by these, it eventually transpired that *all* qualities are secondary, and thus, for the purposes of science, occult. That is to say, they are presumed to be unknowable and without causal significance. The only difference between them and what had originally been dismissed as occult qualities was that the latter were deemed to be, if at all, objective or "natural," while the former were now called subjective or "human." Either way only the measurable is real, and what seems to be the world we live in is "real" only so far as it is measurable. In other words the only really primary objective, and nonoccult, quality is—quantity.

It does look as if, in its relentless pursuit of accuracy at all costs, our Western science has followed, with the help of René Descartes, the advice given to the man who asked how to catch a lion. The answer was: "Catch two lions and let one escape." Certainly it was these presuppositions, as they filtered through into the conscious and subconscious minds of the mass of individuals at a pace accelerated by the growing popularity of science following its dazzling technological achievements—it was these presuppositions that underlay the linguistic phenomenon detected by Pearsall Smith. Perhaps first detected by him.

But if the assumption that what used to be regarded as objective qualities are in fact simply our subjective values is in general a subconscious one, it is by no means so in all cases. There are places where it is a very conscious one and I fear one of those places is education. I am not thinking only of the sciences, or of such provinces as behavioral psychology, but also of education in the humanities. It is no accident that C. S. Lewis opened his three Riddell

Lectures, published under the title *The Abolition of Man,* with a quotation from a school textbook on English literature, where, in connection with an anecdote about Coleridge, the youthful reader was instructed:

> When the man said *This is sublime,* he appeared to be making a remark about the waterfall . . . Actually . . . he was not making a remark about the waterfall, but a remark about his own feelings. What he was saying was really *I have feelings associated in my mind with the word "Sublime,"* or shortly, *I have sublime feelings.*

From this Lewis goes on to demonstrate how this assumption of the subjectivity of natural qualities has led, by a kind of osmosis, to the like assumption of the subjectivity of all human values, including of course ethical ones, and of their ultimately groundless relativity; and to predict the consequence indicated in his title if the process is not arrested. (Incidentally the little book is, in my opinion, one of the best things Lewis did, and might with advantage be made compulsory reading for all educators.) How often we hear an adult aftermath of that sort of teaching in the cliché vocabulary of popular argument on any question where a conflict has arisen between utilitarian considerations and those of quality or ethics—conservation, vivisection, abortion, euthanasia, sex equality, nuclear power, whatever it happens to be. "Rational" always implies value free, and its opposite is always "emotive." As if the two were alternatives, and mutually exclusive! As if so-called value judgments were really judgments in the logical sense at all! Whereas it must be obvious to an unspoiled mind that values can never be conclusions *at* which reason arrives. They are premises *from* which it has to start. If ethical premises are really our subjective values, it will only be when some values are perceived to be as independent of our personal convenience and security as natural qualities that humanity's Gadarene slither downhill can hope to be arrested and reversed.

Perhaps one could sum up what I have been trying to say in some such terms as these: People used to talk about beautiful and ugly, noble and beastly, right and wrong; but that could only go on as long as there was confidence that qualities are objectively real. The current preference for "values" has come about because the term is one that neatly avoids any such ontological commitment. We have spent three or four hundred years learning to perceive the subjective ingredient in all that looks so very objective; the task now, for the sciences as well as the humanities, is to learn to perceive the objective ingredient in all that looks so very subjective.

Has then the whole process been just a deplorable aberration, and is it the duty of the teaching profession to lead its students back to the state of mind that prevailed before the scientific revolution? I do not think so. The plain fact is that qualities and values *are* subjective as well as objective; indeed, they are the bridge from the one to the other or, better still, the tension between the two poles of which consciousness consists. But it is equally plain to me that a growing awareness of the subjective element in them has decoyed us into an overemphasis on it, which is amounting in our time to our losing sight of the other pole altogether. It is therefore the objective element that needs emphasizing today, not the subjective. And such is the general blindness to it that the first necessary step is to draw attention to the fact that there *is* an objective element; or, in other words, that there are qualities as well as values. It is not by distinguishing them as "human" that we shall ever recover, either for ourselves or our students, a belief in the reality of values. Loss of belief in their objective validity followed from loss of belief in objective qualities. I am convinced that its recovery can only take effect in the same sequence.

I have no doubt that there is more than one way of attempting this recovery. My own experience is that one very helpful way is via the contemplation of language. And I stress: the contemplation, not the "analysis." There are reasons for it. It is not so easy, without some philosophical training, to become aware of that subtle interpenetration between subject and object of which perception and consciousness in general consist. *With* philosophical training on the other hand, it is all too easy to jump out of naive realism the whole way with a single bound into either subjective idealism at one extreme or theoretical materialism at the other. If on the other hand we turn our attention away from such matters as perception and natural qualities and human values and on to the nature of *meaning*, we are on less tricky ground. There the interpenetration between what is common to all and what is peculiar to myself is almost unavoidably evident. When I speak, there can be no doubt about the personal nature of the event; but equally there can be no doubt of its involving a transpersonal element, inasmuch as the words I speak have meanings that I did not originate. Moreover, if qualities are indeed the bridge between subject and object, it is by the medium of words that they become so. Viewed historically, all words, however abstract, however subjective, are seen to have a sensuous and phenomenal ingredient. It was in the process of *naming* nature that man became aware of her, and therefore no longer merely a part of her. And every growing child repeats that process. Words and their meanings are to qualities what numbers are to quantities.

You will have noticed that I am now speaking of *words* rather than *language*. I do so because contemplation, as contrasted with analysis, of language does entail paying more attention to individual words than to grammar, syntax, and structure. The loss of interest in precisely this aspect of language, which has characterized recent linguistic studies, may, I think, be seen as part of the general development I have been tracing. It was loss of confidence in objective quality that led to loss of confidence in meaning—to such an extent that it is sometimes maintained nowadays that a word outside a sentence *has* no meaning; and that for that reason we must confine our attention wholly to sentences. I confess that, when I hear people saying things like that, I sometimes wonder what they suppose lexicographers have been doing all this time. But let that pass. Let me rather quote the seventeenth-century theologian and philosopher Richard Baxter, writing in the introduction to one of his books:

> . . . as big as the Book is, I must tell the Reader that the style is as far from redundancies (though some things be oft repeated) that, if he will not chew the particular words, but swallow them whole, and bestow his labour only on the sentences, I shall suppose that he hath not read the book.

For the reasons I have been trying to outline, I would suggest, not as a nostrum that will solve all our difficulties but as one useful path to be explored, that, within the humanities, a good deal more attention might be paid than has hitherto been the case to the study of language, or rather of words. I should like to conclude this paper with a very sketchy indication—hardly more than an allusion, I fear—to certain wider considerations that seem to me to bear on this issue of contemplative language study. One of them looks to the past and the other to the future.

The *historical* study of words, and particularly of the changes that have been going on in their meanings, has two benefits to bestow. In the first place it can bring home to the student, with all the impact of a discovery, the fact that our twentieth-century way of thinking and perceiving and relating ourselves to nature is not *the* way of doing all that, but only one very recent way; a way that, compared with another much older and much longer-lived way, has certain definite advantages but also certain increasingly evident disadvantages. If they are led by this discovery to so much as raise the question of the relation of both ways to truth itself, then surely we have already unfixed one of those hampering presuppositions in the way of acquiring new knowledge with which I began. This much at least will have been achieved, whether or not, as in my own case, it should lead further to an unshakable conviction that the actual course of natural and human evolution must be conceived, not in terms of the Darwinian model, but rather in terms of an evolution of consciousness, proceeding gradually from peripheral diffusion to central focus.

If on the other hand the approach to language is made with our eyes on the future rather than the past, then it will not be its history (though it will be impossible to leave that out of account) that will principally engage our attention, but its function as symbol, or as a system of symbols. Most of what has been written—and a great deal has been written in the last few decades—on that subject seems to me to have been unduly limited by just those old presuppositions. But there are signs of its opening up. The most valuable part of Paul Ricoeur's recent book *Freud and Philosophy*, for instance, is the first part, which deals with symbolism in general, essays a new definition of it, and in the domain of language seeks to undermine the assumed necessity of such things as "univocity" and "single reference," without sacrificing their significance as instruments of cognition. I am, as I say, alluding rather than reporting. What I am dimly looking forward to—or toward—is a gradual change in the whole relation between language and those who speak and write it, between language and consciousness itself; a change that could only follow from an habitual awareness in the speaker's mind that it is in the very nature of words that they use the material to name the immaterial, or if you prefer it, the phenomenal to name the noumenal—and indeed the numinous.

I am beginning to feel as Wordsworth must have been feeling when he produced that sublimely poetic phrase that occurs, if I remember right, in *The Prelude:* "My drift, I fear, is scarcely obvious." I know it. I know only too well that there are all manner of other presuppositions to be excavated and carted away before a new insight of the kind I am envisaging—that is, a true marriage between value and quality—could come about. Probably the most formidable of these is the almost universal assumption that thinking is a function of the physical brain; whereas the guests at that wedding, if it is ever celebrated, will indeed be well aware that consciousness is now, and will more and more become, the source of qualities as well as values. But they will also be in no doubt that consciousness resembles a spark located within the brain much less than it resembles a diffused light focused into the whole body from without. To expatiate on that prophecy would, I fear, require another paper at least as long as this one. Perhaps the issue it raises will turn out to be one of those with which the symposium as a whole cannot avoid concerning itself.

Beyond the Modern Western Mind Set

HUSTON SMITH

Hamline University

In "Excluded Knowledge," an essay from a 1979 issue of *Teachers College Record*,[1] I argued that world views arise from epistemologies, which in turn are generated by the motivations that control them. In the seventeenth century Europe hit on an epistemology (empiricism, the scientific method[2]) that augmented its control dramatically—over nature to start with, but who knew where such control might eventually reach? This increase in our power pleased us to the point that we gave this way of knowing right of way. And with that move the die was cast with respect to world view. Empiricism proceeds through sense knowledge, and that which connects with our senses is matter. I do not say that the world view this epistemology has generated is materialism (the view that nothing but matter exists), for our thoughts and feelings are, on the one hand, too conspicuous to be denied, and on the other too different from what we experience matter to be, to be reduced to it. It is safer to dub our modern Western world view naturalism, this being defined as the view that (a) nothing that lacks a material component exists, and (b) in what does exist the physical component has the final say.[3]

It is ironic that the science that lured us into this world view now seems to be abandoning it. With each successive probe, matter had been growing more ethereal even before Einstein discovered that mass and energy are convertible. What this energy is no one quite knows. If a thimbleful of vacuum contains more energy than all the atomic energy in the universe,[4] it cannot be less powerful than when it is impounded in mass; but as the reference to vacuum emphasizes, in its free state it seems less substantial. Priestley and Boscovitch argued early on that Newton's acceptance of the Greek view that atoms are impenetrable was simple-minded; they are better conceived as mathematical points surrounded by fields of forces that repel up to a point, then attract with the inverse square of the distance. Now that we have split atoms we know that Priestley and Boscovitch were wrong; atoms do have size. But their point may still hold for electrons. Some current experiments suggest that they have a finite size, others that they do not. If something has no size, or no definite position as in the case of particles before they are subject to position measurements, are they still matter? The message that reaches us from frontier physics seems to be that the further we track matter toward its causal origins, the more it sheds the attributes it wears in the "middle region" of size that our senses register, until at some vanishing point on the horizon it seems to drop these attributes altogether to become something we can scarcely guess—disappearing, perhaps, into David Bohm's implicate order.[5]

This ghostly writing has been on the wall for the better part of our century, but it has not shaken our naturalism, which bids to exit this century more entrenched, if anything, than when it entered it. This is because matter remains what we can get at and control. The problem lies deeper than willfulness—wanting to have our way over nature—for even our search for disinterested truth is drawn to naturalism and empiricism. Control includes, importantly, the controlled experiment, and this, more than any other form of validation, inspires confidence. Bertrand Russell's mid-century BBC pronouncement that "what science cannot tell us, mankind cannot know" is absurd as it stands, but if we amend it to read "cannot collectively know for sure," it becomes less so. Propositionalized, this introductory point can be indicated as follows:

Matter is that which (with whatever required amplification) registers on our senses.

Our senses are where our worlds overlap.

The parts of our worlds that overlap are the parts we trust most, for we are social creatures: down isolation's path lies madness.

It is all so plausible. To restate the point only slightly:

Seeing is believing, touching is truth (an old American proverb).

Science's extension of our seeing and touching has augmented our power and enabled us to solve certain problems spectacularly.

With the collectivizing of society we look increasingly to government to solve our problems, while the government relies on science to help it do so.

Everywhere accent falls on the sense domain. It would be surprising if naturalism were not our world view and empiricism our favored noetic probe.

But problems abound. "Our society is not working well and all signs indicate it will work less well in the future," sociologist Robert Bellah told the Woodstock Symposium on which this volume is based. We need to look at these problems, but first I should describe more systematically the outlook that contributes to them.

I. WHAT THE MODERN WESTERN MIND SET IS

I think I see more clearly now than when I wrote either "Excluded Knowledge" or the book out of which that essay derived, *Forgotten Truth*,[6] what the modern Western mind set (hereafter MWM) is. The clue to it can be stated in a single sentence: *An epistemology that aims relentlessly at control rules out the possibility of transcendence in principle.*[7] By transcendence I mean something that is better than we are by every measure of value we know and some that elude us. To expect a transcendental object to appear on a viewing screen wired by an epistemology that aims at control would be tantamount to expecting the melody as well as the lyrics of a song to issue from a printout typewriter. We can "put nature to the rack," as Bacon advised, because it is inferior to us; possessing in its parts at least neither mind nor freedom in the genuine sense, these parts can be pushed around. But if things that are superior to us exist—extraterrestrial intelligences superior to our own? angels? God?—these are not going to fit into our controlled experiments.[8] It is they who dance circles around us, not we them. It being as impossible for us to acquire Gellner's "effective knowledge" (see footnote 7) over them as it is to nail a drop of mercury with our thumb, an epistemology that drives single-mindedly toward effective knowledge is not going to allow transcendent realities to exist.[9]

It follows that accounting can proceed only from the bottom up—from inferior to superior, from less to more. Chronologically and developmentally the more comes after the less; causally it comes out of the less, the only other determining principle allowed being chance, which of course is a non-principle, the absence of a principle. In biology (with Darwin) higher forms come after and out of the lower; in sociology (with Marx) the classless society comes after and out of class struggle; in psychology (with Freud) the rational ego comes after and out of the irrational id. Even when the higher has appeared, the thrust is to understand and interpret its workings in terms of the lower. The name for this mode of explanation is, of course, reductionism,[10] and the growth of the MWM can be correlated with its advance. For Newton, stars became machines. For Descartes animals were machines. For Hobbes society is a machine. For La Mettrie the human body is a machine. For Pavlov and Skinner, human behavior is mechanical.

> How many boxes,
> How many stars;
> How long, O Lord,
> Till they open the bars.[11]

This reductionistic momentum has not abated. Beginning with consciousness, we find Daniel Dennett telling us that "materialism in one form or another is the reigning orthodoxy among philosophers of mind"[12] and Carl Sagan saying in his best-selling *The Dragons of Eden* that his "fundamental premise about the brain is that its workings—what we sometimes call 'mind'—are a consequence of its anatomy and physiology and nothing more."[13] On our way from psychology to biology we cross sociology, where attempts to explain human behavior in terms of continuities with lower forms of life have spawned a vigorous subdiscipline, sociobiology. As this is currently one of the liveliest cross-disciplinary subjects on university campuses, I shall reserve it for separate treatment and pass on to biology. "Biologists," Harold Morowitz, professor of molecular biophysics and biochemistry at Yale tells us, "have been moving relentlessly toward . . . hard core materialism."[14] Francis Crick, codiscoverer of DNA, agrees: "The ultimate aim of the modern movement in biology is to explain all biology in terms of physics and chemistry."[15] Going back to Morowitz: As "physiologists study the activity of living cells in terms of processes carried out by organelles and other subcellular entities, the study of life at all levels, from social to molecular behavior, has in modern times relied on reductionism as the chief explanatory concept."[16] In nonlife, too, we may add; in geology, for example, the formations and properties of minerals are described using the features of the constituent crystals. To close the loop by returning to the top of the ladder, we find that not just mind in general but its finest achievements are approached from below. Ethnocriticism has emerged as the attempt to understand works of art in terms of animal behavior. A sample on my desk proposes to shed light on three literary classics—Molière's *The Would-be Gentleman*, Diderot's *Rameau's Nephew*, and Zola's *Germinal*—by showing that "play" serves the same function in these works as it does in the animal kingdom. "Culture has to do the same job that instinct had been doing."[17]

This spot-check shows how widely the reductionistic approach is invoked, but I promised to say something about sociobiology. So let me conclude this section on what the MWM is with a quick look at the way reductionism proceeds in its province.

The Naked Ape and *Territorial Imperative* are discounted for the glib way they transposed raw, isolated data from one species to another, but their search for biological roots of human behavior continues to be pushed to the hilt. Whether through Pavlov's dogs, Skinner's pigeons and rats, or Lorenz's greylag geese, the hope everywhere is to discover continuities, for only in lower registers are explanations for our basic propensities available. Piaget details continuities in play[18] and speech, seeing the latter as deriving from structures of thought that have their roots in sensorimotor mechanisms that are deeper than linguistics.[19] John Bowlby's fifteen-year, three-volume study *Attachment and Loss* is a detailed effort to bridge the gap between innate patterns of attachment in mammals and the attachment/loss complex in the human baby. Let me be clear: Insofar as such studies simply indicate traits we share with other life forms, they do no harm and indeed some good, for until recently the modern world has made too much of the human/subhuman divide. And there are practical lessons to be learned from the similarities: Bowlby's findings on the crucial role of early emotional attachments in the development of life forms generally, for example, might induce us to pay more attention to this area as we relate to our own children. If his study had concluded simply that "the basic structure of man's behavioral equipment resembles that of infrahuman species," there could be no objection. What must be watched is the sentence that follows, where he moves from the observation that "the early form is not superseded" to the inference that "it [the infrahuman form] shall *determine* the overall pattern."[20] Here the inferior-causes-superior assumption appears in full display.

It is Harvard's Edward O. Wilson, though, who has moved sociobiology onto the pages of *The New York Review of Books* and made it a lively public topic, so his views deserve a paragraph or two in their own right. Like other sociobiologists, he draws on data from life forms generally to reason that human behavior, including actions and choices traditionally explained in terms of idealism and disinterested love of others, is ultimately to be understood as genetically determined. Even when we behave "nobly" we are in fact responding to genetic conditioning that moves us to seek our own interests or those of our kinship group.[21]

Wilson divides altruism into two kinds. "Soft-core" altruism looks like it is directed toward the welfare of others but actually redounds circuitously to its agent's benefit. Hard-core altruism is likewise disguised self-interest, but here the interested agent is not the individual organism, who may even sacrifice his life; it is the species whose will prevails. From the species's point of view individuals exist merely to produce genes and serve as their temporary carriers: "The organism is only DNA's way of making more DNA."[22] As mutual aid between its members helps a species to survive, genes that induce the hypothalamus and limbic systems of the brain to entertain warm feelings for one's fellows have a "Darwinian edge" and turn out to be winners. *This* is why we lay down our lives for our friends;[23] our genes prompt us to do so.

While the West's "brain," which for present purposes we can equate with the modern university, rolls ever further down the reductionistic path, other centers of society—our emotions, for example, as they find expression through our artists, and our wills, as evidenced in part by rise in crime and senseless vandalism—protest. These other centers of our selves feel that they are being dragged, kicking and screaming, down an ever-darkening tunnel. We need to listen to their protests, for they force us to ask if it is possible to move toward a world view that, without compromising reason or evidence in the slightest, would allow more room to the sides of our selves that our current world view constricts.

II. THE NEED FOR A DIFFERENT OUTLOOK

When individuals suffer the loss of something that implicates their sense of self—a spouse, a child, whatever it is that gives their life its focus and meaning—they grow ill; not invariably, but in greater proportion. They become more prone to cancer, for one thing. Here is a clear and direct causal flow from mind to matter. In dynamics it parallels exactly the way hypnosis can remove warts, and placebos cause the brain to secrete more pain-relieving endorphins. In all these cases a mental change effects a bodily one. But the MWM does not know what to do with mind; Barbara Brown tells of a symposium in which a scientist reacted to the suggestion that the mind is emerging as a new tool for medicine by roaring to the audience, "Talking about mind will set medicine back fifty years!"[24] We understand something of how the brain works, and, yes, through depth psychology something of how the mind works too. But when it comes to infusing the mind with motivation and meaning, the MWM is helpless.

In itself this can be excused, since anyone who claimed to have techniques for such infusion would be a charlatan. What is not attractive is the way the MWM works to erode the meaning lives already have. D. and C. Johnson report a pattern of disorder among Sioux Indians called *tawatl ye sni*, "totally discouraged." The syndrome involves feelings of helplessness and thoughts of death: "There is no way out . . . there's nothing he can do."[25] Conditions on the Dakota reservations doubtless go a long way toward accounting for this syndrome, but it would be naive to think that the near collapse of the Native American world view is not also a factor. The six-volume *Handbook of Cross-Cultural Psychology*, which includes the Johnsons' study, illustrates how the MWM facilitates this collapse.[26.] If the Sioux feels himself to be in touch with higher forces, this is because his "reality bounds are not as firmly established as is the case in certain Western societies."[27] If he senses his life to be in the hands of a higher power—well, this "actually serves a useful function in alleviating the stress of life."[28] The clinical, patronizing term for this function is, of course, compensation.

The maladies in our personal lives have become psychological and so have moved into an area we have abandoned. That psychology courses remain the most popular college electives and *Psychology Today* is a booming success does not counter this observation. As the passage on reductionism in the preceding section indicates, we have abandoned the mind by converting to efforts to understand it in terms of things other than itself and lower than itself.

The consequences of this abandonment for our civilization as a whole are difficult to assess. Who is to tell us? Let me opt this time around for Alexander Solzhenitsyn, focusing on his 1978 commencement address at Harvard University.[29] As an exile, he is not likely to downgrade us in favor of Soviet Russia; he sees socialism of any type and shade as leading to a total destruction of the human spirit and to a leveling of mankind into death. But as an outside observer he may be able to see us more objectively than we see ourselves. And what he sees in the West today is "spiritual exhaustion."[30]

> How short a time ago . . . the small world of modern Europe was easily seizing colonies all over the globe. . . . It all seemed an overwhelming success. . . . Western society expanded in a triumph of human independence and power. And all of a sudden the twentieth century brought the clear realization of this society's fragility.[31]

If Solzhenitsyn saw only political factors as responsible for this twentieth-century reversal I would not be quoting him here. As it is, his diagnosis points directly to the concern of this essay.

> How did the West decline from its triumphal march to its present debility? Have there been fatal turns and losses of direction in its development? It

does not seem so. The West kept advancing steadily in accordance with its proclaimed social intentions, hand in hand with a dazzling progress in technology. And all of a sudden it found itself in its present state of weakness.

This means that the mistake must be at the root, at the very foundations of thought in modern times. I refer to *the prevailing Western view of the world* which was born in the Renaissance and has found political expression since the Age of Enlightenment.[32]

Clearly Solzhenitsyn is referring to what I am calling the MWM. He identifies this mind set as "rationalistic humanism or humanistic autonomy: the proclaimed and practiced *autonomy* of man *from any higher force* above him."[33] If superior forces are not allowed—current epistemology has no way to register them, I have argued—then human life has no alternative but to appear autonomous. If we are surprised to find Solzhenitsyn blaming this presumed autonomy for the fact that the Western world has lost its civic courage—"a fact which cannot be disputed is the weakening of human personality in the West," he tells us[34]—it is because, mechanists that we have largely and unconsciously become,[35] we assume that if superior forces exist they would tyrannize; we take their absence to be liberating. It seems not to occur to us that such forces might empower us. Submission was the very name of the religion that surfaced through the Koran (Islam = submission), yet its entry into history occasioned the greatest political explosion the world has known. If mention of this fact automatically triggers our fears of fanaticism, this simply shows us another defense our agnostic reflex has erected against the possibility of there being something that, better than we are in every respect, could infuse us with goodness as well as power were we open to the transfusion. It is usually said that the Copernican revolution humbled man by displacing him from the center of the universe, but this spatial dislodgment was nothing compared with the arrogance that followed in its wake, the arrogance of assuming that nothing exists that quite equals ourselves. For is it not we who ride the crest of evolution's advance? And what source of worth is there save evolution? For the MWM the question is rhetorical.

Mention of the individual and collective problems that the MWM contributes to has its place, but to seek a different outlook in order to allay them will not work. For this understandable (but in the end poorly conceived) motivation reinforces three assumptions of the very mind set it seeks to replace.

The first of these is the assumption that history can be controlled. (That preoccupation with control again.) Do *X*, and *Y* will follow; adopt a different world view and a better world will result. Realistically there seems to be little evidence that history can be constructively controlled, though our destructive power might increase to the point where a madman could end it summarily.

Working hand in glove with this assumption that history can be controlled is a second: the assumption that happiness can be bestowed. Heirs to any better world we might create would be happier than we are—this is what "better world" means—so in creating such a world we would hand happiness to those who are born into it. But this is not how life works. Comfort can be handed to us inasmuch as physical discomforts, at least, can be alleviated from without; if we are hungry food can be given us, if we are in pain, anodynes provided. Happiness, though, is different. Happiness cannot be bestowed from the outside or passively received from within. It must be won. It follows that it is impossible to do as much for another as one can do for oneself—save one's soul, for example, however one wishes to parse that phrase. If it sounds sanctimonious, it can be paired with its Zen variant: "No one can go to the bathroom for you."

The third dubious assumption underlying the "better world" rationale for a new outlook is the notion that truth is instrumental.[36] Here again the prometheanism of modernity comes squarely to view: Truth is seen as what will take us where we want to go. In the punchy formula of its distinctively modern, pragmatic definition, truth is what works. As a partial truth this is unexceptionable; the pragmatic attitude is an appropriate part of life, the *yang* part of its *yin/yang* whole—we were not born for idleness. But to make it the whole of life, and the version of truth it sponsors the whole of truth, is a trap so obvious that it took the bait of science's success to lure us into it. Truths in the plural are indeed instrumental; they can and should be chosen for ends we have in mind. But with truth in the singular—a person's or a people's final surmise as to the way things are—it is otherwise. Truth in this final, last-ditch sense is like love. If one loves for any reason save the beloved's intrinsic lovableness, it is not true love. Comparably, to hold X to be true for any reason save that in fact it is so is a contradiction in terms. Suppose that to the observation that "all men must die" the response were to be, "But surely that can't be true, for it makes people sad and fatalistic." To suspect that one is holding a belief for any reason save that it is true is instantly to undermine it.

"There is no right higher than that of the Truth," a maxim from India reminds us. It follows that we owe it to the truth to accept it; metaphysics may not be moralized. Truth has no obligation to accommodate itself to us; it is we who must fashion ourselves to it. The appropriate reason for changing our outlook is not to create a better world or save the one we have. It is to see more clearly things as they are. All other considerations are secondary.

III. THE APPROACH TO A REVISED OUTLOOK THROUGH LOGIC

Kilimanjaro is the highest mountain in Africa. A number of years ago the frozen carcass of a mountain leopard was found near its 19,565 foot snow-clad summit. No one seems to know what it was doing at that altitude.

Perhaps it was curious. We have seen that no prudential reason for changing our mind set will do; in the end we must want a better one solely for the more accurate view it affords. But how can an improved outlook be acquired? To move from captivity toward a freedom we have yet to understand may be the most difficult task the mind can set for itself.

Let us begin with purely logical possibilities. Being no more than possibilities these will not persuade—that they are possible does not mean that they are true. But even to entertain alternatives to the MWM is a step toward loosening its hold on us, and if we can show that they are not inherently unreasonable, this will be an even longer step. It is as if, faced with a stake that has been driven deep into the ground, we begin in this section to rock it back and forth to loosen the hard earth around it. Not until the next section will we try to pull it up.

In Section 1 we saw that exercise of newly discovered ways of controlling nature established an epistemology that produced the MWM. It follows that if we were to approach the world with intent other than to control it, it would show us a different guise. The opposite of the will to control is the wish to participate—a genuine desire to accent embracing *yin* over abrasive *yang* so that domination will not preclude partnership or assertiveness stymie co-operation. Such an alternative starting point would generate a whole new sequence, which can be contrasted visually with that of the MWM as follows:

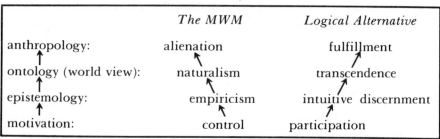

	The MWM	*Logical Alternative*
anthropology:	alienation	fulfillment
ontology (world view):	naturalism	transcendence
epistemology:	empiricism	intuitive discernment
motivation:	control	participation

The payoff of the revised starting point would be an ampler view of reality, and as it turns out to include things that are superior to us, "transcendence" is a fitting name for it. Its greater inclusiveness gives it a starting edge over the MWM, for the fact that every advance in science's understanding of nature has shown it to contain more than we had suspected suggests that a generous ontological vision, too, stands a better chance of being right than does a paltry one. But I leave that as no more than a passing observation. The trickiest link in the right-hand chain is its epistemology. Refusing to accept as truth's final arbiter the controlled experiment (or even objectivity, the consensus requirements of which push it relentlessly, as we have seen, toward sense-verificational empiricism), this alternate epistemology is faced with the problem of distinguishing between veridical discernments and ones that are deceptive. It is not within the scope of this essay to develop this alternative model systematically. I shall refer to it occasionally in what follows, but I introduce it mainly to limber up our imaginations—to keep them supple against an ossifying shell that threatens to become so strong that only the crowbar of historical events could break it.

There is another way to show that the MWM is not the only way to look at the world. Even if we accept the modern world's penchant for control we face a choice, for that road quickly forks. Control over what—the world or ourselves? Ernest Gellner has told us that to qualify as "genuine" knowledge, the MWM requires that knowledge be "effective."[37] But to repeat: effective for what? For changing the objective, external world, or things within ourselves —the dispositions and predilections that constitute our characters and make us the persons we are? As self-transformation was not what interested the founding fathers of the MWM—Bacon's "knowledge is power" was not aimed at power for self-improvement—this mind set has not proved to be sophisticated in handling this side of the question. It does not have a great deal to say on how we might break out of our self-centeredness and relate lovingly to the world at large. Secretly it may wonder if there *is* much to say on this topic; as evidence, note the inverse ratio between prestige and attention to self-change in academic departments of psychology as we pass from experimental and cognitive psychology to clinical psychology, then humanistic psychology, and then transpersonal psychology. When the MWM has its way completely, as in the deterministic behaviorism of B. F. Skinner, self-change is not even admitted as a possibility.

This has produced a paradox. Out of the practical side of our mouths we continue to urge people to exercise their freedom and take responsibility, fearing that if they do not our society may come apart at the seams; Solzhenitsyn is not alone in warning of "spiritual exhaustion." Meanwhile, out of the theoretical side of our mouths we serve notice on these attributes and place them in jeopardy. In the natural sciences where I place Skinner's model of man, human beings are not free at all; Heisenberg's indeterminacy principle has not made the slightest difference here. As for the social sciences, they remain dedicated to explaining human behavior in terms of the stimuli that provoke it. (Is the victim the murdered man or the man who murdered him, the latter having been victimized by society?) Even in the humanities, according to the latest avant-garde literary movement, it is not man who speaks; rather, it is language, and beneath it matter, that speak through him— I am referring to Deconstructionism as headed by Derrida, Foucault, and the late Roland Barthes. Everywhere the individual subject is devalorized in favor of contexts that call the tunes and pull the strings. It is what comes our way that is accented, not what we do with it.

Living as we do in a civilization that prides itself on using everything at its disposal—its resources, its invention, every scrap of information its computers can deposit in their databanks—it is not idle to ask if our most valuable unused resource may not be the capacity of persons to recognize themselves as responsible agents; selves who ask not that the world deliver things into their laps, but that it provide a matrix for their moral and spiritual development—

structures on which character can climb if it resolves to do so. There is a knowledge that is effective for this kind of climbing, but like poetry in the MWM, it is an outcast knowledge.

IV. FROM LOGIC TO IMAGERY

Logic can show us that if we were to approach the world with an eye to embracing rather than controlling it, or asking how it might school us rather than serve us, it would show us a different guise. But what that guise would be it cannot say. For this latter report, insight is required. And insight, as David Bohm has noted,

> announces itself in mental images. Newton's conception of gravity and Einstein's notion of the constant speed of light came to them as perceptions, as images, not as hypotheses or conclusions drawn from logical deduction. Formal logic is secondary to insight [via images] and is never the source of new knowledge.[38]

To add a third example to the two Bohm mentions, the image of a randomly branching tree not only crystallized Darwin's theory of natural selection but guided him through his successive formulations of it. His notebooks show him drawing it repeatedly, lavishing on it a care for representation and detail that shows clearly his need to steep his mind in the image if he were to wring from it everything it had to offer.[39]

So I, too, reach for an image that picks up with our realization that there *is* a different world that awaits discovery and moves us toward picturing what that world might be like. The one I choose appears in a wise and beautiful book by Gai Eaton, *The King of the Castle,* and I quote it in full.

> Let us imagine a summer landscape, bounded only by our limited vision but in truth unbounded; a landscape of hills and valleys, forests and rivers, but containing also every feature that an inventive mind might bring to thought. Let us suppose that somewhere in this measureless extension a child has been blowing bubbles for the sheer joy of seeing them carried on the breeze, catching the sunlight, drifting between earth and sky. And then let us compare all that we know of our world, the earth and what it contains, the sun, the moon and the stars, to one such bubble, a single one. It is there in our imagined landscape. It exists. But it is a very small thing, and in a few moments it is gone.

This, at least, is one way of indicating the traditional or—taking the word in its widest sense—the religious view of our world and of how it is related to all that lies beyond it. Perhaps the image may be pursued a step further. The bubble's skin reflects what lies outside and is, at the same time, transparent. Those who live within may be aware of the landscape in quite different ways. Those whose sight is weak or untrained may still surmise its existence and, believing what they are told by others who see more clearly, have faith in it. Secondly, there are some who will perceive within the bubble itself reflections of what lies outside and begin to realise that everything within is neither more nor less than a reflection and has no existence in its own right. Thirdly, as by a miracle of sight, there will be a few for whom transparency is real and actual. Their vision pierces the thin membrane which to others seems opaque and, beyond faith, they see what is to be seen.[40]

The balance of this essay touches on several points this image raises, but before I proceed to them let me enter a covering observation. It is not possible to adjudicate between contending outlooks objectively, but it is possible to say which is the more interesting. And on this count Eaton's image wins over the MWM hands down, for it allows for everything in the latter and vastly more besides. Specifically, it directs us toward a reality whose qualitative reaches outstrip what the MWM discerns in the way that the latter's quantitative features—the size of the universe it sees, and its other countable features— exceed what Ptolemy had in mind.

V. THE IMAGE EXPLORED

Remembering that we are tracking truth not for its practical consequences but for its intrinsic worth while expecting that each turn in the road will open onto vistas more interesting than the ones before,[41] I proceed now to touch on five points latent in the image I have chosen as guide. The first relates to our ability to see beyond the obvious.

1. *The Possibility of Certitude*

Last spring I received a letter from a young man who had been reading the book in which the image I am working with appeared. "When at one point the author spoke of 'the inrush of the Real,'" he wrote, "I felt that happening to me."

This is an important experience. The word "inrush" implies confidence, while the capitalization of the word "Real" indicates that it pertains here to matters that are important.

There is no way that the MWM can validate both those points.[42] Karl Popper spoke for that mind set when he opened a colloquium at M.I.T. several years ago by saying, "Were it not for science, the skeptics would win hands down." Humanists tend to concur. The Deconstructionists to whom I have already referred are the current elite in the humanities, and the whole of their powerful artillery is aimed, ultimately, at the presumption that thought can amount to more than myth or ideology in the disparaging senses of these words. Reasons are rationalizations. In science we can verify hypotheses; elsewhere we must remain in doubt.

Meanwhile we must live, and this calls for choices and guidelines for making them, ones we consider dependable. It is no use to play games with oneself here, pretending that something is true while knowing that in all likelihood it is not,[43] but as I am trying to steer clear of prudential considerations I shall not dwell on this impasse. Time is better spent on why we think rationality drives toward skepticism, to see if we have that point straight.

There are times that visit us all when we feel at sea about almost everything. T. S. Eliot described them well when he wrote:

> The circle of our understanding
> Is a very restricted area.
> Except for a limited number
> Of strictly practical purposes
> We do not know what we are doing;
> And even, when you think of it,
> We do not know much about thinking.
> What is happening outside of the circle?
> And what is the meaning of happening?
> What ambush lies beyond the heather
> And behind the Standing Stones?
> Beyond the Heaviside Layer
> And behind the smiling Moon?
> And what is being done to us?
> And what are we, and what are we doing?
> To each and all of these questions
> There is no conceivable answer.[44]

When these states come over us they must be respected: faced honestly and stayed with, to learn from them what we can. What is not required is the use of intelligence to glorify (and in certain versions of existentialism, romanticize) these states as if they constitute the acme of human authenticity rather than the mental counterpart of the common cold, or in severe instances the flu, to which we periodically succumb. To level the sharpest charge possible, the relentless championing of relativism, which in its cultural, historical, psychological, social, or existential form underlies all contemporary skepticism, is in the end naive.

Relativism sets out to reduce every kind of absoluteness to a relativity while making an illogical exception for its own case.[45] In effect, it declares it to be true that there is no such thing as truth; that it is absolutely true that only the relatively true exists. This is like saying that language does not exist, or writing that there is no such thing as script. Total relativism is an incoherent position. Its absurdity lies in its claim to be unique in escaping, as if by enchantment, from a relativity that is declared alone to be possible.

Relativism holds that one can never escape human subjectivity. If that were true, the statement itself would have no objective value; it would fall by its own verdict. It happens, however, that human beings are quite capable of breaking out of subjectivity; were we unable to do so we would not know what subjectivity is. A dog *is* enclosed in its subjectivity, the proof being that it is unaware of its condition, for, unlike a man or a woman, it does not possess the gift of objectivity.

If Freudian psychology declares that rationality is but a hypocritical cloak for repressed, unconscious drives, this statement falls under the same reproach; were Freudianism right on this point it would itself be no more than a front for id-inspired impulses. There is no need to run through the variations of relativism that arise from other versions of psychologizing, historicizing, sociologizing, or evolutionizing. Suffice it to say that few things are more absurd than to use the mind to accuse the mind, not just of some specific mistake but in its entirety. If we are able to doubt, this is because we know its opposite; the very notion of illusion proves our access to reality in some degree.

Our minds were made to know, and they "flourish"—no one has said this better than Aristotle—when they work meaningfully at that function. They need not be overweening nor claim omniscience; indeed, one of the important things they can know is their place. But that place exists, and it is not confined to the laboratory. To see, as E. F. Schumacher reminded us shortly before his death, that "only those questions which *cannot* be answered with [laboratory] 'precision' have any real significance"[46] is the first step toward knowledge about those questions themselves.

The most unnoticed reason for current skepticism is our assumption that earlier ages were mistaken. If their outlooks were erroneous, it stands to reason that ensuing eras will show ours to be mistaken too; so runs this argument, which is so taken for granted that it is seldom even voiced. But if we could see that our forebears were not mistaken—they erred in details, but not in their basic surmises, which were so much alike that in *Forgotten Truth* I referred to them as "the human unanimity"—a major impediment to confidence in our global understandings would be removed. The next step would be to separate the reliability of our knowledge from questions of omniscience, to counter the suspicion that if we cannot know everything, what we do know must be tainted. I need not know the position of San Francisco relative to everything in the universe, much less what space and position finally mean, to be certain that, given the present position of our planet's poles, it lies predominantly west of Syracuse. From such simple beginnings we should be able to go on to separate the relativities that should give us pause from ones that are irrelevant, or worse—like sand thrown in the face of desert pilgrims.

2. *A True Infinite*

I have spent the time I did on certitude because there is not a great deal of point in asking how we might understand things differently if we have little confidence in understanding generally. On what a revalidated understanding might encompass, I shall be brief. There is space to do little more than point out several possibilities the post-MWM might explore.

An over-the-shoulder glance at the road we have come gives a lay of the land. That the region of reality the MWM has mapped with virtual certainty—its physical domain—has proved to be incomparably more interesting than we had suspected gives us reason to think that comparable extravagance awaits our astonished discovery in its other regions as well. And as I see no better star to steer by—better either in what it promises or in reasons for adopting it—I proceed to sketch the contours of the most interesting world I can imagine.[47]

Eaton's soap bubbles floating in a stupendous landscape are again our guide. The entire universe the MWM knows—eight billion galaxies with over eight billion stars in each—is contained in one of those bubbles, so we pass now to the landscape that envelops them. It would be a mistake to approach that landscape quantitatively, as if its size were what mattered. That size is not irrelevant—vastness has a majesty of its own—but it is the qualitative features of the surround that the image dwells on: its hills and valleys, its forests and rivers, its sunlight and breezes, as these would show themselves not to a civil engineer or surveyor, but to an artist, a naturalist, or an awe-struck mountaineer.

The MWM has an awesome instrument to register the quantitative marvels of reality, but its qualitative spectrum it cannot track—not beyond the cutoff point of human experience. So it acknowledges no field or center of awareness—no intelligence, "heart," sensibility, whatever term one prefers— that exceeds ours in the way human consciousness exceeds that of minnows or zebras. Eaton's image challenges this myopia; those who are confined by this anthropocentrism, "this bubble's skin," are persons "whose sight is weak or untrained." Gazing on the landscape as a whole, an observer would doubtless delight in our bubble were he to notice it, but "it is a very small thing," besides which most of its beauty derives from the way it "reflects what is outside" and enhances the majesty of the latter by its contrasting smallness.

The environment in question, we are told, is "in truth unbounded," which is to say infinite. The word is important in the MWM, but only in the sense in which it is used in physics and mathematics. And as these disciplines are interested only in the way the concept applies to sets and numbers, it is not a true infinite they are occupied with. From a metaphysical standpoint a mathematical infinite is blatantly finite, for its disregards everything in the world save several of its most abstract features. Solzhenitsyn is right: "The concept of a supreme *complete* entity" does not figure in the modern outlook. He thinks its presence would "restrain our passions and irresponsibility."[48] I am proposing that it would render our world more interesting.

3. Downward Causation

In the image we are working with everything in the bubble of our universe is the consequence of things superior to it. The bubble comes into being because a child wants it to, and its properties—the colors that glisten on its iridescent surface—are occasioned by the brighter colors in the world around it. Causation throughout is downward—from superior to inferior, from what is more to what is less.

The West has, of course, known a philosophy of this sort; Aristotle was the first to state it explicitly. "If anyone wishes to think philosophically, Aristotle is the teacher to begin with," a book at hand advises,[49] and it is especially appropriate to invoke him here because he was not overly other-wordly; it was nature that engrossed him, even as it does us. Yet attraction seemed to him a better model for causation than propulsion; things are lured more than they are driven.

Note to begin with how pleasing this sense of causation is, this notion that things move by being drawn toward what exceeds them and will fulfill them to the degree that they refashion themselves to its likeness. For Aristotle, the entire universe was thus animated. Everything reaches toward its better in the effort to acquire for itself its virtues, as tennis players seek out opponents who play better than they do, children are drawn to slightly older playmates, and dogs prefer human company to their own kind—everywhere the compelling lure of that which we instinctively admire because of its manifest superiority. Aristotle's universe is like a pyramid of magnets. Those on each tier are attracted to the tier above while being empowered by that tier to attract the magnets below them. At the apex stands the only completely actual reality there is, the divine Prime and Unmoved Mover.

Grounded (or stuck, as one is sometimes tempted to say) in the MWM, we cannot today endorse this vision as true, but if our blinders have not grown grotesque we can at least respect its grandeur. In the terms of our image, the thought of bubbles blown for a child's delight has far more charm than the explanation (accurate, of course, but sufficient?) that credits them to the viscous properties of molecules. Extended to the cosmos, the child's delight translates into *lila*, the Indian notion of all creation as God's play, but here the human domain is enough. It may not be diversionary simply to pause for a moment to experience how good the notion of "downward causation" (as I am calling this principle of persuasion from above) might feel. To have a model that inspires, that shows us what we would like to become while at the same time infusing us with the strength needed to approximate it, is as important a condition as life affords.

It is also one that, ontologically speaking, the MWM precludes. There is no way that mind set can allow the possibility that the universe might be ordered teleologically, in the fashion just described. For to announce again the *leitmotif* of this essay, the MWM is a conceptual balloon inflated by knowledge of the sort that facilitates control, and such knowledge is necessarily limited (as we have seen) to things that are inferior to us. Jacques Monod puts the point in a nutshell: "The cornerstone of the scientific method is . . . the *systematic* denial . . . of final causes."[50] It should not escape us that such causes are not denied because they have been found *not* to exist; only because they have not been *found* to exist. But how *could* they have been found when search for them is excluded on principle—*"systematic* denial" is Monod's term; even the emphasis is his. The unspoken, but in no wise obscure, reason for rejecting final causes out of hand is that every glance in their direction would divert us from the efficient causes the MWM is bent on getting its hands on.

It is all very clear, and also ironical. For if the only way we are permitted to account for ontological novelty—new things coming into being—is through antecedent inferiors, what is the logical terminus of this downspout that evolution converts into an upspout? We do not have to guess at the answer, for the leading philosopher of science of our generation has told us, having made it the cornerstone of his life's work. "The basic theme of Karl Popper's philosophy," his biographer and foremost expositor writes, "is that something can come from nothing."[51]

Quite apart from whether this notion has a shred of explanatory power, is it intuitively believable?

4. *The Self/World Divide*

In the mid-1970s a graduate student in psychology at New York University ran an experiment involving college undergraduates who were taking a six-week summer course in business law. Dividing them into two groups, he had both groups gaze at what looked like a blank screen for a minute or so before each class session. Four times in the course of that minute a momentary, tachistoscopic message appeared on the screen, but as its four micro-seconds duration was too brief for it to be recognized, all that the students consciously saw was a flicker of light. The messages that were flashed to the two groups differed; for the control group it was "People Are Walking," whereas the experimental group was treated to "Mommie and I Are One." The groups had been matched for grade-point average, but when the scores of the blindly marked final examination were tabulated, the "Mommie and I" group was found to have scored almost a full letter grade higher in the course than did the control group, the numerical averages being 90.4% and 82.7% respectively.[52]

Such is the increase in power and effectiveness that can accrue when one feels tuned to one's world, for the tachistoscopic message is presumed to activate an early and powerful level of consciousness where Mommie represented (and in that layer of consciousness still represents) the world at large. Some psychologists dispute this interpretation, insisting that the only way information can enter the nervous system is through the conscious mind, but if they are right, from whence comes the improved performances? As of this writing eight studies along the lines of the one described have been conducted, and whether the subjects were trying to lose weight, stop smoking, get good grades, or improve their mental health the results have been positive.[53] A book that summarizes the entire field of research is in press. It speaks so directly to this section of my paper that its title, *The Search for Oneness*,[54] could have served for my heading.

It hardly seems necessary to say more on this point. So much is self-evident that I feel I need only arrange the pieces.

a. No other culture in history has tried to live by an outlook that isolates the human species from its matrix to the degree that ours does. Whereas formerly men and women sensed themselves to be distinguished from the rest of reality by no more than a bubble's skin, a film so thin as to be transparent (to call again on Eaton's image), we now face the impermeable wall of Descartes's disjunction. Once he categorically isolated matter from mind, science was able to seize that matter like a fumbled football and run with it. The tracks it has left inscribe a cosmos Manfred Stanley has described as follows: It is a world

> denuded of all humanly recognizable qualities; beauty and ugliness, love and hate, passion and fulfillment, salvation and damnation. . . . Such matters [have of course] remained existential realities of human life, [but] the scientific world view makes it illegitimate to speak of them as being "objectively" part of the world, forcing us instead to define such emotional experiences as "merely subjective" projections of people's inner lives. . . . All that which is basic to the specifically human [is] forced back upon the precincts of the "subjective" which, in turn, is pushed by the modern scientific view ever more into the province of dreams and illusions.[55]

b. The consequence of this fateful divorce, so obvious that Professor Stanley refers to it as now "a Sunday-supplement commonplace," is

> a spiritual malaise that has come to be called alienation. . . . The world, once an "enchanted garden," to use Max Weber's memorable phrase, has now become disenchanted, deprived of purpose and direction, bereft—in these senses—of life itself.[56]

> The dehumanizing price [of this outlook] is that our identities, freedom, norms, are no longer underwritten by our vision and comprehension of things. On the contrary we are doomed to suffer from a tension between cognition [what we believe to be true] and identity [who we sense ourselves to be].[57]

c. We have not been drawn into this alienated outlook because it is true, but by historical choice or accident; specifically, this essay has argued, by the way Western civilization has responded to its invention of modern science.

> It was Kant's merit to see that this compulsion [to see things this way] is in us, not in things. It was Weber's to see that it is historically a specific kind of mind, not mind as such, which is subject to this compulsion.[58]

Here, more than on any other point considered in this paper, we may be beginning to see light at the end of the tunnel, for our ecological crisis is all but forcing us to reexamine the Cartesian premise we have built on for four hundred years. I by-pass here the radical proposal, ventured by counter-cultural scientists like Frithjof Capra, that Mahayana Buddhism, which includes an important idealist component, provides the best philosophical model for quantum physics that is currently available, in favor of more modest suggestions that emanate from scientists who are more established. Gregory Bateson subtitled *Mind and Nature*, his last book, "A Necessary Unity"; and biologist Alex Comfort argues in his *I and That* that though the self/world (I/That) divide is to some extent inevitable, it can hypertrophy, and in our minds has done so. Finally, there is this suggestive statement by Lewis Thomas:

> It may turn out that consciousness is a much more generalized mechanism, shared round not only among ourselves but with all the other conjoined things of the biosphere. Thus, since we are not, perhaps, so absolutely central, we may be able to get a look at it, but we will need a new technology for this kind of neurobiology; in which case we will likely find that we have a whole eternity of astonishment stretching out ahead of us. Always assuming, of course, that we're still here.[59]

5. *We Have What We Need*

Once, when it had become clear that the days of Suzuki Roshi, founder of the San Francisco Zen Center, were numbered, his dharma heir, Richard Baker, asked him in distress, "How will we manage without you?" The Roshi answered, "Never forget: Everything you need you already have." There is an echo of this in *The Autobiography of Malcolm X*. Describing his prison conversion to Islam and the difficulty he had in getting knees to bend in prayer that till then had bent only to jimmy locks, Malcolm remarks: "I was going through the hardest thing, also the greatest thing, for any human being to do; to accept that which is already within you, and around you."[60]

It is difficult to think of a presumption more foreign to the MWM than this one. In Eaton's image nothing turns on time, for the limitless landscape is there from the start, waiting to be seen by anyone who looks outside his bubble and adjusts his vision to the reaches that extend beyond it. In the MWM, however, the case is the opposite. There time is decisive. Buckminster Fuller refers to "our failed yesterday and our half-successful today." All eyes are on tomorrow.

Partisans of the MWM are quick to object that if the Roshi's claim were taken seriously it would cut the nerve of social concern. The objection leaves the Roshi's own energetic life an anomaly, but let that pass. Once in the course of a television interview on "progress" I asked Reinhold Niebuhr if relinquishing the dream of historical progress would defuse social action. He answered with a question of his own: "To take his work seriously, need a doctor believe that he is eradicating disease?" We are back at the point that was made in Section 2. All myths are tied to the Golden Age of their origin, and in the case of the MWM it was an age when technology seemed to be effecting historical progress. So the MWM continues this mystique, focusing on society rather than the individual (specifically, on what society might *give* the individual), and on the future rather than the present (on what society might provide individuals with *tomorrow* that it cannot provide today).

This is why in the context of the MWM the heading of this section sounds bizarre. If we think of what we need as a happiness that is handed to us by society, then to say that "we have what we need" is patently false, for our society obviously hands us no such thing. But that society *can* hand people happiness is an illusion that was earlier indicated. Whether it can provide individuals on average with more opportunity than it now does to work out their own salvation, I leave as an open question.

VI. CONCLUSION

Do I expect our outlook to change in the directions I have tried to imagine? Not soon, and never for everyone.

The first half of that answer needs no elaboration. It is obvious that the MWM is not about to collapse in the way an avalanche of snow periodically slides off a roof. Section 1 of this essay was given to showing how firmly entrenched it still is.

The second half of my answer, though, may seem enigmatic, so let me conclude by making it less so. To revert for a last time to Gai Eaton's image, let us recall that those who live within its child-blown balloon can be aware of its surrounding landscape in different ways. Some merely surmise its existence. Others recognize its reflections on their bubble's surface, while still others, having a talent for the long look, pierce with their vision the bubble's membrane, which to others is opaque, and see what is to be seen.

This is not an egalitarian picture, ranking persons as it does by their respective powers of sight. But then, who claims that at face value our world is egalitarian? Only in its hidden harmony, in the respect in which we can all work on our power to see, is there the prospect that we are alike.

If the wisdom of the ages is indeed wisdom and teaches us anything, it is that the outlook I have been reaching for is, details aside, the most advanced to which mind can aspire; it represents, we might say, the higher mathematics of the human spirit. Civilizations and cultures can encourage their peoples to advance in its direction, but to dream of an age wherein everyone would enter it lockstep would be to perpetuate one of the errors of the MWM itself, its excessively temporal view of historical progress.

> Because I do not hope to turn again
> Because I do not hope
> Because I do not hope to turn.[61]

If it is too much to hope that our Western outlook will turn concertedly in the directions I have noted, it is not too much to hope that it will encourage, more than in this century it has, those who choose to do so.

Footnotes

1   Huston Smith, "Excluded Knowledge: A Critique of the Modern Western Mind Set," *Teachers College Record* 80, no. 3 (February 1979): 419-45.

2   I am not overlooking the rational, mathematical component in science, but the crucial role of the controlled experiment gives empiricism the edge. One thinks of the opposition as fine a mind as Chomsky's faces because his "Cartesian" linguistics leans toward rationalism.

3   A fragment from Willard Quine shows how tightly the steps in the sequence outlined in this paragraph lock together: (a) Because science is the best procedure we know for getting us to where we want to go (this premise is not stated here, but it underlies Quine's entire corpus), (b) "epistemology is best looked upon . . . as an enterprise within natural science. [And as] science tells us that our only source of information about the external world is through the impact of light rays and molecules upon our sensory surfaces," (c) no prescience is required to see naturalism just around the corner. The quotation is from Quine's essay in *Mind and Language*, Samuel Guttenplan, ed. (Oxford: Clarendon Press, 1975), pp. 65-81.

4   See John Wheeler's address to the American Physical Society in January 1967 as summarized in Walter Sullivan, "Smallest of the Small," *New York Times*, 5 February 1967. The basic principle involved is that "the amount of energy associated with light corpuscles increases *as the size is reduced.* . . . The energy necessary to create a proton is contained in a light pulse only about 10-13 centimeters in diameter. An the energy of a million protons would be contained in a light pulse *a million times smaller* (Arthur Young, *Which Way Out?* [Berkeley: Robert Briggs Associates, 1980], p. 2).

5   David Bohm, *Wholeness and the Implicate Order* (London: Routledge & Kegan Paul, 1980). Professor Bohm was in the audience when the initial draft of this paper was presented. When I came to this line I was gratified to see him nod in agreement.

6   Huston Smith, *Forgotten Truth* (New York: Harper & Row, 1976).

7   That modern epistemology so aims was a major thesis of "Excluded Knowledge." I shall not reproduce the evidence I there marshalled for that thesis; it will be enough to repeat Ernest Gellner's summary verdict in his *Legitimation of Belief* ([London: Cambridge University Press, 1974], pp. 206-07): "We have become habituated to and dependent on effective knowledge [read: knowledge that enables us to control], and have bound ourselves to this kind of genuine explanation. . . . What . . . this . . . compulsion . . . amounts to is in the end simple: if there is to be effective knowledge or explanation *at all*, it must [pass the tests of empiricism and mechanism], for any other kind of 'explanation' . . . is *ipso facto* powerless."

8   Human beings must be kept in the dark if they are to be subjects for controlled experiments directed at domains in which they are free. But transcendental subjects, if they exist, cannot be kept in the dark. By definition they know more than we do.

9   Signs of this are everywhere. "If anything characterizes 'modernity,' it is loss of faith in transcendence, in a reality that encompasses but surpasses our quotidian affairs," a contributor to *The Chronicle of Higher Education* wrote in its January 9, 1978, issue (page 18). A participant in the Woodstock Symposium, Owen Barfield, has noted the consequences of this for his own field, that of letters. "The eighteenth century essay was allowed . . . to 'bring in' religion [in the word I am using here, "transcendence"]. That is exactly what the twentieth century was *not* allowed to do. Not on any account" (*Journal of the American Academy of Religion*, 47/2, Supplement [June 1979]: 221-22).

10   The belief that human activities can be "reduced" to—for example, explained by—the behavior of lower animals and that these in turn can be reduced to the physical laws that govern inanimate matter. For a full-scale crititique of this belief see Arthur Koestler and James Smythies, *Beyond Reductionism* (New York: Macmillan, 1970).

11   I do not know the author of this quatrain. It was chalked on the blackboard at a meeting of graduate students I attended last year.

12   Daniel Dennett, "Review of *The Self and its Brain* by Karl Popper and John Eccles," *The Journal of Philosophy* 76, no. 2 (February 1979): 97.

13 Carl Sagan, *The Dragons of Eden* (New York: Ballantine Books, 1978), p. 10.

14 Harold Morowitz, "Rediscovering the Mind," *Psychology Today* 14, no. 2 (August 1980): 14.

15 Francis Crick, *Of Molecules and Men* (Seattle: University of Washington Press, 1966).

16 Morowitz, "Rediscovering the Mind," p. 12.

17 Annette J. Smith, "Playing with Play: A Test Case of 'Ethocriticism,'" *Journal of Biological Structures* 1, no. 11 (1978): 199.

18 Jean Piaget, *Play, Dreams and Imitation in Childhood* (London: Routledge & Kegan Paul, 1951).

19 D. Elkins, ed., *Six Psychological Studies* (New York: Random House, 1967).

20 John Bowlby, *Attachment and Loss*, vol. I (New York: Basic Books, 1969), emphasis added.

21 "The emotions we feel, which in exceptional individuals may climax in total self-sacrifice, stem ultimately from hereditary units that were implanted by the favoring of relatives during a period of hundreds of thousands of generations" (Edward O. Wilson, "Altruism," *Harvard Magazine*, November-December 1978).

22 Edward O. Wilson, *Sociobiology: The Abridged Edition* (Cambridge: Harvard University Press, 1980), p. 3.

23 These friends cannot be four-footed, feathered, or furry, though—much less leafy and flowery. To be kind to the point of sacrificing human interests for these—restraining our predatory impulses towards the whales, say—is irrational, for in genetic ethics (the opening section of *Sociobiology* is titled "The Morality of the Gene") "rational" is what favors species survival.

It is irrational to defer to other species unless there is a gene that has caught on to the fact that species need environments to sustain them—I enter this suggestion of my own to caricature the lengths to which sociobiology has already stretched evidence in the interests of theory (see Marvin Harris, *Cultural Materialism;* Richard Dawkins, *The Selfish Gene;* and Stuart Hampshire, "The Illusion of Sociobiology," *The New York Review of Books*, October 12, 1978). Wilson is now quoted as saying that by "gene" he does not mean the actual physical entities we can see with electron microscopes. Officially he claims only that biological findings might *plausibly* be used to explain human behavior. But his suggestion meshes so neatly with current styles of explanation that a dropped hint is enough to place its author in vast demand. Sociologists and psychologists are already working with sociobiological hypotheses as if they were tested theories—Pierre van den Berghe and David Barash are examples.

24 Barbara Brown, *Supermind* (New York: Harper & Row, 1980), p. 199.

25 D. and C. Johnson, "Totally Discouraged: A Depressive Syndrome of the Dakota Sioux," *Transcultural Psychiatric Research Review*, no. 2 (1965): 141-43.

26 Or the collapse of any worldview with a religious component, for that matter. Edward Wilson says sociobiology is forced to conclude that "the predisposition to religious belief is the most complex and powerful force in the human mind," but whereas elsewhere complexity is a biological virtue, here it shows only that the religious impulse is "in all probability ineradicable" (Edward O. Wilson, *On Human Nature* [New York: Bantam Books, 1978], p. 176).

27 Anthony Marsella, "Depressive Experience and Disorder across Cultures," in *Handbook of Cross-Cultural Psychology*, ed. Harry Triandis and Jurgis Draguns, vol. VI (Boston: Allyn & Bacon, 1980), p. 254. I am indebted to Kendra Smith for pointing me to the references in this section.

28 Ibid., p. 255.

29 Alexander Solzhenitsyn, published as *A World Split Apart* (New York: Harper & Row, 1978).

30 Ibid., p. 35.

31 Ibid., p. 5.

32 Ibid., p. 47, emphasis added.

33 Ibid., pp. 47-49, emphasis added. "It could also be called anthropocentricity," he adds, "with man seen as the center of all," p. 49.

On the day that I found myself writing these lines a letter reached me from a former student, Will Fitzhugh, relating an anecdote from his freshman philosophy course at Harvard University. It seems that when Emerson Hall (where the class met) was built, the Philosophy Department selected for the motto to be inscribed on its main wall, "Man is the Measure of all things." President Eliot, however, was of a different mind and what actually appeared was, "What is man that Thou art mindful of him?"

The occasion for the student's note to me was a return visit to his alma mater. He found that vines had obscured the inscription, leaving only three words visible, those words being "that Thou art," the claim (in its Vedantic formulation) that man is indissolubly joined to the Absolute. I shall return to that in Section V-4 below.

34   Ibid., p. 35.

35   I refer the reader to what Gellner calls the "mechanistic insistence" of an epistemology that aims at power; see footnote 9. The phrase "mechanistic insistence" appears in Gellner, *Legitimation of Belief*, p. 207.

36   In Joseph Weizenbaum, *Computer Power and Human Reason: From Judgment to Calculation* (San Francisco: W. H. Freeman, 1976). Weizenbaum, another participant in the Woodstock Symposium, warns of "the imperialism of instrumental reason" in our time.

37   See supra, footnote 7, or the original in Gellner, *Legitimation of Belief*, pp. 206-07.

38   Statement by David Bohm at the Woodstock Symposium "Knowledge, Education, and Human Values," 1980.

39   See Howard E. Gruber, "Darwin's 'Tree of Nature' and other Images of wide Scope," in *On Aesthetics in Science*, Judith Wechsler (Cambridge: M.I.T. Press, 1978).

Images figured prominently in the Woodstock Symposium. Peter Abbs followed David Bohm to argue the need for education "to restore the power of the living image, to confer on it a high epistemological status, to put it along side concept as one of the key ways in which we symbolize and then come to know our world."

40   Gai Eaton, *The King of the Castle* (London: The Bodley Head, 1977), pp. 11-12.

41   On this latter point I take my cue from science, with Fred Hoyle its spokesman: "No literary imagination could have invented a story one-hundredth part as fantastic as the sober facts that have been unearthed. . . . If there is one important result that comes out of our inquiry into the nature of the Universe it is this: when by patient inquiry we learn the answer to any problem, we always find, both as a whole and in detail, that the answer thus revealed is finer in concept and design that anything we could ever have arrived at by random guess" Fred Hoyle (*The Nature of the University* [New York: New American Library,· 1950], pp. 120, 128).

42   Edward Norman says "there is no doubt that in developed societies education has contributed to the decline of religious belief," to which Robert Bellah adds that the decline is not in religious belief only. "The deepest indictment of the university," he told the Woodstock Symposium, "is that it erodes belief" generally. Norman's statement appears in his *Christianity and the World Order* (New York: Oxford University Press, 1979), p. 6.

43   Sociobiology provides an instance of such game playing. On the one hand we are told that as human beings have been programmed by their evolutionary history to be incorrigible mythmakers, we require conceptual systems that engage our loyalties; while on the other, that these systems must "satisfy our urge for knowledge" (paraphrase of Edward O. Wilson, in *Religious Studies Review* 5, no. 2 [April 1980]: 102). Whether a conceptual system our knowledge tells us is a myth *can* engage our loyalties is never squarely faced.

44   T. S. Eliot, "The Family Reunion," in his *Complete Poems and Plays* (New York: Harcourt, Brace & World, 1971), p. 291.

45   Frithjof Schuon's essay "The Contradition of Relativism" in his *Logic and Transcendence* (New York: Harper & Row, 1975) has helped me crystallize the thoughts I set down in the next several paragraphs.

46   E. F. Schumacher, *A Guide for the Perplexed* (New York: Harper & Row, 1977), p. 5

47   I suspect that the approach I am following—my methodology if you will—is clear by now, but let me state it explicitly. In place of our usual tendency to begin with the accepted world and

add to it only what collective evidence requires, I am asking if it would harm us to conjure the most interesting world we can and then drop from it what reason erases. There is some resemblance to Anselm's *credo ut intelligam*, "I believe in order to understand." Or as Wilfred Smith, using current idiom to get at what *credo* meant in the Middle Ages, paraphrases Anselm, "I get involved in order to understand."

48 Solzhenitsyn, *A World Split Apart*, p. 57; emphasis added.

49 Mortimer Adler, *Aristotle for Everybody* (New York: Bantam Books, 1980), p. 174.

50 Jacques Monod, *Chance and Necessity* (New York: Vintage Books, 1972), p. 21.

51 W. W. Bartley, III, in *The Philosophy of Karl Popper*, Paul Schilpp (La Salle, Ill.: Open Court, 1974), vol. II, p. 675.

52 K. Parker, "The Effects of Subliminal Merging Stimuli on the Academic Performance of College Students" (Ph.D. diss., New York University, 1977). Reported in Lloyd Silverman, "Two Unconscious Fantasies and Mediators of Successful Psychotherapy," *Psychotherapy: Theory, Research and Practice* 16, no. 2 (Summer 1979): 220.

53 Lloyd Silverman, "A Comprehensive Report of Studies Using the Subliminal Psychodynamic Activation Method," issued by the New York Veterans Administration Regional Office and Research Center for Mental Health, New York University, 1980, p. 14.

54 L. H. Silverman, F. Lachmann, and R. Milich, *The Search for Oneness* (New York: International Universities Press, in press). I am indebted to a former student, Robert Ebert, for calling my attention to this whole matter.

55 Manfred Stanley, "Beyond Progress: Three Post-Political Futures," in *Images of the Future*, ed. Robert Bundy (Buffalo: Prometheus Books, 1976), pp. 115–16. I have used this and the two quotations that follow in other essays, but enter them again because I have encountered no others, penned from within the MWM itself, that bring out the issues quite as crisply.

56 Ibid.,

57 Gellner, *Legitimation of Belief*, p. 207.

58 Ibid., pp. 206–07.

59 Lewis Thomas, *The Medusa and the Snail* (New York: Viking Press, 1979), p. 87.

60 Malcolm X, *The Autobiography of Malcolm X* (New York: Grove Press, 1964), p. 164.

61 T. S. Eliot, "Ash-Wednesday," in his *Complete Poems and Plays*, p. 60.

Towards a Living Universe

KATHLEEN RAINE
London, England

Every civilization is grounded in certain premises but it is precisely of these that we are least aware. Yet those who find meaning in Plato's fable of the alternation of ages of gold and iron, or in "The Great Year of the Ancients" see in the alternation or progression of historic "ages" precisely a reversal or a change of premises. Some see in the precession of the equinox from the sign of Pisces to Aquarius such a reversal. Others without recourse to symbol have reached a similar conclusion; for when the implications of certain assumptions—in our own case those of the natural sciences—have been fully unfolded and explored, other assumptions, other premises become necessary. Many, not least among the scientists themselves, are now calling in question the basic premise of the natural sciences, that the universe is a self-contained material system acting autonomously as a mechanism, according to "laws of nature."

Yeats, one of the first great voices to proclaim, at the beginning of this century, a reversal of the age, described the centuries of science, on which those who see in human history a steady progression from ignorance to knowledge, a "conquest" of nature and the ascent of man to the top of the tree of natural evolution, so pride themselves, the "three provincial centuries," a mere deviation from a human norm whose premises—and whose fruits therefore—are of quite another kind.

Technology and its products are to the mass of mankind the obvious and incontrovertible vindication of science. But there is a growing realization that the naive premises of materialism are applicable within certain limits only. The pursuit of "matter" into its ultimate origins has resulted only in the discovery that what to the senses seems so solid is in reality something intangible, one might say immaterial. The end of the history of scientific investigation would seem to be a dematerialisation of matter itself.

So our New Age seems likely to begin with a reversal of premises, a return to metaphysical orthodoxy: that is, the assumption that not matter but mind is the ground of our universe, and that, in consequence, the natural universe can no longer be seen as a mechanism (however complex) but, as Plato called the world, an immortal and blessed God, a living being.

The fruits of these two views of reality will be as different as their premises. The fruits of materialist science are utilities; those of the spirit are the qualities and values of life. It is the great merit of scientific thought that the laws of the natural order are respected throughout the whole field of natural science. The coherence, the ordered harmony of the scientific world-picture is truly a wonderful speculation of nature. What is in question—as Owen Barfield many years ago set forth in his book *Saving the Appearances*—is the nature and context of that speculation. The implications of an account of the universe which excludes mind, or soul, or spirit—excludes whatever is not of a material order—have in the long run proved disastrous. Naive materialism nevertheless remains the irreligion of the masses in this world of material wealth and spiritual indigence. For the price paid for our prestigious material civilization is that we are, in comparison with many backward races, spiritual savages. Blake himself pointed to the American Indians as a race who have more in common with Homer's world than have the scholars who study "the classics"; and that the Brahmans of India are "naked civilized men" whose inner culture is in marked contrast with that of our own "trousered apes" who have rejected as primitive ignorance that dream of divine descent which haunts every mythological—that is to say imaginative—account of our origin and nature. The fields of the arts, religion and moral values, and metaphysics have become debased in proportion to the incursions of scientific standards and assumptions into their respective fields. Since scientific standards of measurement are inapplicable to whatever is not of a material order there have ceased to be any standards at all in whatever belongs to what is (pejoratively) called the "subjective." And yet other civilisations have recognised the laws of mind as the most real, the most universal of all things. In the arts and in criticism of the arts (not to mention behavioural psychology and other bastard sciences) the distinction between the significant and the meaningless, and even of the pathological, has been virtually lost. Our age can gape at the great works of the past—megalithic circles, the pyramids, the Parthenon, Chartres, the Alhambra, or comparable works of poetry, music, or painting. But with our vast technical skill we ourselves do not possess the knowledge to create such works; for that knowledge was a spiritual knowledge. Do we even possess the knowledge necessary to understand these "monuments of unageing intellect"? Perhaps science is itself the one significant work of imagination our spiritually forgetful culture has produced.

If a New Age means anything it means a change of premises, and the consequent recovery of a whole body of knowledge excluded by materialist science as irrelevant: a knowledge no less exact, no less extensive, structured, and objective than the laws of nature: knowledge of man's inner worlds, of the imagination. Many are now turning to the Far East, to those philosophies based on the premise that mind or spirit is the ground. But the West has its own tradition, of Greek philosophy, united in Christian theology with the Jewish prophetic affirmation of a "living God." From this norm post-Cartesian thought has deviated; but the threads of tradition are never quite lost. I myself discovered this knowledge, excluded as irrelevant by materialist humanism, in the course of my studies of William Blake, who is a key figure in the reaffirmation and recovery of the perennial wisdom. His prophetic voice was unheard by his contemporaries, but speaks eloquently to our own, better able than the nineteenth century to appreciate the force of his arguments, the truth of his vision, and the reality of those inner worlds it was his prophetic mission to reopen.

Blake was not an "original" thinker, nor would he have wished to be so in the modern sense. Rather he gathered up the threads of the excluded knowledge—gnosticism, alchemy, the mythologies of many races. He was in principle eclectic, believing as he did that the human Imagination is itself the source of all religions and all mythologies. In these he found traces of what he regarded as the universal religion of mankind, which he called the Everlasting Gospel or "the religion of Jesus" (by which he did not necessarily mean the religion of the Christian Church) who is, in Blake's terms, the Imagination itself. But two of his principal sources were Neoplatonism and the writings of Swedenborg; and these we shall presently consider.

Blake's fundamental objection to the scientific philosophy, "natural religion"—and the objection is still valid—is that the universe of material science is devoid of life. It is located outside the perceiving mind in "a void outside existence" (that is, outside living consciousness) in "non-entity's dark void," "a soul-shuddering vacuum" filled with "voids and solids." This lifeless universe outside the human Imagination is created by the "wrenching apart" of the "eternal mind" resulting, on the one hand, in an externalized "nature" devoid of life, and on the other a "shrinking" of humanity from the boundless being of Imagination into the "mortal worm" of "sixty winters" and "seventy inches long," an insignificant part of the externalized nature this wrenching apart has created. In this fall from the infinity and expansiveness of the Imagination into a world of matter man becomes "a little grovelling root outside of himself"; for the human imagination is not contained by a material universe, but contains and is coextensive with whatever it perceives and experiences. Thus Blake held the materialist view of nature to be both false, and destructive to humanity. Nature, no longer within the human imagination, has an existence merely quantitative, and becomes a spiritual desert, "a wondrous rocky World of cruel destiny,/Rocks piled on rocks reaching the stars," which Blake calls

A building of eternal death, whose proportions are eternal despair. (K.702)[1]

With the "shrinking" of eye and ear from imaginative to natural vision, the sun and moon are "hurried afar into an unknown Night,"

. . . the Sun is shrunk: the Heavens are shrunk
Away into the far remote, and the Trees & Mountains wither'd
Into indefinite cloudy shadows. . . .
The Stars flee remote; the heaven is iron, the earth is sulphur,
And all the mountains & hills shrink up like a withering gourd. (K.703)

Externalized nature becomes an "unfathomable non-ens." The rationalist thought of Bacon, Newton, and Locke alienates man from his universe. All nature "flees" from man into externality; the animals "wander away" in "sullen droves," and as with the natural world so with human cities:

The Cities & Villages of Albion become Rock & Sand Unhumanized. (K.697)

The astonishing writings of Emanuel Swedenborg reopened in the eighteenth century those inner worlds which post-Cartesian science had thought dispensable. Blake and his wife were members of the Swedenborgian Society; and Blake's seemingly original "system" is, in its essentials, that of Swedenborg's New Church—a fact which Blake scholars, including myself, have been slow to recognise. Indeed the only interpreter of Blake who has not made this mistake is his first and greatest disciple, Yeats. Yet Swedenborg represents in its most pure form the alternative view of the world which in our own time can no longer be brushed aside.

Swedenborg was a geologist and assessor of minerals to the Swedish government, a distinguished and respected man of science; nevertheless after the "opening" of his inner perceptions, which took place in middle life, he saw the world as a purely mental phenomenon. There are, he says, three worlds, the celestial, the spiritual, and the world of "uses," the natural world. These degrees correspond to the Platonic, Kabbalistic and other cosmologies and doubtless to the actual structure of the mental universe; and—again like other systems—the degrees are not a continuous gradation, but "discrete," a point on which Blake, and Yeats also, insists. In countless passages throughout his work Swedenborg insists that whereas all in the mental worlds is alive, all in "nature," Blake's world "outside existence"—is "fixed and dead," a view, as we shall later see, shared by Plotinus and the Neoplatonists:

. . . for all that is created, in itself is inanimate and dead but things are made alive by the fact that the Divine is in them, and that they are in the Divine. (*Divine Love and Wisdom* 53)[2]

Of nature he writes that "in herself she is dead, and no more contributes to produce these things (that is the appearances) than the instrument to produce the work of the artificer." (*DLW*.340). This divine artificer, called by Swedenborg, and Blake after him, the "Divine Body," is present in humanity as the "Divine Humanity," called by Swedenborg the Lord and by Blake the Imagination. God, according to Swedenborg, is life in its twofold aspects of love and wisdom.

Blake in the *Book of Los* describes in mythological symbol the creation of a "dead" sun in the fixed and dead spaces of the "deeps" of the Newtonian universe formed by the "wrenching apart" of human consciousness. This natural sun Blake says gives "no light." In the same way he mythologizes the dry bones of a statement by Swedenborg that "space in the natural world may also be called dead" (*DLW*.156) in contrast with the imaginative spaces of the mental world, which are flexible according to thought. By this Blake by no means understands only the imagined spaces of dreams and inner reverie; for we also imaginatively perceive the outer world. His two mythological figures Los (time) and Enitharmon (space) create these imaginative extensions and durations we inhabit:

> For Los & Enitharmon walk'd forth on the dewy Earth
> Contracting or expanding their all flexible senses
> At will to murmur in the flowers small as the honey bee,
> At will to stretch across the heavens & step from star to star. (K.288)

We all possessed as children this imaginative faculty of entering imaginary caverns and burning mountains in the fire, or losing ourselves in a miniature forest of grass. That is imaginative space and cannot be measured. Blake mythologizes the effect of the "wrenching apart" which separates the merely quantifiable spaces of nature from the Imagination, describing how Enitharmon becomes frozen into deadly rigidity:

> . . . Enitharmon stretched on the dreamy Earth
> Felt her immortal limbs freeze, stiffening, pale, inflexible. (K.305)

So Los and Enitharmon are "shrunk into fixed space" and

> Their senses unexpansive in one stedfast bulk remain (K.305)

in externalized nature whose state Blake follows Swedenborg in describing as "eternal death."

Into this externality sun and moon, mountains and fields and animals "wander away into a distant night, separated from man." So nature is externalized to become the "dark Abyss" "outside existence." Thus both Blake and Swedenborg are concerned with the human consequences of abstracting a material universe from a living mind. Blake by no means calls in question Newton's mathematics; he depicts the human consequences of the abstraction of matter from mind in the portrait he paints of Urizen, the usurping rational faculty who builds for himself a hell of lifeless nature, a "ruined world" where

> . . . A Rock, a Cloud, a Mountain
> Were now not Vocal as in Climes of happy Eternity
> Where the lamb replies to the infant voice, & the lion to the man of years,
> Giving them sweet instructions; where the Cloud, the River & the Field
> Talk with the husbandman & shepherd. (K.315)

Nature "talks" to man in the sense that perception itself is experienced as meaning.

The separation of a universe of matter from the universe of life is for both these visionaries the tragedy of our civilisation, dooming us to an existence in a world of inanimate objects devoid of qualities or meaning; René Guénon wrote a book entitled *The Reign of Quantity*, and this reign had already been foreseen by Blake who denounced as "Satanic" the reverence paid to "length bredth and highth" under the domination of the mind of the ratio. In the world of the Imagination "everything that lives is Holy." The rational mind can know nothing of the sacred, which is immeasurable and exists only as an experience.

Locke had argued—and his supposition remains the basis of behaviourist psychology and of naive materialism generally—that the human senses are passive recipients of stimuli from a "real" material order exterior to us and to which our senses are merely a passive mirror, Flaubert's "mirror dawdling down a lane." For the imaginative tradition the reverse is true—"nature" is the mirror in which Imagination beholds herself.

Swedenborg also answered in detail Locke's view of the passive role of the senses before an externalised nature. In his pedantic way, Swedenborg insists, as Plotinus does, that the forms we perceive reside in the percipient and not in an external nature; and such is the importance of this point that I quote, without apology, Swedenborg's laboured argument:

> A man has five external senses which are called touch, taste, smell, hearing, and sight. The subject of touch is in the skin with which a man is encompassed: the very substance and form of the skin cause it to feel the things applied to it: the sense of touch is not in the things which are applied, but it is the substance and form of the skin, which are the subject; this sense is merely an affection of the subject from the things applied. It is the same with taste; this sense is only an affection of the substance and form belonging to the tongue; the tongue is the subject. The same is the case with smell; it is well known that odour affects the nostrils, and that it is in the nostrils, and that it is an affection of them by odoriferous particles touching them. It is the same with the sense of hearing: it appears as if the hearing is in the ear, and is an affection of its substance and form; that the hearing is at a distance from the ear is an appearance. The same is the case with sight: when a man sees objects at a distance, it appears as if the sight were there; and yet it is the eye which is the subject, and is likewise and af fection of the subject . . . It may appear from all this that the affection of the substance and form which causes sense is not anything separate from the subject, but only causes a change in it, the subject remaining the subject then as before, and afterwards. (*DLW*.41)

In other words whatever we behold as if an external universe is in reality subjective—within the consciousness of the beholder; a very obvious truth which Western scientific thought has continued to overlook. So Blake wrote "Forms must be apprehended by Sense or the Eye of the Imagination" (K.775). The forms which we perceive as external nature are in reality within the perceiving mind. That mind cannot perceive otherwise than in accordance with its innate structure.

The Imagination or Divine Body—man's real body—is of an immaterial nature and the *mundus imaginalis* is man's proper world; not as an "afterlife" (called by Blake "an allegoric abode where existence has never come") but as the place where we actually are. Swedenborg wrote ". . . man is a spirit; from that he thinks and wills: wherefore the spiritual world is where man is, and in no way far from him . . . every man as to the interiors of his mind is in that world" (*DLW*.92). Swedenborg insists again and again that the divine body is neither large nor small since it exists otherwise than in natural space. Thus the Imagination is at once mind and its universe. The created world is itself an image of consciousness and Swedenborg argues that everything in nature— the dead world—is an image or reflection of this living world of consciousness. It is not mind but nature which is the mirror, in which objects have only an apparent existence. This view, shared within the whole Platonic tradition (of which Swedenborg is himself a remote recipient) is in total opposition to the view of causality which sees mind as an epiphenomenon of bodily organs and functions:

> For the dead thing to act upon the living thing, or for the dead force to act upon the living force, or, what is the same, for the rational to act upon the spiritual, is entirely contrary to order. (*DLW*.166)

This world is, according to Swedenborg (again like the Platonic philosophers) the *ultimum opus* in which all things end and upon which they rest.

Blake writes of "Eden, the land of life"; and mankind's exile from Eden is, quite specifically, exile from the *mundus imaginalis* in which "all things exist in their eternal forms." Thus the breaking of the Platonic unity of being, the separation between knowledge and its object made by Aristotle as a convenience for discursive thought, ends in a dehumanization of the natural universe and, ultimately, of humanity also. Our positivist science (like a conquering army which brings devastation in its wake) seeks in our own time to quantify consciousness itself, equating mind with brain, and thought with a mechanical process which can be carried out by computers. As Blake long ago wrote of the English national being, "his machines are woven with his life." The thing itself, life, becomes an irrelevance within the vast, self-contained and perfectly functioning mechanism of an externalized nature.

Underlying all later affirmations (in the West) of a living universe is the Platonic tradition. With every return to a philosophy which gives primacy to mind comes a return to the Platonic succession. Blake's acquaintance and contemporary Thomas Taylor the Platonist played, through his many translations and commentaries on the Neoplatonic writers, and above all Plotinus, a part no less important than Blake's in establishing the ground for a return to the Platonic succession. His writings provided the basis of the American Transcendentalist movement, and were later an important element in the Theosophical movement and in the Irish renaissance. The Platonic philosophy, coherent and lucid, considers matter as the last effect of a descending chain of causes originating in a divine source, through the intelligible world of "reason" by way of the "seminal reasons" of individual souls of every species, which in turn inform the world of matter, itself devoid of form, but the mirror, as it were, in which the intelligible world beholds itself. Among Taylor's paraphrase translations of Plotinus is Ennead III Book 8 *On Nature, Contemplation, and The One*. Since it was through Taylor that both Blake and the American Transcendentalists received this sublime teaching of Plotinus, I shall use his version in presenting the Platonic view of the universe.

Like Swedenborg, Plotinus calls the material universe both "dead" and without the power of causality, which belongs only to Intellect, the living principle. He calls matter a "non-ens" whose existence is only equivocal. Matter can be said to exist only insofar as it is the recipient of forms (the "seminal reasons"—*rationes seminales*) but (and modern physics would support Plotinus' argument) unknowable in its ultimate nature because by definition without form. And Plotinus summarizes his view of the forms we discover in the external world:

> Reason, therefore, extrinsically produced according to a visible form, is the last reason, generated, as it were, in the shade of the first, destitute of life, and incapable of forming another reason. But reason endued with life, and which is as it were the sister of that which fabricates form, and possesses the same power, generates that reason which is the last in the effects.[3] (*Enn.*205)

—that is to say, in matter. Blake, with his gift for grasping the essence, summarizes Plotinus' teaching—and indeed Swedenborg's also—in his own affirmation

> And every Natural Effect has a Spiritual Cause, and Not
> A Natural; for a Natural Cause only seems; it is a Delusion
> of Ulro & a ratio of the perishing Vegetable Memory. (K.513)

(Ulro is Blake's and Swedenborg's lifeless world "outside existence.")

According to Plotinus "Nature" is reason, is form, and the mother of the multitude of "seminal reasons" of the diverse multitude of creatures—plants, animals and all the rest—which derive the inherent reasons responsible for the unfolding of their diverse forms from the overruling "reason" of "nature" considered as a whole. Thus the phrase "mother nature"—or Spenser's Dame Nature—is by no means a personification of a mechanism but in the most literal sense true since Nature is "endued with life" and in this sense not a thing but a Person. The parent-reason of "Nature" generates her innumerable offspring while "abiding in the mean time permanent in itself."

The Darwinian scheme of evolution which we all learned at school as the very canon of scientific orthodoxy concluded from the serial unfolding and

diversification of natural species in time that natural causality which the
Platonists deny; but if time be merely relative to our own situation within it
Plato may be nearer the truth when (in the Timaeus) he describes this world as
a "moving image of eternity, unfolding according to number of eternity
abiding in one." From a non-temporal point of view all is simultaneously
present, effects already implicit in their "seminal reasons." Plotinus, developing this Platonic theme, sees Nature operating, not as the blind mechanism of
"natural selection" postulated by Darwin, (a kind of hit-or-miss process
whose beginning is in chaos and whose end is indeterminate) but conceives
the operation of Nature as "contemplation" of what eternally exists. And he
considers

> what is the speculation of earth, and trees, and plants, and after what man-
> ner we may be able to reduce that which is produced in these into the energy
> of speculation; and lastly, how nature, which is said to be void of imagina-
> tion and reason, possesses contemplation in herself, and yet operates from
> contemplation she does not possess. (*Enn.*201)

(The word "speculation" is here not used in the modern sense, as more or less
synonymous with a reasonable guess but in its literal sense, of looking into a
mirror—*speculum*—in which reality is contemplated.) Plotinus concludes
that Nature contemplates herself in an endless reverie of her innate "reason":

> But does nature operate from contemplation? From contemplation entirely.
> But what if after a certain manner she contemplates herself? For she is the
> effect of contemplation, and is contemplative of something . . . such as she
> is, such she fabricates. (*Enn.*206–07)

Nature is said to contemplate "a soul more powerful and vivid" which does
not operate in matter but resides in the intelligible world. Nature is not fully
conscious, as intellect is, and in a beautiful image Plotinus describes Nature as
a dreamer, whose dream is the "spectacle" of natural forms:

> And if any one is desirous of assigning to nature a certain apprehension or
> sensation, he ought not to attribute to her a knowledge of the same kind as
> that of other beings, but in the same manner as if the knowledge of a man
> dreaming should be compared with the perceptions of the vigilant: for con-
> templating her spectacle she reposes; a spectacle produced in herself, be-
> cause she abides in and with herself and becomes her own spectacle and a
> quiet contemplation, though more debile and obscure; for the soul from
> which she is produced is endued with a more efficacious perception, and
> nature is only the image of another's contemplation. (*Enn.*210)

Thus the image of nature as a mirror—Jakob Boehme's "vegetable glass,"
Blake's "looking-glass of Enitharmon"—goes back to the Platonic tradition.
Plotinus develops the myth of Narcissus, who falls in love with his image
reflected in water, as the soul which falls in love with its bodily image and is in

consequence turned into what Blake calls a "human vegetable"—losing his humanity. Yeats summarises the doctrine in his line

Mirror on mirror mirrored is all the show.

That which Nature contemplates in order to produce her "spectacle" is soul, which is "full of speculative forms." Thus

Indeed all things proceed in a beautiful and quiet order . . . The intellectual soul of the world contemplates indeed a sublime spectacle, and that which she thus contemplates, because it rises higher than soul, generates that which is posterior to itself, and thus contemplation begets contemplation, so that neither has speculation or spectacle any bound, and on this account they proceed through all things. (*Enn.*215)

This dreaming figure of Nature (generative and therefore feminine) survives or re-emerges in the *anima mundi* of the alchemical and Rosicrucian tradition, *natura naturans*. Robert Fludd, in his *Mosaicall Philosophy,* wrote

The Platonists did call the general vertue, which did engender and preserve all things, the *Anima Mundi*, or *the soul of the world*. And to this their opinions, the *Arabic Astrologians* do seem to adhere: forasmuch as they did maintain, that every particular thing in the world hath his distinct and peculiar soul from this vivifying spirit. (II.I.IV.)

And Fludd quotes the Greek saying that the world is "full of Gods."
This allusion to the "Arabic Astrologians" points forward to Henry Corbin's work in our own time on Iranian mystical theology; and Fludd enumerates the sources of the tradition he represented in his generation

. . . Mercurius Trismegistus [that is the Hermetica] Theophrastus, Avicenna, Algazel, as well all the Stoiks, and Peripatetiks, . . . Zoroaster and Heraclitus the Ephesian, conclude that the soul of the world is that catholick invisible fire, of which and by the action whereof, all things are generated and brought forth from puissance into act. (II.I.IV)

The soul of the world Fludd equates with the angel Metatron and with the Divine Wisdom of the Scriptures:

The Cabalist's tenent is, that the great Angell whom they term Mitattron . . . is that very same catholick Spirit, which doth animate the whole world, and thereupon *Rabbi Moses* does averre it to be *Intellectus agens, or the general intellectuall agent, from which all particular forms do flow.* And they say, that from this universall angelicall Spirit, all singular vertues as well animall, as vitall and naturall, do proceed, which also they call Angells, whereof there are an infinite number in respect of our capacity. (II.I.IV)

Fludd goes on to equate the soul of the world with the Wisdom of the

Scriptures, whose "spirit filleth the whole world" and indeed (being in this respect close to Blake, who would have read the *Mosaicall Philosophy* and may have been directly indebted to Fludd) with

> *that Christ which filleth all things, who is all in all,* as the Apostle sayeth, who *in the beginning made the earth, and the heavens were the work of his hands;* And after his creation of all things he doth (as St. Paul telleth us Heb.i.) *bear up, suffer and sustain all things by the vivifying virtue of this Word.*

And Fludd continues:

> But each Philosopher cannot but acknowledg that *Anima* is nothing else, but that which doth animate or vivifie a body or spirit. Why then should not the catholick divine spirit which filleth all, and operateth all, and in all, be tearmed the fountain of the worlds life, by which it liveth, moveth, and hath its being, and consequently the essentiall life, and Centrall or mental soul of the world, moving the created humid spirit thereof, no otherwise, then the spirit which God breathed into *Adam,* did move and operate, in and by the Organ of the created aire? (II.I.IV)

Plotinus also says that "in every soul there is the same spectacle." There is no question of "subjectivity" in the modern sense. If the view of Locke, continued in our own time by the behaviourist schools, that all knowledge comes through the senses and refers to an externalized world, of which every individual is a passive mirror, were true, then subjectivity would indeed be, in Blake's words, "a fortuitous concourse of memorys accumulated and lost." But if, on the contrary, the "seminal reasons" of all creatures individually "speculate" the universal "reason" of Nature, then it is the "latent reasons" residing in the soul which unfold in energy and action. Self-knowledge is the soul's desire—to behold her latent reasons externally and "as if different from herself." This is the root of her speculation; but she "cannot produce what she has not received" and she "perceives what she possesses." But in so doing—so Plotinus puts it—she has "relinquished part of herself" into externality, as that "spectacle" in which soul sees itself in generated beings.

Again Blake has summarized this philosophy—which reached him indeed also through Swedenborg—with his inimitable aphoristic clarity:

> . . . in your own Bosom you bear your Heaven
> And Earth & all you behold; tho' it appears Without, it is Within,
> In your Imagination, of which this World of Mortality is but a Shadow.
> (K.709)

This might be—perhaps in fact is—Blake's summary of Plotinus' *On Nature, Contemplation, and the One.*

Thus Plotinus presents us with a living universe in which there is neither distinction nor separation between knowing and being; since "in intellect essence is the same as intellection. For it cannot be any longer said that *this* is one and *that* another." Coleridge, great philosopher of the Imagination, for whom also Plotinus was supreme, wrote of "the adorable I AM" in which knowledge and being are one and indistinguishable. Thus the *unus mundus* is restored, in whose unity of being Blake's "wrenching apart" of the natural universe and the mind which beholds it is healed.

To conclude this summary of Plotinus' teaching concerning Nature; we see him in the following passage reaching the affirmation characteristic of Christian, Jewish and Islamic thought, that the universal living mind or spirit the Greeks call Intellect must be considered as a Person—the only and supreme Person of the universe. For what constitutes a "person" if not life, knowledge, and that unity of being which belongs by definition to "the Good Itself" and which is, for the Platonists, also "the One":

> Intellect indeed is beautiful, and the most beautiful of all things, being situated in a pure light and in a pure splendour, and comprehending in itself the nature of beings, of which indeed this our beautiful material world is but a shadow and image; but intellect, that true intelligible world, is situated in universal splendour, living in itself a blessed life, and containing nothing unintelligible, nothing dark, nothing without measure; which divine world whoever perceives will be immediately astonished, if, as is requisite, he profoundly and intimately merges himself into its inmost recesses and becomes one with its all beauteous nature. And as he who diligently surveys the heavens, and contemplates the splendor of the stars, should immediately think upon and search after their artificer, so it is requisite that he who beholds and admires the intelligible world, should diligently inquire after its author, investigating who he is, where he resides, and how he produced such an offspring as intellect, a son beautiful and pure, and full of ineffable fire. But his father is neither intellect nor a son, but superior to both; for intellect has a posterior subsistence, and is indigent of nourishment and intelligence, being situated the next in order to that nature which is superior to every kind of want. Intellect, however, possesses true plenitude and intelligence, because it possesses the first of all things; but that which is prior to intellect is neither indigent nor possesses; for if this were the case, it would not be *the good itself*. (*Enn.*245)

Thus Intellect, as the "son" of "the good itself" is the same as the Johannine Logos, called alike by Blake and Swedenborg the Divine Body, and the Divine Human. In the Christian creed also it is said that it is "the Son" "by whom all things were made"; in Blake's terms "Jesus, the Imagination"; a concept which goes far to restore Christendom's garbled and distorted version of the teaching of the philosophers. "All things exist in the Human Imagination," which Blake calls "the Divine Image":

The Eternal Body of Man is The Imagination, that is,
God himself
The Divine Body } יֵ[ו]שׁוּ, Jesus: we are his Members.

(K.776)

The fact that Blake and Swedenborg, from whom he derives his Christian theology, have nothing to say (as Plotinus and Plato have) of that which is the "father" of Intellect or Imagination does nothing to lessen the truth or the value of what both these visionaries have to say about the "son"—the *mundus imaginalis*, even though this is in fact the one epithet Blake never does apply to his "Jesus the Imagination" who for him is, simply, "God."

Blake's criticism of Locke and of "natural religion" was that natural science, by relegating mind to the role of a mere passive recipient of stimuli from a mechanized nature, allows no active role for consciousness. He foresaw what has in fact taken place in our own century: that those who call "rocks the atomic origins of existence" must come to see life itself as mere mechanism, an elaborate system of conditioned reflexes which enable us to survive and perform complex operations; but what are the values—indeed what is the value—of a quantified humanity?

Those, by contrast, who take intellect, spirit, life under whatever name—God, Intellect, Imagination—as primary are concerned with values because these are inherent in the nature of mind as such. As quantity is the essence of scientific measurement, so love and wisdom, joy and sorrow, beauty, meaning, knowledge, the sense of the holy—these are the qualities of life, of the *sat-chit-ananda* which is the irreducible base of traditional cosmology. Science precludes by definition life's highest experience of value, the sense of the sacred: Blake's "Every thing that Lives is Holy!" is in scientific terms meaningless, an attribution of an imaginary quality to a natural process. But for life, regarded not as biochemistry but as a consciousness, the sense of the holy has the reality of an experience. Is it therefore reasonable to claim for a system which precludes all that belongs to human experience as such a truth and a reality greater than that which it precludes? It is not, as some who concern themselves with so-called "supernature"—telepathy and ESP and so on— would have us believe, that science has not "as yet" accounted for mental phenomena: such a transposition of experience into quantity is not in its nature possible. We may measure the brain-waves of the dreamer but that does not give us the dream.

Attempts have been made by natural scientists to restore the wholeness and unity of the *unus mundus* in their own terms; but because, as we have seen, this attempt implies the exclusion of those meanings and values proper to inner experience, and which alone call into play the whole gamut of our innate potentiality, these attempts must fail. The solutions offered by behavioural psychology and the like would be laughable were they not also tragic. But whereas the lesser cannot include the greater, the imaginative universe by no means excludes that of science, which becomes, as we have seen from Plotinus, the mirror of intellect itself. Quantity itself becomes what Blake calls "humanized." In its return to Imagination ". . . the all tremendous unfathomable Non-Ens/Of Death was seen in regenerations terrific." By "death" Blake means of course the "dead" universe of matter; his use of Plotinus's word "non-ens" indicates his source.

Thus the nature of the experience is itself determined by our view of it; and those who conceive themselves to be obsolescent parts in a material universe devoid of life forego the whole range of those unquantifiable values which constitute the universe of Imagination:

. . . What seems to Be, Is, To those to whom
It seems to Be, & is productive of the most dreadful
Consequences to those to whom it seems to Be, even of
Torments, Despair, Eternal Death. (K.663)

Blake in no way exaggerates the human consequences of those ideologies which reduce all to mechanistic terms: love to biochemistry, the moral sense to imprinted behaviour patterns, and so on, the higher being in every case reduced to the lower, a value to a material cause. The end is the spiritual *nihil* which those who subscribe to such ideologies avoid only by allowing themselves blind-spots, areas of illogicality or unawareness, pain-killers and palliatives, that way of life T. S. Eliot describes as "distracted from distraction" or lives of "quiet desperation." I do not wish to underrate the intellectual satisfaction many find in contemplating the ordered complexity of the physical universe; but history seems to bear out Blake's judgment that "the same dull round, even of a universe, would soon become a mill with complicated wheels" (K.97).

Plotinus, like Blake and like the Vedas, equates felicity—"bliss"—with "life" which has in all creatures, so he argues, "a certain end" in which, when accomplished, "nature makes a stop, as having accomplished the whole of their existence, and filled it with all that is wanting from beginning to end." (*Enn*.I.4.) The "seminal reasons" of animals and plants find their fulfilment within the terms of their simpler states of consciousness; but human beings, precluded by some ideology from experiencing whatever lies within our capacity can never experience the "felicity" or "bliss" proper to human existence. "More! More! is the cry of the mistaken soul" Blake writes; "less than All cannot satisfy Man" (K.97). It is science which asks for "more" while "All" is the capacity of mankind's boundless Imagination.

Ruskin, a man of the nineteenth century, wrote of the "pathetic fallacy," by which he meant the arbitrary attribution to inanimate objects or phenomena —storms, rainbows, the sun and so forth—of conscious feelings which are merely "projected" (as we would say) upon them by the experiencer. And doubtless a writer who does regard nature as an inanimate system and then proceeds to pretend that it is alive is being doubly dishonest and is likely to be a bad writer. But in the *unus mundus* of the Imagination "nature is one continued vision of the Imagination." Man and his universe cannot be separated. Cloud and mountain do really "talk" to the husbandman and the shepherd, for they communicate meaning.

I have entitled this paper "Towards a Living Universe" but have spoken rather of a departure from than an advance towards such a universe, once normal to humankind, and still envisaged and experienced by the Eastern theologies of Hinduism, Buddhism and Sufism, for all of which the primacy of life and of the *mundus imaginalis* over "matter" is self-evident. It is therefore not surprising that growing numbers in the West are turning towards those ancient treasuries of spiritual knowledge. But truth belongs neither to the past nor to the future, but is always itself. The nature of things does not change with our ideologies; Tradition does not reach us from some golden age, neither does it concern itself with any future Utopia; it teaches what is eternal in the human imagination; its relevance is at all times immediate.

Henry Corbin has performed for Iranian mysticism a service comparable to that of Thomas Taylor for the Platonic philosophers at the turn of the eighteenth century. He understood the relevance, the timeliness of the thought of the Mazdean and Sufi mystics in a West forced to reconsider the premises of naive materialism. I remember his describing Swedenborg as "the Buddha of the West"; and Swedenborg's radical calling in question of the premises of materialism justified the comparison. Corbin was a friend of C. G. Jung and a member of the Eranos circle; and it is in the context of the contemporary re-opening of the world of psyche (with a consequent re-examination of metaphysical premises) that Corbin has re-presented the Iranian mystical tradition relating to the *mundus imaginalis,* the world of *hurqalya.* Like Blake, like Swedenborg, like Plotinus, this tradition teaches that man's body is a mental body and his universe a mental universe. Like these also the Iranian tradition (whose roots also are of course in Platonism) understands the world to be informed with life.

Robert Fludd had long before quoted Alguzel (Lib i Chris) in his own *Mosaicall Philosophy,* in which is embodied the counter-tradition to Aristotelian naturalism:

> Some say that whatsoever filleth the Heaven, the Aire, the Earth, and wide Seas, is stirred up by a soul, through the vertue whereof all things in the world do live; and also that the world itself doth exist by it. But because there is not any bodily substance that is void of a soul, and that the world and every particular thereof doth consist of a body, therefore there is an intermediate spirit betwixt this soul and body, which they neither call a soul or a body, but a mean substance, participating of them both to reduce both extreames together into one. (II.I.IV)

Islamic angelology considers not only natural but also mental orders of beings; and indeed this view follows from the understanding that not matter but life is the substance and place of the cosmos; the world, as the Greeks also held, is "full of Gods." A quotation from Corbin's *Corps Spirituelle et Terre Céleste* summarizes the view I have attempted to indicate in the title of this paper:

> The encounter with the Earth not as a sum of physical facts but in the person of its Angel is essentially an event of the psyche; it cannot "take place" either in the realm of impersonal abstract concepts nor on the level of simple sense-experience. The earth must be perceived not by the senses at all but by means of a primordial Image; and because that Image has the aspect of a personal countenance it will present itself as a "symbolic correspondence" with the image proper to itself which the soul bears in its inmost ground. The Angel of the Earth is to be met with in that intermediate universe which is neither that of the essences considered by philosophy, nor the sense-data with which material science busies itself; a universe of imaginal Forms, the *mundus imaginalis* experienced as so many personal presences.

> If we are to grasp the meanings which constitute that universe in which Earth is figured, meditated, and encountered in the person of its Angel, we must understand that the questions to be answered concern not essences ("what is it?") but persons rather ("who is it?" or *"to whom* does it correspond?")—for example *who* is the Earth, *who* are the waters, plants, mountains, or *to whom* do they correspond? The answer to these questions renders present an imaginal Form, and that imaginal form invariably corresponds to some state of being. Therefore we must here understand the phenomenon of Earth as an angelophany or mental apparition of its Angel, within the totality of the fundamental Mazdean angelology, which imparts to its cosmology and its science alike a structure such that these constitute an answer to the question "who?"[4] (*CSTC* 32)

Corbin comments that these angelic and archangelic forms correspond much more closely to the *Diis Angeli* of Proclus than they do to the angelic "messengers" of the Bible and the Koran:

> On this point I am convinced that the Neoplatonists (whom it has long been fashionable to deride) were much nearer to the Iranian angelology and understood better the theurgic and demiurgic rôle of these celestial entities than do those philosophic improvizations to which histories of religion are prone, lacking as they do the requisite categories. We must follow a precise tradition if we wish to understand, for example, what the Angels of the Earth represent to Mazdean piety. (*CSTC* 33)

Such are Blake's "angels stationed in hawthorn bowers" or his lark that is "a mighty angel" or his sun which is "an Innumerable company of the Heavenly host crying 'Holy, Holy, Holy is the Lord God Almighty'" (K.617). To give

Blake the last word I quote from his great poem on the living universe of the Imagination *Milton*:

Thou seest the Constellations in the deep & wondrous Night:
They rise in order and continue their immortal courses
Upon the mountain & in vales with harp & heavenly song,
With flute & clarion, with cups & measures fill'd with foaming wine.
Glitt'ring the streams reflect the Vision of beatitude,
And the calm Ocean joys beneath & smooths his awful waves:
These are the Sons of Los, & these the Labourers of the Vintage.
Thou seest the gorgeous clothed Flies that dance & sport in summer
Upon the sunny brooks & meadows: every one the dance
Knows in its intricate mazes of delight artful to weave:
Each one to sound his instruments of music in the dance,
To touch each other & recede, to cross & change & return:
These are the Children of Los; thou seest the Trees on mountains,
The wind blows heavy, loud they thunder thro' the darksom sky,
Uttering prophecies & speaking instructive words to the sons
Of men: These are the Sons of Los: These the Visions of Eternity,
But we see as it were only the hem of their garments
When with our vegetable eyes we view these wondrous Visions. (K.511-12)

Footnotes

1   Page references to the Oxford Standard Edition of Blake, edited by Geoffrey Keynes, are indicated by K followed by the page number. See Geoffrey Keynes, editor, *Blake, Complete Writings* (London: Oxford University Press, 1966).

2   References to Swedenborg's writings are indicated by *DLW* followed by the paragraph number.

3   References to Plotinus' *Ennead* III are indicated by *Enn.* followed by the paragraph number.

4   References to Henry Corbin, *Corps Spirituelle et Terre Céleste* (Paris: 1979, 2nd ed.) are indicated in text by *CSTC* followed by the page number.

Education and the Living Image: Reflections on Imagery, Fantasy, and the Art of Recognition

PETER ABBS
University of Sussex

In this paper I want to open up a field of great importance to education, a field that has been greatly neglected not only in our own century but at least since the time of the Renaissance, namely, the place of the arts in education, and, more specifically, the place of the image in education. I believe that in Western civilization we have valued concept at the expense of image and that this has culminated in an extraordinary alienation of man from the sources of his own being. Inasmuch as our schools, colleges, and universities engender only an abstract and quantitative mode of understanding, the memorizing of inert knowledge crudely measured through a plethora of mechanical examinations, they are responsible for passing on some of the darkest pathologies in Western civilization. In this paper my intention is to restore the power of the living image, to confer on it a high epistemological status, to put it alongside concept as one of the key ways in which we symbolize and thus come to know our human world. Because of the broad nature of my argument I will not make many references to schools and classrooms, yet I am most anxious that these connections be made, for the implications of my argument for teaching and learning are many and of the utmost consequence. I hope to develop this side of the argument more fully at a later date but nevertheless I will take the bull by both its horns at the end of this paper and briefly indicate what I consider to be the most important connections between my defense of the image and a true understanding of the educational process.

"No more great dreamers; no more great dreams. . . . Is it really such a great dream to parcel up a building or a mountain?"[1] So the painter Josef Herman has remarked in response to the nullity of much contemporary art. The emphasis on the word "dream" is, I think, significant, because dreams are made up of the spontaneous imagery of the unconscious mind, imagery unmediated by intellect, imagery that, in Jungian language, we might say constitutes the symbolic equivalent of emotion and instinct. The artist is close to the dreamer in the sense that he is an active collaborator in the extraordinary process through which instinct and bodily function are converted into image and fantasy—and herein lies his great educational role.

For if there is a formal and reciprocal relationship between image and instinct, it follows that the development of an image can not only release powerful flows of instinctual energy but can also redirect that energy along new routes.

Let me condense part of the main argument of this paper into three propositions:

First proposition: that the image-making propensity lies at the very heart of our biological nature. Images, we might say, form the first language of humankind. We are taught how to speak, but we are not taught how to dream.

Second proposition: that through conscious collaboration with the unconscious image-making forces (images, in this context, being the symbolic and spontaneous expression of instinct and emotion), we can refine, broaden, and deepen our own natures.

Third proposition: that the arts—which are devoted to the development and re-creation of metaphors—have, therefore, a unique part to play in the evolution of individual consciousness.

James Hillman writes: "What we do within our imagination is of instinctual significance. . . . By working on imagination, we are taking part in nature in here."[2] Idolatry, then, was not perhaps such a perversion of human consciousness. Through a worship of images and ikons people were able to make immediate contact with their own instinctual energies, their own submerged identities, their own dreams. When we look at the metaphoric exuberance of an Indian temple or a Gothic cathedral and we consider our own bleak award-winning architecture, with its glass, steel, and concrete blocks, we cannot but be aware of the nature of our loss, for without a rich plurality of images and ikons we cannot easily locate those inward states of being that the symbols are outer representations of. An environment functional in design tends to make humanity functional in nature. Our inwardness, being unrepresented, becomes difficult to grasp. Paradoxically, in a sterile cement and glass environment we become less than we are. If a house is only "a machine for living in" (Corbusier) the danger is that the inhabitants of that house become automatons.

Yet why has metaphor become so neglected as a means of knowledge and understanding? And to what extent can the power of metaphor be demonstrated? These are the questions I want to meet in this paper. I want, first, to indicate some reasons for the inferior status of metaphor in Western civilization and then move to show, in a more positive manner, the actual power of fantasy *to cognize* human reality. I want to affirm the cognitive and creative power of fantasy, for I believe that if this is recognized the value of the arts will be immediately perceived, and perhaps even a way forward for contemporary art be discerned.

In *Reclamations* I attempted to show how certain negative features of Western philosophy lead to a general misunderstanding of art and metaphor.[3] Particularly since the Renaissance, philosophers both in the rationalist stream and in the empiricist stream have tended to reject the arts as superficial pursuits, as decorations and diversions rather than powerful and necessary sallies into the hinterland of consciousness. If, as with the rationalists, the world is known only through the categories of pure reason, then it must follow that all the other dramatis personae who compete for a hearing in the active theater of the psyche are judged as "subjective," "emotive," "fantastic," "illusory," "unreal," not to be heeded. Hegel saw an inevitable contradiction between the sensuous base of art and the conceptual base of art and in his Platonic maxim "the Rational is the Real: the Real is the Rational" implicitly judged art as less important and confirmed on a grand scale the bias of Western civilization. If, on the other hand, as with the empiricists, the world is known only through experimental science and if, therefore, the main purpose of philosophy is to cleanse the language so that it can be used more and more clinically and accurately by the scientist, then in this counter-tradition also it can be seen how a similar rejection of the inward life of feeling and imagination developed.

Locke, in his desire for a simple language of sign-object equivalence, attacked metaphor. Hume wanted to commit to the flames all those books devoid of deductive reasoning or experimental reasoning, for lacking such qualities they could only embody "sophistry and illusion." Bentham, we are told by John Stuart Mill, held that "words . . . were perverted from their proper office when they were employed in uttering anything but precise logical truth!"[4] James Mill, who was converted to utilitarianism by Bentham and who was responsible for creating one of the most inhuman educational programs ever devised, regarded all intense feelings as pathological phenomena. "For passionate emotions of all sorts, and of everything which has been said or written in exaltation of them, he professed the greatest contempt. He regarded them as a form of madness."[5] With such a tradition behind it, it is not surprising that in our own century logical positivism made the word "emotive" a term of abuse and has culminated in a fascination with "language games" with no interest in what lies beneath the game in the deep preconceptual sources of our being.

As I argued more fully in *Reclamations*, both traditions of philosophy, the rationalist and the empiricist, excluded from their analysis the immense and rich complexity of actual experience. While both in different ways undoubtedly contributed much to the advance of science and technology, they tended to thin out and reduce our understanding of the psyche. They neglected both ontology and aesthetics. In my previous analysis I put it this way:

> We are not pure minds nor are we bundles of sense perceptions. To insist that we are is to distort the nature of what is. Our experience is elusive,

many-stranded, ever-changing, problematic, unfolding; it includes often simultaneously, thought, feeling, imagination and sensation in one creative manifold. We are creative centres constructing a world we can inhabit out of a world which is terrifyingly dense and seemingly indifferent. Through the powers of symbolism, and particularly through the powers of language, we are able to grasp our own inner being and assert values, beliefs and aspirations. These are meaningful simply because they arise out of our existence in personal and endless attempts to clarify, to contain, to understand. The arts are valuable because they are an essential part of the existential quest for meaning and because they keep sharp and subtle the various tools necessary for the task.[6]

I wanted in the context of *Reclamations* to establish a more comprehensive sense of meaning that would include all the wealth of the creative arts, the wealth that derives from the contemplation of completed works of art as well as the wealth that comes through the process in which they are made. In this paper I am anxious to establish the power of the image in the psyche and to confer on it a high epistemological status, that is, that through the image we *cognize* experiential truths that, perhaps, could not be recognized through any other means. I also want to establish the idea defined at the opening of my paper, that through the creative elaboration of the psyche's spontaneous imagery we can become agents in our own development. It is important to stress that my arguments for imagery are not intended to deny the importance of experimental reasoning or deductive reasoning for in themselves they represent noble achievements; their form and procedures are an essential part of our heritage. The problem is that rational categories have claimed a monopoly in interpretation and have thus excluded other more primitive and existential modes of symbolic elaboration and exploration. There is, perhaps, bound to be a certain tension between imagistic and conceptual forms because the psyche would seem to yearn for unity, and always struggles to reduce the many to the one. The philosopher shouts "concept"; the painter, "image." Neither heeds the other. The truth would require us to embrace both—yet what can be painlessly expressed in an abstract proposition cannot be converted by incantation into an immediate experience. In life, we seem to work through one dominant mode or the other. We dream in images. We argue in concepts. We strive for a synthesis that invariably eludes us. The challenge is one of accepting in the same existence a plurality of competing forces, to allow both the images and the concepts, to let the bright metaphors and the abstract voices emerge, on their own terms, from the complex and many-faceted psyche. When the images and colors have been banned—and when it can be shown that these have a primary connection with instinct and feeling—then the historical moment has been reached for a defense of idolatry, but such a defense should entail an attack only on *the excesses of reason, the hubris of reason*, not on reason itself. The true dialectic consists in the tense holding of opposites, not in their exclusion or their integration, but in the hard-won recognition of their necessary differences. We cannot afford to choose between *mythos* and *logos*. We need both, however difficult the achievement, however contentious the outcome. To heighten the inward dialectical process, it is time, as I argued in "Education, Symbol and Myth," to reintroduce the suppressed images of the gods and goddesses, of Eros, Pan, Aphrodite, Prometheus, Hermes, Poseidon, Dionysius, Hephaistos, and many others; images that are as contemporary as they are archaic, for they lie at the very root of the soul, embodying permanent images of behavior and the enduring impulses of mankind.[7] It is time also *to look at* fantasies of the psyche and to see what, at critical moments, they reveal. Having, to some extent, established the former elsewhere, I wish here to turn to the latter, the revelatory potential of fantasy.

I will take for examples experiences recorded in autobiography and biography. The first involves the fantasy of a young boy in psychotherapy. The second is taken from the autobiography of Yvonne Stevenson and records the dramatic experience of a young woman trying to free herself from a highly repressive background. The third example comes from one of my students, who was working on a one-term course that included the task of writing an autobiography. The fourth and last example comes from the fascinating but not well-known autobiography of Edwin Muir. I have chosen these autobiographies for no better reason than that they were at hand when I began to explore this theme and that, I think, they admirably demonstrate my general thesis. There is no doubt in my mind that many other autobiographies would yield further examples of fantasy in its educative role (as well as its destructive role); indeed, the most unlikely autobiography in this area of fantasy, that of John Stuart Mill, demonstrates the fact that, at times, fantasy (serving the purpose of a creative unconscious) can see deeper and further than that sharpest of agents, the analytical intellect.

The first example, then, is taken from *Dibs: In Search of Self,* a detailed description of a young boy's psychotherapy. Dibs is the son of two distinguished parents; in the public account his father is presented as a renowned scientist, his mother a surgeon. The parents, while well adapted to the public world of professional work, are in no way adapted to their own emotional natures. They are bitterly disappointed with their child, alarmed by his irrationality, depressed by his seeming lack of talent. They are embarrassed, as it were, by his infantilism and even lock him away when their distinguished guests visit them. Although his mother succeeds in teaching him to read at the age of two, he is regarded as stupid, clumsy, and maladjusted. At five, although attending a conventional school, Dibs is unable to relate to other children and recoils from his teachers. It is at this point that his psychotherapy begins. A large part of his therapy, a therapy that would seem to have been remarkably successful, consists of playing (for one hour a week under the guidance of Virginia Axline, who is both the psychotherapist and the author of the book) at a sand pit and with a doll's house. In one of the crucial sessions he works out, through the elaboration of fantasy in play, the true nature of his feelings. His fantasy provides a concise image of his own state and includes within it a creative answer. It is an unsophisticated example of the revelatory power of imagery that I am now attempting to define. To understand its nature, we will need to quote a lengthy section from the book.

Dibs has emptied the doll's house of its four dolls, the mother doll, the sister doll, the father doll (who has gone to buy a microscope for his son) and the boy doll (who has gone out "because he doesn't like the locked doors"). The fantasy continues with the return of the father doll:

Dibs got up and paced the room glancing at me from time to time. Then he knelt down beside the house again and picked up the father doll. "He called and called to the boy and the boy came running in." Dibs brought the boy doll back beside the father. "But the boy ran in so fast he bumped into the table and upset the lamp. The father cried out that the boy was stupid. A stupid, silly, careless boy! 'Why did you do that?' he demanded, but the boy wouldn't answer him. The father was very angry and told the boy to go to his room. He said he was a stupid, silly child and he was ashamed of him."

Dibs was tensed up, immersed in this scene he was playing out. He looked up at me and must have felt that I was as deeply in the experience as he was. "The boy slipped out of the house and hid," Dibs whispered. "The father didn't notice what happened. Then . . ." He got up and hurried across the room after the mother doll and brought her back to the house. "The mother was finished with her park visit and so she came back. The father was still very angry and he told the mother what the stupid boy had done. And the mother said 'Oh dear! Oh dear! What is the matter with him?' Then all of a sudden a boy giant came along. He was so big nobody could ever hurt him." Dibs stood up. "This giant boy saw the mother and father in the house and he heard what angry things they said. So he decided to teach them a lesson. He went all around the house and he locked every window and every door so they could not get out. They were both locked in."

He looked up at me. His face was pale and grim. "You see what is happening?" he said.

"Yes. I see what is happening. The father and mother are locked in the house by the giant boy."

"Then the father says he is going to smoke his pipe and he gets some matches and he strikes a match and drops it on the floor and the room catches on fire. The house is on fire! The house is on fire! And they cannot get out. They are locked in the house and the fire is burning faster and faster. The little boy sees them in the house where they are locked in and burning and he says 'Let them burn! Let them burn!'" Dibs made quick darting snatches at the mother and father doll as though he would save them, but he drew back and shielded his face as though the fire he imagined was very real and burning him as he attempted to save the father and mother.

"They scream and cry and beat on the door. They want to get out. But the house is burning and they are locked in and they can't get out. They scream and cry for help."

Dibs clasped his hands together and tears streamed down his face. "I weep! I weep!" he cried to me. "Because of this I weep!"

"Do you weep because the mother and father are locked in the house and can't get out and the house is burning?" I asked.

"Oh no!" Dibs replied. A sob caught his voice and broke it. He stumbled across the room to me and flung his arms around my neck while he wept bitter tears.

"I weep because I feel again the hurt of doors closed and locked against me," he sobbed. I put my arm around him.

"You are feeling again the way you used to feel when you were so alone?" I said.

Dibs glanced back at the doll's house. He brushed away his tears and stood there breathing heavily. "The boy will save them," he said. He went to the boy doll and took him to the house. "I'll save you! I'll save you!" he cried. "I'll unlock the doors and let you out. And so the little boy unlocked the doors and put the fire out and his father and mother were safe."

He came back to me and touched my hand. He smiled wanly. "I saved them," he said, "I didn't let them get all burned up and hurt."

"You helped them. You saved them," I said.

Dibs sat down at the table, staring straight ahead. "They used to lock me in my room," he said. "They don't do it any more, but they used to."

"They did? But not any more?"

"Not any more," Dibs said, and a trembling sigh escaped him. "Papa really did give me a microscope and I have lots of fun with it." He got up from the table and went across the playroom to the spot where he had put the sister doll. He carried her back to the doll's house and put all four dolls in chairs in the living room.[8]

The metaphor speaks eloquently enough; it enacts faithfully the boy's own emotion, his feelings of anger and bitterness, as well as his ambivalent desires for revenge and reconciliation. Like a dream it would seem to issue spontaneously from some creative integrating force at the center of the child. Simultaneously it reveals and partially heals. At the end of the hour Dibs even considers relinquishing his comforter, the baby bottle he still needs for emotional sustenance. He said:

"I'm a big boy now. I don't need the baby bottle."

"You don't need the baby bottle any more?" I commented.

Dibs grinned. "Unless I sometimes want to be a baby again," he said. "However I feel. However I feel, I will be."

He spread wide his arms in an expansive gesture. "Cock-a-doodle-do," he crowed. "Cock-a-doodle-do!"

He was relaxed and happy now. When he left the playroom he seemed to leave behind him the sorrowful feelings he had uprooted there.[9]

The fantasy also anticipates the future sequence of events, for Dibs, by insisting on his own feelings and his own core of identity, eventually succeeds in drawing his parents into a recognition not only of him, a six-year-old child, but also the suppressed and deprived nature of their own fantasy and feeling experiences. His search for self compels them to enter into a relationship where intellect and achievement are not the only criteria for being. "I saved them," he said, "I didn't let them get all burned up and hurt." In the concluding act of the fantasy Dibs is responsible for returning all four characters, mother, father, sister, and himself, to "the living room." In a sense this is what he was able to do as a result of the fantasy in his actual life. Fantasy can thus anticipate and prepare for "reality."

The second example of thinking through imagery is taken from Yvonne Stevenson's autobiography, *Hot-House Plant*. It is a dramatic example. It does not represent the vague if continuous image-making energies of the psyche; rather it shows this natural process brought to a pitch of intensity and to a level of experience one might characterize as visionary. The vision manifests to the psyche all that has been previously ignored, suppressed, undervalued, and negated. But in its very "abnormality" it points to an innate propensity of the mind to create images charged with inner meaning and the power to heal. Its abnormality points to a normal process of the psyche. Once again, it will be necessary to quote at some length. And we will find, as with the case of Dibs, that the process is largely self-explanatory. All I am urging is that we should recognize this distinct manifestation of the psyche for what it is: a possible way of knowing, a possible mode of integrating, and, therefore, a possible means of education.

The visionary experience comes toward the end of the autobiography as, in many ways, the final act of clarification forcing the author to see the limitations imposed by her restricted childhood (the daughter of a vicar, the pupil of two private single-sex church schools) and to recognize dimensions of human experience other than that of self-sacrificial service and self-immolation. Her whole personality had, in truth, contracted to that of a fierce Puritan conscience. "I had always" she writes, "ignored the little voice 'I want.'" This process of self-recognition had already begun at the age of nineteen when she met another student at college who persuaded her to consider, among other things, "the unity of opposites." But intellectual discussion, while opening up, cannot resolve the complex dilemmas of a life divided between the identity that has evolved to meet the past and an identity that has not found itself and yet longs to be itself. Propositions tend to work somewhat outside the bewildering currents of contradictory feeling that flow through a person brought up in one philosophy of abnegation and desirous of another philosophy, more affirmative, more inclusive of self. Such propositions need complementing by a stronger and deeper experience involving body, feeling, and imagination. Such an experience Yvonne Stevenson undergoes and describes in her autobiography.

The visionary passage comes in the autobiographical narrative just after Yvonne Stevenson has related how she had failed miserably her intermediate examinations, examinations in subjects she had never actively chosen but had passively submitted to. She is returning from a walk through the rose gardens, a walk she has made at her mother's suggestions (the "good" compliant girl again?). During this walk she has found herself loathing the formal perfectionism of the rose garden and also—the outer landscape and the inner mirroring each other—the perfectionism of her own personality:

And then suddenly it all came to me. A great inner voice boomed at me. "You have gone wrong TRYING TO BE GOOD and thus breaking the laws of nature."

The violence of this thought was so great that my legs gave way, and I found myself scrabbling on the ground.

"Pretend you have lost something," I ordered myself, and I began feverishly turning over the grass.

"No. People will offer to help. And you look quite mad. Get away from here. Get back to your own room." I got up and began running.

"Not so fast. You look quite mad. Everybody will stare."

Grappling with my self-composure, I was suddenly aware that in the sky there was a vision for me to look at, as soon as I could concentrate on it—a vision of my imagination, nevertheless a new "picture" to study. For picture it was. There seemed to be a gap in the sky, through which I could see dark rumbling clouds pierced by vivid blues and purples. These lowering colours became concentrated into a large, black mass, situated slightly to the right. This I knew was "God," the real God behind everything—Fate—for across it, in white shining letters, was written "The Laws of Nature." It was Nature, then. This black, seething mass had the shape of an octopus, and one wavy limb was stretched out sideways into the left of the picture. Seated on this black "paw" of the monster was the Christian Trinity, tiny, shining figures of God the Father, Jesus Christ and the Holy Ghost. With a kind of sneering leer, the black monster crumpled up his paw and they were gone. Then he turned his expression to me, though he had no face, and from behind the white lettering came a voice saying: "I know of no labels. What I have made I have made. Courage and cowardice, love and jealousy. Cruelty. What you call Good and what you call Bad. To me everything has its place in my scheme. It is sin to break my laws. You have broken the laws of nature. I did not create you to be good. I CREATED YOU AS I CREATED YOU."[10]

In a state of agitation, compulsively repeating to herself as she walks "A perfect fool . . . a perfect fool . . . a perfect fool," she returns quickly to the solitude of her own college room where the second act of the inward drama begins:

As soon as I was alone forces greater than myself took control of me. I found myself with my hands raised slightly above my head, my eyes closed; and I was squirming my body, shoulders and head sideways as if I were trying to lower myself through a narrow hole. As I "fell free" (though still standing), I opened my eyes and "saw" the inner flank of a great, black hairy leg. Gasping with surprise, I twisted my head up and "saw," towering over me, the legs apart, a huge gorilla-like monster, with a round face and gentle, benign expression. I recognized at once what it represented to me—the evolutionary scale—the laws of nature—man's predecessor, the hairy ape. I knew then that I had just fallen from between its legs.

"I have been born again!" I whispered aloud. "I am part of nature now. A human animal. That means I must join myself up to my body. There must be no longer a division of the neck." I stepped onto the hearthrug, turned round with my back to the fire, and stood very straight.

"Yes, that's it. I will entrust myself to the laws of nature, since I'm part of nature. And the laws of nature will guide me through my body; they will send me their messages, up through my neck to my head, and I will no longer use my head alone—my reason—and neglect the feelings in my body."[11]

At this point she pauses, savoring, she writes, "this new sensation which was upon me," this feeling of being "all of one piece," united. Then, without any sense of choice but rather of submitting to a drama deeper than her highly developed will power, she is drawn into the third and last act:

I paused, and for a moment savored this new sensation that was upon me— that of being joined up at the neck so that I was all of one piece. Suddenly I felt strange forces, like little wires, pulling me forwards and downwards. In a loud voice I said: "I know what I have to do." A deep, black pit had appeared before me, and these little wiry forces were urging me to step into it. Once more the blackness represented the laws of nature, my new allegiance.

With a kind of joy I said to myself: "I shall dare to. And since I am a part of nature it's bound to be all right." I stepped into the air and into the pit. At that I began to have the sensation of slowly falling—down a lighted tunnel.

"I am like Alice in Wonderland," I thought, and went on floating down until I suddenly landed in a heap of dry twigs and leaves.

"Now what do I do? Alice had a white rabbit to guide her!" And then I remembered my new guide. What did my *body* want to do? It was straining forward, wanting to run—for a long, straight corridor had suddenly appeared before me.

"I must run and run," I said to myself, and began running along at great speed. And there, at the end of the corridor, no bigger than a tiny speck, was an image of my mother, kneeling down on one knee, with her arms outstretched, shouting to me, "I love you *whatever* you're like, however naughty you are. Whether you're good or naughty I love you just as much." I began changing into a smaller and smaller little girl until I was of a size to fit her kneeling height, and was approaching her to within about twenty yards, when suddenly she disappeared and was replaced by a new figure— that of myself at the age of fourteen, standing to one side and gazing with horror at that group of Sixth Formers in my first boarding school. The head girl in the centre of the group was saying angrily, "What she wants is a thorough squashing. To be treated like a new girl. . . ." The moment when something inside me had snapped as if breaking apart.

"It is *myself*, it is *myself*, that I must make friends with!" I cried aloud, and rushed up to that fourteen-year old girl. I turned her round to face me and clasped her in my arms, as if I were the mother. Still crying, "It is myself, it is myself!" I staggered over to the bed and sat down, clutching my own stomach as if clutching myself to myself. I then sat gasping for breath, panting, wet with sweat, wet from head to foot.[12]

The self-realization is immediate, physical, emotional, and conceptual, all inextricably bound and flowing together through one single experience. As she rocks to and fro, with her eyes half-closed, she accuses herself of betrayal. "Six years! Six years ago I abandoned you. Abandoned my own feelings." Slowly the outer world, which has been totally eclipsed by the power of her own fantasy, acting as if "out there," projected on the world's face, slowly the outer world returns, almost with a comparable revelatory force because it is a new world that is witnessed.

Then I became aware of the sound of tennis being played in the court below my window. I opened my eyes fully and looked across the room. I had to jam the side of my hand into my mouth to stop myself from screaming. The room looked different! It was three-dimensional and in colour! Before it had always appeared more flat and in a kind of black and grey way. The colours were there, of course, and yet they had *not* been there, they had not intruded right into my consciousness.[13]

I trust I have quoted enough from *Hot-House Plant* to give the reader a sufficient grasp of Yvonne Stevenson's experience. For a full understanding, of course, the reader must turn to the autobiography itself. I do not want to labor here the manifest/latent content of the dramatic fantasy; I want, rather, to make a number of conceptual points about the actual nature of the fantasy and its educative power.

First, we can see that images represent a preconceptual form of knowing. They possess meaning, a meaning that, in Yvonne Stevenson's case, is very quickly made conceptually apparent: "In white shining letters was written 'The Laws of Nature.'"

Second, we can see that fantasy tends to project itself from what we might call "inner space" to "outer space." The images come from out of the sky. The deep black pit is there before her. What is within is experienced as being out there (it is clearly a similar process to that by which mythic images are projected across the face of the universe).

Third, the images, at least at critical moments (such as those of Dibs and Yvonne Stevenson) are not only seen but are actively undergone. The whole body has to encounter them.

Fourth, the kind of knowledge locked within the dramatic sequence of the imagery is existential in character, that is, it reveals a personal truth, not a scientific truth. The gorilla god is not to be given ontological status but psychological meaning for it pertains, first and foremost, to the unique condition of Yvonne Stevenson. Another individual might well need to encounter a numinous god. The truth of imagery is personal in nature, but nonetheless real for that.

Fifth, imagery, being primarily the language of feeling and all those meanings that are accessible only through feeling, is often, in its spontaneous and strange eruptions, serving some deeper purpose, that of selfhood: a theme to which I will return briefly at the end of this paper.

I want now to take two examples that may seem more literary, but in being "literary" it is hoped they will show how close the activity of artistic making invariably is to the indigenous processes of the human mind. From the perspective of this article, art is the formal elaboration and refinement of all the elusive, dramatic, ever-changing feeling, mood, and phantasmagoria thrown up by the conscious, semiconscious, and unconscious psyche. The arts provide the ritualized forms of feeling, make visible the rhythms of breath and blood, hold up for contemplation the ceaseless imagery of the active imagination; they return us to ourselves not, in essence, changed, but more coherent, more complete, at a higher level of integration. It is for this reason that Suzanne Langer asking the questions "Who knows what feeling is like? Who has a naive but intimate and expert knowledge of feeling?" answered with the following reply:

Above all, probably, the people who make its image—artists, whose entire work is the making of forms which express the nature of feeling. Feeling is like the dynamic and rhythmic structures created by artists: artistic form is always the form of felt life, whether of impressions, emotion, overt action, thought, dream or even obscure organic process rising to a high level and going into the psychical phase, perhaps acutely, perhaps barely and vaguely.[14]

In some of my courses at the University of Sussex I ask my students to write an autobiography. I have written about the importance of such work elsewhere.[15] It must suffice to say here that most students tackle such work in the traditional linear narrative, working chronologically from one significant event to the next. Recently, however, one of the students, while ultimately succumbing to the power of the traditional form, began to see beyond it, began to see a way of representing experience other than through the category of historical time. She discovered metaphor. In a letter accompanying her lengthy autobiography, Jacqueline Langlois wrote: "Poetry is perhaps the most natural expression for autobiography." She also attempted an analysis of the strengths and weaknesses of her own writing:

I would like to say a little about how I tried to write, and the different frameworks that entered and started warring with one another.

The first piece was the introductory "how can I tell you best who I am?" p. 2, which took me a long time, but which I liked. But I wrote it *before* the work was done. It was anticipatory and what happened was that I felt by page 34, when it was getting unspeakably dull, that the following pages just did not live up to its promise. I was all there on p. 2. By p. 4, looking back I can see that I was just manufacturing, not spinning any more. Maybe this is what disturbs me most. My heart is now pulsating from the work, but the work itself lacks a lot of heart, except in patches. Ugh! The whole thing has tired me out!

Writing this introduction was perhaps the best thing. The intensity of my feelings drove my language into metaphor. It was very exciting because the metaphors just took over and I found myself in a different plane of consciousness.

The "personas" passage that "ghosts" starts off with immediately wanted to turn itself into poetry and go down into it's own realm instead of moving along into the autobiography elle-même."[16]

"The intensity of my feelings drove my language into metaphor." The passage "immediately wanted to turn itself into poetry and go down into its own realm." Here we find again intense feeling manifesting itself not as recall but as metaphor, as a new series of relationships and connections illuminating self and the world in which it lives. As we shall see, in the sequence in which the writer felt "all there," the self has become part of a myth, the autobiography part of a universal biography.

Here are pages 2 and 3 of the autobiography, ending where the subsequent descent into linear rather than mythic time becomes apparent.

How can I tell you best who I am? Each my word an inkling for your portrait. I will give you my soul if you don't lose it. A beautiful piece of work this, but some of the silken threads may have been stolen, I cannot tell.

The real piece of work is spun from my own silk and sometimes it shines with God's own colours, but much is soiled and torn I can't give you this one—it is not in my hands to give. I can only get it when I die. Roll on delivery day!

Sometimes I search for days through the archives, but I can't tell which is the right document. "Come on!" I shout, "give me back what is mine!" Miritrovo nel una selva selvaggia[17] and I can't get out!" The guru at the door says that all the documents used to be filed in the Ancient of Days, but when God was born, the angels around him started to whisper and all the papers blew away. So, now, no-one can find their documents, unless they are very clever.

"That's no good to me! I'm not clever and if I don't get a light for this damn pestilence of vapours[18] soon I am going to get asthma! I mean it!"

To start the weaving of this tapestry, I had first to throw a pebble into a pond. This pebble was an immaculate conception—just the right weight and completely round. I dropped it neatly into the water. But when it touched the water's surface it grew into a huge ragged boulder and waves drove higher than my boat and I felt sick because the horizon had gone.

When the storm had abated I felt much better and the sea was calm, although it is always dangerous.

I was able to consult the ship's log:
"December 4th 1979 A.D. Vessel launched 4th August 1957. Vessel still intact, although she proved frail in certain adverse circumstances and nearly went down in a bad storm at the beginning of the year, because I hadn't got all the tools to repair the bodywork that had slowly been eroding over the years, particularly the recent years. Luckily, I was able to bring her into port and she was given a major overhaul. She was not seaworthy for six months afterwards . . ."

. . . no I wasn't! At least in this I know what it is to be adult. I know what it is to be suicidal.

When I was little, I was safe. Now I am dangerous.

I am still so uncertain why I cracked up and so aware of what feel like fundamental weaknesses.[19]

At this point the narrative begins to unpack the metaphor and lay it out. The autobiography becomes explanatory, rational. The writing enters the linear mode: *A* then *B* then *C* then *D*. Of course, there is an important place for such discursive proceedings, but, in this context, the writer experienced the form as artificial, as distorting and false. It led to what she described in her own letters as "a listless chronology," a documentary recording that by rendering the surface of experience somehow missed its essence, giving the hard husk but not the inner fruit. How, then, is it that the metaphoric and the poetic have a meaningfulness not open to faithful factual chronology? Is it that the individual detail becomes absorbed into a holding archetype? The ordinary, the trivial, the peculiar is lifted up and, without being negated, raised onto the high level of symbolic adventure. What might otherwise have been merely odd now becomes representative and suffering is placed in a comprehensive pattern that both contains and supports it. The fantasy that can spontaneously draw on the rich deposits of the inherited culture—on Hamlet and on Dante, for example—is a fantasy that not only heals the wounds of the individual but also brings comfort to that same individual by making the person feel a member of that very culture and, through that culture, a member of the human race. Is it this insight that lies quietly below the suggestion that poetry is the most natural expression for autobiography?

The last example I want to take is from the poet Edwin Muir's autobiography. In this undervalued account of his own development as a person and as a poet, Edwin Muir describes the genesis of one of his poems. He recalls how one day at the age of seven he ran away from Freddie Sinclair, who threatened to fight him. He ran with an excessive sense of fear ("What I was so afraid of I did not know; it was not Freddie, but something else; yet I could no more have turned and faced him than I could have stopped the sun revolving").[20] And mingled with the fear was a sense of shame. He felt that everyone in the village could see his cowardice and his panic: an event and an apprehension common enough, and yet, as Edwin Muir points out, it took him thirty years to objectify the experience through mythic imagery and in this manner to possess it. Edwin Muir's commentary here is both fascinating in its own right and highly pertinent to our inquiry. He writes:

> I got rid of that terror almost thirty years later in a poem describing Achilles chasing Hector round Troy, in which I pictured Hector returning after his death to run the deadly race over again. In the poem I imagined Hector as noticing with intense, dreamlike precision certain little things, not the huge simplified things which my conscious memory tells me I noticed in my own flight. The story is put in Hector's mouth:

> The grasses puff a little dust
> Where my footsteps fall,
> I cast a shadow as I pass
> The little wayside wall.

> The strip of grass on either hand
> Sparkles in the light,

I only see that little space
To the left and to the right

And in that space our shadows run
His shadow there and mine
The little knolls, the tossing weeds,
The grasses frail and fine.

That is how the image came to me, quite spontaneously: I wrote the poem down, almost complete, at one sitting. But I have wondered since whether the intense concentration on little things, seen for a moment as the fugitive fled past them, may not be a deeper memory of that day preserved in a part of the mind which I cannot tap for ordinary purposes. In any case the poem cleared my conscience. I saw that my shame was a fantastically elongated shadow of a childish moment, imperfectly remembered; an untapped part of my mind supplied what my conscious recollection left out, and I could at last see the incident whole by seeing it as happening, on a great and tragic scale, to someone else. After I had written the poem the flight itself was changed, and with that my feelings towards it.[21]

In brief, the original experience of panic and flight is transformed by being imaginatively comprehended through an analogous mythic experience. As the imagery crystallizes so the original feelings are changed. "I could at last see the incident whole by seeing it as happening, on a great and tragic scale, to someone else." Through the healing power of metaphor the experience has been truly integrated and transcended. Furthermore, we must note, as with Dibs and Yvonne Stevenson, the imagery is given; it spontaneously arises as a completed gestalt to the surface of consciousness.

Edwin Muir, reflecting further on the experience, continues:

I think there must be a mind within our minds which cannot rest until it has worked out, even against our conscious will, the unresolved questions of our past; it brings up these questions when our will is least watchful, in sleep or in moments of intense contemplation. My feeling about the Achilles and Hector poem is not of a suppression suddenly removed, but rather of something which had worked itself out. Such events happen again and again in everyone's life; they may happen in dreams; they always happen unexpectedly, surprising us if we are conscious of them at the time. It is an experience as definite as conviction of sin; it is like a warning from a part of us which we have ignored, and at the same time like an answer to a question which we had not asked, or an unsolicited act of help where no help was known to be. These solutions of the past projected into the present, deliberately announced as if they were a sibylline declaration that life has a meaning, impress me more deeply than any other kind of experience with the conviction that life does have a meaning quite apart from the thousand meanings which the conscious mind attributes to it: an unexpected and yet incontestable meaning which runs in the teeth of ordinary experience, perfectly coherent, yet depending on a different system of connected relations from that by which we consciously live.[22]

The experience points to a creative coordinating energy with its own center largely beyond the manipulation of the will and often out of the reach of ego-consciousness, that consciousness which has developed in us to meet what we imagine to be the expectations of those who surround us. In ego-consciousness our life exists only in the imagined consciousness of the respected other and, beyond that, in the imagined collectivity of norms, standards, and tacit assumptions. In poetic consciousness, where the energy of dream and metaphor resides, lies the hidden self that longs to exist on terms innate to its own condition. We will turn soon to consider the self that fantasy serves (or rather can serve—for some fantasies may destroy the self and others be little more than escape fantasies fed into the psyche by the manipulative media).

In our examples we have moved from fantasy to poetry, but then, as the last two passages demonstrate, one moves imperceptively into the other. Emotion, we might say, is the condition for fantasy and fantasy the condition for most of the arts. If Dibs had possessed the technical skill, he could have developed his archetypal fantasy of anger turning into vengeance and vengeance turning into the desire for reconciliation into a powerful play. Indeed, as the use of the words in ordinary language reveals, the play of the child and the play of the dramatist and the play of mind over experience share many characteristic qualities. And Edwin Muir's account of the genesis of his Achilles and Hector ballad reveals that the poetic process and the fantasy process may often be one and the same. The arts do not lie on the far side of life, are not simply matters of either genius or skill; rather, they reside at the center of ordinary existence, a formal elaboration of deep processes at work in every one. The necessity of art is the necessity of experience or, more precisely, the necessity of the self seeking for its self.

There is one last point to be made about metaphor. It cannot be converted into the language of discursive symbolism and retain its transforming energy. Just as water is not H_2O but so much more, so the ikon on the wall is not "a symbolic figure" for "religious devotion"; so the Achilles and Hector fantasy is not "a depiction" of "two archetypal heroes." We cannot translate the concrete into the abstract without loss of emotion and inwardness. To conceptually understand a myth is quite different from the experience of living through the same myth. Metaphor is not a clumsy or archaic or precious way of stating a truth that could be expressed more simply through a series of propositions. Metaphor is, on the contrary, a unique and enduring and irreplaceable way of embodying the truths of our inward lives. I hope the examples I have given go some way toward establishing this claim.

I have contended that fantasy erupting from the unconscious may, in its more positive manifestations, be serving the needs of the true self. "It is myself, it is myself, that I must make friends with" concludes Yvonne Stevenson after being dramatically overwhelmed by the images that burst into her guarded consciousness first in the rose garden and then in her room. Also, this recognition of self brings with it a recognition of the suppressed elements; in this case, a new valuation of the body, the senses, and the emotions. "Six years ago I abandoned you. Abandoned my own feelings": The lost is restored to its true place in the hierarchy of being and, even more strangely, the restoration of the suppressed leads to a sudden awareness of the three-dimensionality of the universe and of its extraordinary color. The fantasy has inaugurated a new and enhanced sense of identity and, at the same time, a heightened consciousness of the surrounding world. When I use the word identity to describe the self I do not mean ego: I mean rather that through such an experience as Yvonne Stevenson describes the brittle, defensive, consciously cultivated ego is broken open and that above its shattered remains a deeper and truer configuration of self emerges. Identity refers to authenticity of self—and it must be quite clear from the examples I have given that the unconscious may well be working for identity more than our daily defensive consciousness, which labors to protect rather than to reveal, to manipulate rather than to be. This is what I take Edwin Muir to mean when in the last passage quoted from his autobiography he declares that life has a meaning quite independent of the conscious meanings claimed for it, a meaning "which runs in the teeth of ordinary experience, perfectly coherent, yet depending on a different system of connected relations from that by which we consciously live." It is not a question of being totally passive before the unconscious, but rather of recognizing creative energies in the psyche that are prior to rational conceptualization and of being willing to submit (though not uncritically) to shaping forces operating outside of our analytical reason and our controlling willpower.

I realize that many of the concepts I am putting forward, while far from new, are strangely foreign to most current psychology, sociology, and philosophy. We would seem to live in an age that is predisposed to deny an ontology of self. In common "educated" parlance, human beings are conceived not in terms of authentic existence and struggling identity but more in terms of socially defined and continually changing possibilities. Thus we talk about people's "playing different games," of playing "different roles," adopting "strategies," and "negotiating" reality. The implication is that there is nothing inward, nothing substantial, no permanent self with its own moral imperatives: only a socially constructed game. We are given no sense of an author with authority within; no sense of an identity that is something more than the outcome of innumerable external pressures, whether biological or social.

We find therefore no reference to inwardness or authentic being. The dominant assumptions make either society or biology primary and the individual secondary and derivative. Even before current theories begin to build their edifices they have excluded from their foundations the possibility of intrinsic identity, of an I that at least embryonically is the integrating center of its world. Furthermore the mechanical language generally employed ensures that such a possibility will be permanently excluded. Such theories rob existence of any sense, conceptual or intuitive, of inherent meaning. We are left with the feeling that there is nothing deeper, there is nothing other, there is nothing further. When one mask is taken off there is only a nightmare blankness until the next mask is (quickly) inserted into place. It is no more than a game that is being played out, the rules ultimately arbitrary and secured only by those with the greatest willpower, by those determined "to survive" (another symptomatic word in current vogue).

It is not a question of denying "role play," "survival strategies," or "language games"—they are reasonably accurate descriptive labels for much human behavior, particularly in competitive and materialistic civilizations like our own. It is rather a matter of making a more probing inquiry into human existence. We need to ask the question: Is there a formative principle in the psyche transcending these social pressures and demanding from us a kind of submission? Is there a force that while not synonymous with instinct is yet deeper than ego, a force for individuation? Is there an enduring face behind the sequence of masks? Is there a self beneath the daily adapted self that longs to be and whose language comes to us primarily through image, fantasy, and dreams?

In the context of this paper these questions are not as open as they sound. They are not purely speculative. At an intellectual level we may well require the hypothesis of an innate identity to make adequate sense of human behavior, but at an existential level the hypothesis has to give way to something more elusive, more difficult, more compelling, a personal listening and a personal heeding to what lies below, a creative act of exquisite attention and tentative interpretation working through hunches, intuitive "feel," and occasional moments of revelation. And it is here, in this quest for being, that the language of metaphor comes into its own.

I would like to conclude by briefly stating some of the implications of my argument for education.

In expanding our concept of knowing to include such knowing as can be inwardly acquired through metaphor we dramatically enlarge our view of the curriculum. In particular (although, of course, image is not confined to the arts) we draw the arts into the center of the curriculum. The arts represent a fundamental way of knowing and assimilating experience and therefore must form an essential part of any core curriculum.

Furthermore, our understanding of the arts in education changes. Our emphasis does not fall on "knowledge about" or "history of" but more on the active process of making in relationship to an inward unfolding. The arts are seen as the living symbolic process through which subjectivity is given form, meaning, and coherence. This is not to dismiss cultural heritage or technical "know-how" but to see these elements as serving a deeper process, the movement that in this paper, following Carl Jung, we have called individuation. This process lies at the very heart of the arts and is another way of defining one of the true and enduring ends of education.

At the same time as we emphasize image and the high value of the arts, we emphasize also the place of emotion in understanding. Indeed, *within emotion itself there lies a cognitive dimension*. To exclude emotion from the curriculum is therefore to exclude vital forms of knowing, is to establish an education that stands against the full range of understanding, is to institute a form of schooling that narrows rather than expands the consciousness of the individual. The nature of our argument compels us to contemplate the positive potentialities of emotion within education. We can no longer rest content with an education that would exclude, deny, or merely repress the instinctive and affective domain.

In the arts, the aim of good teaching becomes that of establishing a disinterested space where the student can feel free to symbolize—and thus explore, evaluate, refine, integrate—his own experience. This requires the most delicate qualities in the teacher: an ability to read his environment (as one reads a complex sonnet), an ability to enter the students' space when it is required and to withdraw when it is superfluous or inhibiting, an ability to relate the expression of the individual to the best in the culture—and to do this in the most natural and infectious manner, an ability to create the context of trust and nurture for all his students, an ability, above all, *to be* in his own right and thus to be an image of authentic being for all those in his charge. It will be remembered that it was such an image of being that Socrates represented for his student Alcibiades. The teacher himself embodies what it is to create, to think, to contemplate. In and through his being he represents education as a passion for meaning and a way of relating to the entire universe. For his students—for better and for worse—the teacher is ineluctably an image of what it means to be.

There is no escape from the existential dimension in teaching. The teacher must be a learner and explorer in his own right if he is to be a teacher of others. This truth has important repercussions for our sterile teacher-training programs. Recently I sent an open letter to my English students training to become teachers, in which I said:

I want you to give yourself to the work in hand without practical worries about pedagogy. *I want you to be selfish.* I want you to put to yourself the question "Well, what can I get out of this *for me?*" and not be ashamed. You see this is not irresponsible. Before you can teach well, you must be a self-sustaining individual with your own alert life, quite independent of the classroom. I am convinced that creative teachers are creative because they have kept in touch with their own hidden sources of emotional energy. If you are to remain an alert teacher, you must not live only for the class;

otherwise the level of your consciousness will drop to that of the class and you will then become a companion rather than a guide. You must continue to be an intellectual adventurer, quick to pitch tent on the fluctuating boundaries of the known. You must continue to develop and refine your own talent. And all this, as a *precondition for teaching*.[23]

We can only teach out of our own being—there is nowhere else to teach from. And yet, strangely, we would wish to smother this truth and take refuge in all sorts of technological pseudo answers. In our alienation we turn to computers, teaching machines, mechanical aids, and in doing so pervert the educational process; education in our society thus becomes an instrument destroying those very qualities it should seek to nurture.

I would like to conclude by making three further points. First, I have concentrated on the arts in this paper because the arts are neglected and misunderstood, but I would not like to leave the impression that all my arguments apply only to the arts for I believe many of them have an important bearing on the whole of the curriculum and on all forms of pedagogy. Second I would like to draw attention to our bad habits in language. It is painfully ironic that in the discipline of educational study we have spawned, perhaps more than in any other human study, a barbaric language of jargon and gobbledygook, an iron and cement language that is incapable of grasping the human essence and of making the necessary and subtle discriminations in living experience. As teachers we must find the courage to discard this harsh defensive language and speak, again, the language of human beings, with due simplicity, due passion, due intelligence. In our own cultures we can locate the true voices of individuals speaking of education with the necessary eloquence; in English culture we have, for example, Dickens in *Hard Times*; we have Coleridge, Carlyle, Arnold, Ruskin, D. H. Lawrence, George Orwell, and T. S. Eliot. In American culture we have, among others, Emerson, Thoreau, William James, and Lewis Mumford. With such rich examples in our common-language traditions we have no justification for adopting the degraded machine language of behavioral psychology and quantitative sociology.

Finally I must take on the possible charge of being utopian in parts of this article. My answer to such a criticism is simple. Yes, my answer runs, the argument is partly utopian, but utopia refers, literally, to no place. Utopia is there not to be realized, but as a beckoning finger, an invitation to move into new ground when the old ground has become dusty and exhausted. I believe that the inherited paradigm of the industrial society is now intellectually and emotionally spent. All the informing ideals of technological power and materialist progress have become shot through with ambiguity and contradiction. They now strike the ear with the heaviness of cliché. No intelligent person can give simple assent to the fading assumptions that still largely inform this civilization, a civilization that is perilously close to disaster. At such a moment there is no alternative but to move one's base, to move out into the unknown in search of new patterns, new connections, a new synthesis. At such a moment, utopia beckons, as image, as metaphor—and in the metaphor much is to be cognized.

Footnotes

1   Josef Herman, "Open Letter to *Tract*" published in *Crisis in the Visual Arts, Tract 28* (Sussex: Gryphon Press, 1980), p. 4.

2   James Hillman, *Pan and the Nightmare* (Zurich: Spring Publications, 1972), p. 24.

3   Peter Abbs, *Reclamations* (London: Heinemann Educational Books, 1979).

4   John Stuart Mill, *Autobiography* (New York: First published 1873; Signet ed. 1964), p. 55.

5   Ibid.

6   Abbs, *Reclamations*, pp. 42, 43.

7   Peter Abbs, "Education, Symbol and Myth," in *Myth and Symbol in Education, Tract 29 and 30* (Sussex: Gryphon Press, 1980).

8   Virginia Axline, *Dibs: In Search of Self* (London: Penguin, 1971), pp. 134-36.

9   Ibid., p. 137.

10   Yvonne Stevenson, *The Hot-House Plant* (London: Elek/Pemberton, 1976), p. 142.

11   Ibid., p. 143.

12   Ibid., pp. 143-44.

13   Ibid., p. 144.

14   Suzanne Langer, *Mind: An Essay on Human Feeling*, Vol. I (Baltimore and London: Johns Hopkins University Press, 1962), p. 64.

15   Peter Abbs, *Autobiography in Education* (Sussex: Gryphon Press, 1974).

16   Jacqueline Langlois in unpublished autobiography for University of Sussex contextual course.

17   Taken from the first lines of the Divine Comedy: "I find myself in a dark wood."

18   Hamlet.

19   Langlois unpublished autobiography.

20   Edwin Muir, *An Autobiography* (London: The Hogarth Press, 1980), p. 42.

21   Ibid., p. 43.

22   Ibid., p. 44.

23   Open letter written by the author to University of Sussex Post-graduate Certificate in Education English students, unpublished.

Cultural Vision and the Human Future

ROBERT N. BELLAH

University of California, Berkeley

I share with other contributors to this symposium the conviction that there is something profoundly awry in our modern Western culture and that our contemporary cultural, social, and political difficulties are in part a result of that fact. I share particularly with Huston Smith the hope that premodern and non-Western cultures might have something important to contribute to our getting out of these difficulties. I am convinced that cultural vision has much to do with the human future into which we will move. The problem is: what cultural vision and how do we appropriate it? In this paper I will consider four models for relating cultural vision, or rather the diversity of cultural visions, to the human future.

The first and most pervasive view is that in which the modern West is taken as the most advanced culture and it is the task of other cultures to "catch up" with ours. Not long ago it was common to rank the cultures of the world in terms of how closely they resembled our own. Modern Western culture was seen as the standard of rationality and progress toward which all other cultures are or ought to be approaching. Thus the relation of the modern West and the rest of the world was that of teacher and student, with "us" doing the teaching and "they" doing the learning. In the nineteenth century this pedagogical role was expressed as "the White man's burden." In the 1950s it took the form of what was called "modernization theory." There was no little truth to this model and indeed much of the rest of the world has been eager to absorb aspects of modern Western culture. But it has become increasingly clear that this whole way of thinking is morally suspect: too closely allied with colonialism and imperialism and too profoundly ethnocentric. But even more serious is the fact that this first way of dealing with our problem has run up against doubts about our own project that have made other cultures seem less obviously benighted.

I would like to look for a moment at a rather extreme example of a "backward" culture, the extraordinarily interesting culture of the Australian aborigines. We think about it today differently than we did just a few years ago, in part because we understand it better, but largely because we understand ourselves differently.

Before the Europeans came the aborigines had lived in Australia for at least ten thousand years, and yet through all that time they managed to leave the land almost exactly as they found it. In the words of W. E. H. Stanner:

They are, of course, nomads—hunters and foragers who grow nothing, build nothing, and stay nowhere long. They make almost no physical mark on the environment. Even in the areas which are still inhabited, it takes a knowledgeable eye to detect their recent presence. Within a matter of weeks, the roughly cleared campsites may be erased by sun, rain, and wind. After a year or two there may be nothing to suggest that the country was ever inhabited. Until one stumbles on a few old flint tools, a stone quarry, a shell hidden, a rock painting, or something of the kind, one may think the land had never known the touch of man.[1]

For generations Europeans used to think that making such a faint impression on the landscape was a sure sign of invincible barbarism. But now it is not so obvious. Imagine what a century or two of European occupation has done to the Australian landscape. Perhaps it may dawn on us that it is the native Australians who have a more "civilized" attitude toward nature than the modern inhabitants and it is we who are "barbaric" toward our environment.

Nor must we too quickly condemn that aboriginal society with the word "scarcity," which is used so sweepingly about all premodern societies. Again it is Stanner who sets us straight:

The notion of aboriginal life as always preoccupied with the risk of starvation, as always a hair's breadth from disaster, is as great a caricature as Hobbes' notion of savage life as "poor, nasty, brutish, and short." The best corrective of any such notion is to spend a few nights in an aboriginal camp, and experience directly the unique joy in life which can be attained by a people of few wants, an other worldly cast of mind, and a simple scheme of life which so shapes a day that it ends with communal singing and dancing in the firelight.[2]

It is not my purpose to romanticize primitive life—we have been through the noble savage routine before—nor to replace a pejorative stereotype with an idealized one. Australian aboriginal life is not paradise. There are seasons of the year when most people are mildly hungry. There are bitter quarrels and occasional bloodshed, particularly over women. The old men pretty well monopolize what prestige and power there is in this simple society and women and young people are under their domination. And yet for all that it is not a bad life. It is a life in which all can participate, without a division into a few who are admired and the rest who look on. It is a life of hard work and lean moments but also one of great beauty, lived close to the earth and punctuated by an annual round of rituals that lend drama and meaning to everyday existence. Of the religious life that is so central to Australian aboriginal culture Stanner has written, "It allows them to assent to life, as it is, without morbidity."[3] Few cultures or religions at any level of cultural development can claim more.

I do not then want to reverse recent judgments and proclaim the aborigines our superiors. Yet if we really take all the rhetoric of development and modernization seriously there is something uncomfortable about how close the best of their life is to the best of our own—especially when our own society contains an enormous capacity, and what seems on occasion an enormous desire, for self-destruction, totally lacking in the aboriginal culture. It may be that our society contains resources for self-transformation that are also missing in aboriginal Australia—I do not want to rule that out. Nonetheless a balanced look only enhances the doubts expressed by Robert Heilbroner:

> For some time, observers skeptical of the panacea of growth have wondered why their contemporaries, who were three or five or ten times richer than their grandparents, or great-grandparents, or Pilgrim forebears, did not seem to be three or five or ten times happier or more content or more richly developed as human beings. This skepticism, formerly the preserve of a few "philosophically minded" critics, has now begun, I believe, to enter the consciousness of large numbers of men and women. . . .
>
> The civilizational malaise, in brief, reflects the inability of a civilization directed to material improvement to satisfy the human spirit. To say as much is not to denigrate its achievements, which have been colossal, but to bring to the forefront of our consciousness a fact that I think must be reckoned with in searching the mood of our times. It is that the values of an industrial civilization, which has for two centuries given us not only material advance but also a sense of *élan* and purpose, now seem to be losing their self-evident justification. And yet, the doubts and disillusions are only faint. But they are there, and the stirrings they cause must be added to the unease that is so much a part of our age.[4]

Since Heilbroner wrote, these doubts have been confirmed on a mass basis by public opinion polls. In late 1978, for the first time in our history, a majority of Americans expected their own future to be worse than their past and, even more shocking, their children's lives to be worse than their own. One of the strongest beliefs in our history, namely, that however tough we have had it our children will get a better break, is no longer self-evident. Progress, which has long been in doubt among our intellectuals, is now a shaken idol even among the masses.

Most of the contributors to this symposium agree that something has gone wrong in the modern West. Most point mainly to ideological causes such as materialism and science—at least in the form of empiricism and positivism, a Western "mind set," and so forth. As a sociologist I would like to discuss some of the things that correlate with that ideology that others have not mentioned. Peter Berger said recently that we sociologists are by profession vulgar and talk about things that philosophers, theologians, and poets may sometimes ignore.

I would like to start with a rather blunt social correlate of our ideological distortions, namely capitalism, and capitalism not just as a system of economics but as a system of social and economic power. I would suggest that capitalism entails a number of other vulgar and upsetting things such as exploitation, imperialism, war, and the threat of total nuclear destruction. I might add that I do not use the word capitalism as a term to contrast with the self-styled socialist or communist regimes, which I regard as merely statist versions of capitalism more completely bureaucratized than our own.

There is, nevertheless, a distinction between regimes, even if the major powerful nations of the world all suffer from the same illness. Democratic capitalism is not the worst of systems. It is certainly better than authoritarian or statist capitalism. It produces a rather high level of ethical demand—what David Riesman called a rising standard of loving—that, however, only increases our malaise, for it makes clear how short we fall relative to our expectations. Our present danger, and here I am thinking of American society but Western Europe and Japan are in many ways in the same boat, is that democratic capitalism has a deep built-in instability in that the economic system and the political power that goes with it relentlessly undermine all the moral bases of our democracy. It is this process of undermining that could lead to either cataclysmic nuclear disaster or permanent universal tyranny.

By pointing to social correlates, which I think we ignore at our peril, I do not in the least wish to deny the importance of ideology. Ideas, sentiments, opinions, are important and in many ways central. But by remembering the social situation in which ideology operates we may see certain things we would otherwise overlook.

I want to focus on the dimension of our current ideology that I believe is close to the heart of our distress. That is radical secular individualism and its accompanying egalitarianism. It starts from the assumption that the biological individual is the only human truth. This radical secular individualism is so pervasive that even those of us who would like to combat it, including those of us who have contributed to this symposium, are absolutely permeated by it. By saying that this pervasive set of assumptions is an ideology, which I think it certainly is, I do not mean to view it entirely as a product of intellectual history. It was not simply caused by Descartes, or Hobbes, or "modern science." While intellectuals have certainly made major contributions to this way of thinking, it is certainly not only the result of what certain intellectuals thought and wrote at certain times. What I most want to stress is that this ideology correlates with the way we live. It resonates with our economy, our political system, even with the way we organize our private lives. It is rooted in wholly unconscious preconceptions and practices that pervade us even when we wish ardently that this were not the case. This is because we live in a society in which this is the organizing way of thinking.

We live in a social system that tells us, not just verbally but in the daily practice of life, that we are alone, that we are here to pursue our own interests, that neither anyone nor anything can save us except ourselves. It tells us that we must mistrust every noble impulse we feel because it must be only a form of our own self-seeking. A couple of years ago a friend of mine addressing a class on international human rights at the University of California–Berkeley Law School asked the students why they cared about human rights. The students had a difficult time with the question but concluded that it must be because it was in their interest. I would suggest that as an example of ideology masking human impulses that could not be articulated as such. We live in a society where a book by Robert Ringer entitled *Looking Out for Number One* was a best seller for many weeks and has spawned a whole series of successful imitations. Intellectuals seldom read or mention works of such vulgarity, though they may be telling us something of great importance about our society. But even a distinguished philosophical work like John Rawls's *Theory of Justice* premises the radically self-interested individual as the necessary starting point. Though Rawls's argument far transcends that framework, he believes that in order to be convincing this is where he must start. That fact is as culturally telling as is Robert Ringer's book.

What I am describing cannot be simply categorized as a mind set, though it is that, for there is a whole set of social practices and institutions that breed, support, and reinforce it. The belief in the isolated self is reinforced by what happens to us in our daily experience. I am currently directing a research team that is inquiring into the mores—what Tocqueville called "habits of the heart"—of middle-class white Americans. On the basis of that research, which is as yet in an early stage, as well as other reading and observation, I would say that the problems of life for middle-class Americans are certainly not those of oppression and unfreedom, even though middle-class undergraduates until fairly recently liked to talk in those terms. White middle-class Americans are probably as free, in any possible sense of the word except the highest philosophical and religious meanings, as any group of people has ever been. In many ways our way of life fulfills the wildest dreams of millennia of peasant societies. Most of the world envies us even as they condemn us. What the Vietnamese or Cuban refugees seek here is a concrete sense of material well-being that not all Americans have attained but that most Americans have reached to a degree unique in human history.

But what Heilbroner and others have observed is that together with the full stomach has come the empty soul. For many our freedom is contentless and our daily life barren of meaning. Our research has found that for many Americans occupation causes psychic isolation. Work lacks the articulation with a larger organic society that it often has in other cultures and civilizations. Instead work creates a boredom from which one seeks to escape if one is on the lower rungs, or if one is on the higher rungs it often requires a degree of anxious self-manipulation from which one desperately seeks relief whenever possible. Above all, work does not provide a way to tie one into larger structures of meaning and participation. Public life outside of work is often equally if not more barren, consisting of encounters either with the market, where virtually everything from the most private to the most material needs can be met by the payment of money, or with large impersonal bureaucracies that one learns at best to manipulate. We are studying that still sizable minority of Americans who resist the tendency to locate real life in one's own living room in front of the television screen. There are millions still struggling in one way or another to make a public life in America possible, but the cost is high and "burnout" a constant theme among those who are publicly active.

What life in this extraordinarily rich society lacks above all is what the Australian aborigines have: that round of meaningful action that ties them into society, nature, and the cosmos. For us it is not only nature that has become cold, lifeless, and abstract. Society too is cold, lifeless, and abstract. Even intimate relations grow more and more calculating. One of the things we did not expect is that the word "love" is viewed with suspicion among many of the people we are studying. Love is seen as dangerous because it threatens the autonomy and independence of the individual.

Cumulatively the pressures and tensions of our way of life are very great and require certain reactions in order for us to stay alive and functioning at all. One increasingly important reaction that we are finding among middle-class Americans, in Massachusetts, Pennsylvania, and Georgia as well as in California, is the alleviation of the greyness and deadness of one's daily life by a stress on purely private inner experience.

Owen Barfield in his contribution to this symposium points to the eighteenth century as a time when subjective experience was beginning to be emphasized as expressed in the appearance of such words as "interesting," "entertaining," and "exhilarating." These words, he tells us, point to inner states with no necessary correlate with anything in the external world. Our research is finding an advanced stage of the same tendency. The words that come up again and again in our interviews are "feeling," "creative" and "creativity," "aliveness," "excitement," and "energy." Increasingly we come across rather cryptic phrases like "to get it" or onomatopoetic expressions like "zing." What is striking is that we are discovering a private world of great intensity and no content whatever. There is a vehement insistence on selfhood but it is an absolutely empty self; except for the sheer quantity of excitation there is nothing there at all. Symbolic, ethical, or religious content terms get swallowed up in the language of psychic process. "Creative," for example, would certainly be used more circumspectly in a society that deeply believed in God as the real creator. Among us creative tends to be a contentless quality pointing to the intensity of inner experience.

The extreme individualism of our culture entails a functional, though not always an ethical, egalitarianism. Individuals are both absolutely unique and absolutely interchangeable. There are no organic connections between them that would allow for an ethically meaningful hierarchy. Functions are different and some may supervise others but there is no sense of a whole of which all are parts. There are also no standards from which an ethical hierarchy could be deduced. No unique individual can be judged by any other.

There can be no notion of noble and base. My sensations are as good as your sensations and who is to say anything about better or worse? We maximize individual choice beyond what any traditional society has ever done and then we deny all objective standards of choice. Choice is finally completely private. We stress human rights as our most sacred belief but we define rights as the absence of external limits on individual decision. The ultimate right becomes the right to commit suicide. Who is to tell me I should not?

While this whole system obviously works and a complete collapse is not in sight, the level of dissatisfaction is clearly on the rise. It is not working very well and all the signs are that it is going to be working less well in the years ahead. If, then, we are not moving into a utopia of human happiness and fulfillment, if indeed our society is less and less capable of giving people a sense of meaning about who they are in relation to the world in which they live, then pretty clearly our culture is not the measure for all of the other cultures that have ever been. Let us turn then to the second of our four models of how to relate cultural vision to the human future.

In reaction to the arrogance and self-importance of this first view there developed, at least from the early years of the twentieth century, a doctrine that can be called "cultural relativism." Anthropologists studying quite simple cultures that would have been most despised by the Europocentric theorists of modernization endeavored to show that such cultures had their own unique values that were every bit as worthy of respect as our own. Indeed they argued that since each culture is a self-subsistent whole there are no standards by which to judge between them. While promoting the values of tolerance and pluralism the doctrine of cultural relativism had the ironic result, as Paul Rabinow is currently pointing out, of trivializing the whole enterprise of the study of other cultures. Since all cultures are of equal value and none has anything to learn from any other, why make the effort? Outside a particular cultural context there is nothing that is good, true, or beautiful. There is nothing in the whole range of comparative cultural studies that we need ultimately to take seriously. Therefore a position that started out emphasizing the uniquely different finally levels all to sameness: We are all equally trivial. I would suggest that cultural relativism is finally another example of the radical standardless egalitarianism so central to our current ideology.

Let us turn to the third of our models. There has been for a long time another position critical of ethnocentrism that differs strongly from cultural relativism. This position has been espoused, marginally and fitfully, by those Westerners who have never been happy with our modern "progress." Critical of modern science, materialism, and power seeking, they chose to reverse the roles assigned by the modernizers and saw "us" in need of being taught by "them." It was the spiritual wisdom of India or the natural life of the South Sea Islanders or the aesthetic grace of the Japanese that provided the standard relative to which we had much to learn. For long, only a few romantics, misfits, and spiritual seekers espoused such views because self-confidence in modern progress was almost unquestioned. Today things are different. Uncertainty about the future is endemic in Europe and America, as we have seen. Our own uncertainties are so great that it is enormously tempting to look somewhere else for an answer.

While it is a valid though enormously difficult task to seek from these other cultures a way to change the drift toward death that seems so evident in our own culture, it is quite tempting and much easier to use them simply as palliatives that will allow us to keep going in the same direction. Indeed, it is common in our society to use oriental religions or non-Western philosophies for purely personal ends—exotic forms of energy, creativity, excitement, and zing. That is, I believe, a way of totally perverting those cultures, denying the context out of which they come, using them as a drug to keep people in the very system that is depriving them of meaning rather than giving them a resource for questioning it. Zen Buddhism, for example, requires a commitment to a total way of life, without which it runs the peculiar danger of being turned into a spiritual technology for ulterior ends. Fortunately we have in America today examples of Zen (and other oriental religions) being lived as a way of life, but we also have many examples of utilitarian distortion.

While each of these three approaches to the study of other cultures has its merits, I have tried to show that none is very satisfactory. Is there another approach or is there another dimension to the study of other cultures that would be more fruitful, that would even help to rescue what is of value in the three common approaches discussed above? I think there is. I would suggest that we use the study of other cultures first to learn more about ourselves and that we can begin to consider what we can adopt from outside only on the basis of this deepened self-knowledge. In this perspective, the recent writing of Louis Dumont has been particularly suggestive.

Dumont suggests that we are indeed in trouble and in need of help. In *From Mandeville to Marx* he writes:

> [W]e are witnessing a crisis of the modern ideological paradigm. It is true that the tendency to see crises everywhere is strong in modern ideology and that, if crisis there be, it was not born yesterday but has been there for quite some time; in a wider sense, the crisis is more or less congenial, to the extent that some of us take pride in it. Yet, we may perhaps say that the twentieth-century crisis of the paradigm has recently gone through an intensification, deepening, or generalization.[5]

But, he suggests, the crisis is so close to us, so involved in the very ways we think, that it is peculiarly difficult to define it. Hence, "to isolate our ideology is a sine qua non for transcending it, simply because otherwise we remain caught within it as the very medium of our thought."[6] The only way out of this dilemma, he suggests, is to adopt a comparative perspective. We must take imaginatively the perspective of a radically different culture and then, as it were, look back at the peculiarities of our own. A lifetime of studying traditional India has given Dumont precisely that point of leverage.

Dumont isolates those aspects of modern ideology that differentiate it not only from India but from all traditional cultures, including that of the premodern West. Indeed, it is one of Dumont's points that what we take for granted as "natural" is really a radically aberrant world view shared by no other culture in human history. In essence the rise of what he calls "economic ideology" makes the relation of the isolated individual and nature primary and derives society and culture from that, whereas every traditional culture made society and the relations between individuals primary and derived conceptions of both economics and the individual from the prior social matrix.

Of course we know that radical individualism and a utilitarian attitude toward nature have never become completely dominant, even in the modern West. Older views that saw the end of man in the love of neighbor and the contemplation of God have never entirely died out. There is doubt whether a society based on individualism and utilitarianism alone could even survive. Yet the critical consciousness that seems to flow from individualism and utilitarianism is the source of our greatest achievements as modern men and women.

This formulation of the problem suggests some of the difficulties we face. We need very much to learn from cultural models different from our own recent past, models of how to live that are less personally, socially, and environmentally destructive. Traditional societies throughout the world, including the societies of the premodern West, provide such models. But while we learn from other cultures, we must be aware of our own commitments. Our extremes need balancing polarities that other cultures seem to contain. But there is no other culture that we can uncritically follow, not even our own biblical and classical past, much as we have to learn from them still today. While we must certainly rethink our modern values, we cannot simply jettison them without so great a loss of identity as to make the whole project fruitless.

One of the things that Dumont is saying is that equality and hierarchy, which are only specifications of those more basic terms individuality and wholeness, are among the great polarities of human life. We cannot escape either pole without pathology. In particular that means that in a culture that has gone far in the direction of egalitarian individualism we need to reassert the principle of hierarchy, above all the hierarchy of values. In our society we scarcely know what hierarchy is—we think it means domination. We cry out for community but we do not realize that there is no community without hierarchy, no sense of the whole without an organic structuring of the parts. As a gesture toward recovering the human reality that the word hierarchy has traditionally carried I would like to suggest a current word that we might provisionally substitute at least in some contexts. The word I have in mind that might help to make our meaning clear to contemporaries is the word "ecology"—more particularly the term coined by an associate of mine, William Sullivan, "moral ecology." Moral ecology implies not only interdependence, but standards, priorities, directions of choice that are not private or relativistic—precisely the things we have almost lost.

But clearly we cannot create a moral ecology out of nothing. If there is any chance of changing the direction of our drift it will be because there are groups, communities, traditions, active and alive in our society, for whom this change of direction is a real possibility. We must seek whatever moral ecology actually exists. We must nourish every element of coherent culture and community that is still alive among us. Only coherent persons in coherent relation to one another can challenge the drift to catastrophe in the midst of which we live. There never has been and there never could be a society of pure atomistic individuals. Though that ideological tendency is strong in our society, we could not live without the sources of life that still come to us from the traditional religions and philosophies.

I look in America to two places where there is sufficient coherence to provide the basis for a new direction. One is the civic tradition, where it is still alive, that has its roots all the way back in the ancient Greek polis. It is not identical with abstract liberalism or interest-group politics but still expresses even today a sense of public virtue and concern for the common good. And I would look to the churches and synagogues, which again and again in our history have provided the saving remnant. Religion has always had an ambiguous influence in our society, never more so than today. Yet time and again it is out of the religious communities, often with much opposition within them, that the forces for revitalization and renewal have come. Out of such traditions and communities in the chaotic period we are entering might come the reshaping of our economy and our polity. In a different, more human society science and scientists might find their rightful place as part of a larger whole.

Footnotes

1   W. E. H. Stanner, "The Dreaming," in *Reader in Comparative Religion*, ed. William Lessa and Evon Z. Vogt (New York: Harper & Row, 1958), p. 163.

2   Ibid., p. 166.

3   W. E. H. Stanner, *On Aboriginal Religion*, Oceania Monograph no. 11, University of Sydney, 1966, p. 58.

4   Robert L. Heilbroner, *An Inquiry into the Human Prospect* (New York: W. W. Norton, 1980), pp. 18-19. This essay was written in 1972 and 1973.

5   Louis Dumont, *From Mandeville to Marx* (Chicago: University of Chicago Press, 1977), p. 10.

6   Ibid., p. 27.

Knowledge and Human Values:
A Genealogy of Nihilism

HUBERT L. DREYFUS
University of California, Berkeley

Nihilism in its essence is the fundamental movement in the history of the West. It shows such great profundity that its unfolding can have nothing but world catastrophes as its consequence. . . . Those who fancy themselves free of nihilism perhaps push forward its development most fundamentally.[1]

THEORY AND NIHILISM

Our problem, I take it, is that many people today feel that they have lost a sense of the meaning and seriousness of their lives. Robert Bellah has given us an eloquent and chilling description of contemporary America in which the highest goal now seems to be energy or "zing." Being a philosopher rather than a sociologist, I am now going to give this problem a name, nihilism, and talk about it in a much more abstract and general way than Professor Bellah did. I want to argue that what is at issue is not merely a sickness in American society just beginning to show up in questionnaires, but a condition of Western man that has been gradually revealing itself since Socrates subtly launched nihilism about 300 B.C. Not that our present nihilism is any particular person's fault—not even a very important person like Socrates. He was simply the first symptom. As Nietzsche says in *Twilight of the Idols*, Socrates was merely an Athenian degenerate, a first expression of the decadence that had come over Athens of which we are the final heirs.[2]

When I say that our current condition can be characterized as nihilism I do not mean that we have forgotten or betrayed our values. Thinking that we once had values but that we do not have values now, and that we should regain our values or get new ones, is just another symptom of the trouble. Heidegger, who seems to me to have by far the deepest understanding of nihilism (and glimmers, at least, concerning what to do about it), points out that thinking about our deepest concerns as values *is* nihilism. We will soon see why.

My general point, of which the value question is a special case, is that though we cannot do anything to prevent or cure nihilism—it is much too

I am grateful to Jane Rubin for her insights into nihilism, many of which have found their way into this paper.

wide and deep for that—one thing we *can* do is to develop the deepest possible understanding of our nihilistic situation so that we do not inadvertently contribute to the problem. The most important message of the Heidegger quotation I have used as epigraph is that it is precisely those who fancy themselves free of nihilism who push forward its development most fundamentally. If this is true, we must ask whether what has been going on here at this meeting may not be a sign that our culture has reached what Heidegger considers the penultimate stage of nihilism, and whether our discussion of how to save "human values" in education may not, in fact, be a contribution to the steady infiltration of nihilism into every aspect of our culture.

To answer this question we must first spell out more fully what nihilism is. Nihilism is loss of meaning or seriousness. If nihilism were complete there would be no significant private or public issues. Nothing would have authority for us, would make a claim on us, would demand a commitment from us. In a non-nihilistic age—which Kierkegaard calls a revolutionary age—there is something at stake. There are questions that all can agree are important, even if they violently disagree as to what the answers to these questions are. But in our age, everything is in the process of becoming equal. There is no meaningful difference between political parties, between religious communities, between social causes, between cultural practices—everything is on a par. That means there are no *shared commitments* and, as a result, as Professor Bellah has pointed out, individuals feel isolated and alienated. They feel that their lives have no meaning because the public world has no meaning. They then retreat into their private experiences as the only remaining place to find even zing when everything that is material and social has become completely flat and drab. When all our concerns have thus been reduced to the common denominator of "experience" we will have reached the last stage of nihilism. That is, when there are no shared examples of greatness that focus public concerns and elicit social commitment, people become spectators of fads and public lives, just for the excitement. When there are no religious practices that call forth sacrifice, terror, and awe, people consume everything from drugs and meditation practices to rituals and gurus to give themselves some kind of peak experience. The peak experience takes the place of what was once a relation to something outside the self that defined the real and was therefore holy. The same thing happens when sexual relations no longer seem real or important. Then the participants fall back on private sexual experience. All these attitudes only seem attractive once the shared public world has lost its meaning and reality. Then one thinks (as if somehow it had always been the case and he had just discovered it) that, after all, it is the experience that matters. But sooner or later one finds that although private experience may have "energy" or "spontaneity" or "creativity" it provides nothing in terms of which one can give consistency, meaning, and seriousness to one's life. In fact, once it is the *experience* that matters, *reality* has stopped mattering altogether.

Of course, we would all like to do something to relieve this distress, but, as I have said, that is asking too much. All we can do, at best, is not to contribute to it. The first step, then, in resisting nihilism is to get as clear as possible about what it is. To begin with, it is something that is very deeply rooted in our history. And, as Heidegger points out, only if we find its roots can we avoid confusing its symptoms with the disease itself. "Because we do not experience nihilism as a historical movement that has already long endured, the ground of whose essence lies in metaphysics [i.e., philosophy], we succumb to the ruinous passion for holding phenomena that are already and simply consequences of nihilism for the latter itself. We set forth the consequences and effect as the causes of nihilism."[3] The most prevalent form of this mistake at this meeting is, I think, the double illusion that somehow materialism is the problem because it has caused our loss of values. Materialism is just one symptom of nihilism. Materialism is the view that all meaning has gone from the cosmos, nature, and culture. Materialism is thus not the *cause* of nihilism, but only the other side of the view that all that is meaningful is private experience. Both are symptoms of some underlying problem.

Nihilism is deeper than any of these symptoms. The real danger is not, for example, materialism. Even if science told us that everything was *im*material —that it was process, empty space, spirit, or what have you—it would not make any difference. As long as one believes that science tells us the truth about "everything" there can be no meaningful difference. The *whole of reality* is energy, process, empty space, spirit, etc., and everything is the same. Indeed, such interest in science and whether or not it is materialistic is one important way of *not* facing the real problem. It may be exhilarating to learn that science has recently shifted from a reductionistic materialism to a holistic spiritualism. Those who think that the meaning of their lives depends on what science tells them about reality may now feel lighter and happier, dance more, and generally breathe deep sighs of relief. But that does not touch the problem of nihilism. Likewise, what some have prophesied is certainly alarming. We may, indeed, be twenty years from the destruction of our culture, whether by nuclear bombs, computers' getting out of control, pollution, or some other technological calamity. But on the view I am presenting, the real danger in technology is not that it might completely destroy us, but that it might not. We might find a technological fix for every technological problem until we finally achieve the total domination of the planet—every threat stamped out: no more cavities, no more ringworm, no more stomach aches, no more nuclear bombs—finally health and happiness for all. We may achieve total control of ourselves and our world. Then it will become clear what the real danger was, for there will still be no meaningful difference, and no seriousness. There will be nothing to commit oneself to.

So the question becomes: How did we get ourselves into this nihilistic situation? If technology's threat to our lives and science's crude materialistic view of the universe are only effects, what is the cause? On Heidegger's analysis, which I share and will try to defend, the real cause is something called "theory," which starts with Plato. In Plato's time *theoria* meant contemplation, seeing the systematic order of all of reality. Theory, at the time of Galileo, became science, and science in Nietzsche's time became technology. These are all stages of the working out of the 2,000-year long history of nihilism. But it was all implicit as soon as the Greeks came to believe that the theoretical, detached attitude was our fundamental access to reality.

There are five features of theory that are the deep cause of our current condition. Huston Smith put his finger on the most important one in his discussion of *objectification*. Objectification is nothing new. Objectification starts when Plato posits ideas as ideal *objects* over against a knower who, while not yet understood as a subject, is already understood as other than these ideas that he contemplates. Later with Descartes the knower who turns toward and contemplates the object becomes the subject. It is this basic theoretical split between the knower and the known, not simply its later development as the split between subject and object, that is the root of nihilism. Once one thus distinguishes causes from effects one can see that we are not going to get over nihilism by affirming subjectivity and opposing objectification. Subjects and objects are two sides of the same coin. There is no deeper truth in subjects than in objects. They are both an effect of thinking in terms of theory. Generally, flipping some aspect of the tradition into its opposite will not get you out of problems built into the tradition.

A second cause of our problem, which I think goes back to Socrates instead of to Plato, is *the attempt to make everything explicit*. Socrates had a passion for getting people to articulate completely the principles by which they lived. In one of the first Socratic dialogues, Socrates gets hold of Euthyphro, a religious leader of sorts who thinks he understands piety, and forces him to admit that he cannot give a definition of piety, that is, that he cannot state the necessary and sufficient conditions for something's being a pious action. Euthyphro keeps giving examples of piety—dramatic stories that everybody in Euthyphro's subculture or, indeed, his whole culture would recognize as instances of piety. That is, Euthyphro presents paradigmatic cases of piety, but Socrates will not accept them. Socrates wants *explicit* definitions. He wants to know "the rule by which I can recognize an action as pious."[4] He wants what computer programmers would now call an effective procedure for piety recognition. And since he cannot get one out of Euthyphro, he concludes, quite naturally, given his premises, that Euthyphro does not know what piety is.

Incidentally, there has been much discussion here about why the poets were thrown out of Plato's republic. Plato gives a very clear reason in the *Apology*—a very Socratic reason, in fact. It is not that the poets stand for the wrong things; it is not even that they work up people's feelings, although they may do both. Rather, as Socrates says, he has gone to the poets and asked them to tell him what it is that their poetry means in precise prose and they cannot do it. He concludes that "they understand nothing of what they say."[5] The trouble with the poets is that they cannot make explicit and justify the "principles" expressed in their poetry.

Third, theory, by making everything explicit, takes it out of context. It belongs to the very essence of theory that the theorist must *decontextualize* his subject matter. Again, Plato is the first to have seen this. The myth of the cave stresses the fact that the theorist must remove himself and the object of knowledge from the everyday public shared world (the shadows on the cave's walls) in order to see the Ideas in another world where, of course, they are their own context.

This brings me to the fourth feature of theory. It always forms *a system or a whole*. The Ideas, Plato tells us, are all completely interrelated and all imply each other. The everyday context is left behind as confused and unimportant. It gets bracketed out in the name of obtaining decontextualized elements; then these elements, whether they be Ideas or atoms or whatever you like, are recontextualized into a new whole. Theory thus decontextualizes its object in order to recontextualize it, but, whereas the old context was implicit and open, the new context is explicit and complete—publicly shared commitments and the everyday perceptual world are replaced by an abstract system of ideas. The way this is done is tied up with Socrates' way of questioning Euthyphro. He engages in relentless and pragmatically pointless questioning. This is supposed to get all knowledge out in the open as explicit, decontextualized, and objectified. Then Plato comes along and systematizes the resulting elements in terms of an ultimate ground that is explicit and unquestionable— the Good. Only then, according to the philosophical tradition, do you finally have something solid on which you can build.

All this leads to a fifth and final feature, which Heidegger calls seeing the world as a picture. It takes a long time for this aspect of theory to emerge, but finally in the Classical Age the subject stands outside of and over against whatever it is he knows, and sees it as an objective, explicit, context-free, total picture. Plato's introduction of theory was already implicitly nihilistic according to Heidegger, but only with this idea of reality as a world view does the nihilism become explicit.

This final stage in which the world becomes a picture gets us back to the relation between nihilism and the belief in values. Values are objective, explicit options that we can stand outside of, picture, and choose among. The essence of a value is that it is something that is completely independent of us, able to be seen by us, evaluated, and then chosen or rejected. The Ideas were already in a sense values. Values have an interesting history, as Mr. Barfield has pointed out. (Heidegger would add that once you see what values are, you will see that this history is inevitable.) One starts with objective values, which Barfield calls "quality." These values seem to have some kind of independent status. Later we arrive at the notion that we must *choose* our values. They are still objective, but now they are taken to be over against us and so no longer believed to have any claim on us. We have to decide which ones we want to adopt. Once we get the idea that there is a plurality of values and that we choose which ones will have a claim on us, we are ripe for the modern idea, first found in Nietzsche, that we *posit* our values—that is, that valuing is something we do and value is the result of what we do. Once we see that sets of values or mind sets or world pictures are simply posited they lose all authority for us and, far from giving meaning to our lives, they show us that our lives have no intrinsic meaning.

This very idea of a mind set is completely Western. A mind set is a table of values or a belief system. It suggests that somehow what people live in terms of is in their minds. It is the most recent version of the world as a picture. One gets the notion that Europeans have a mind set, the Greeks had a mind set, Buddhists have a mind set, and so forth. We have all these pictures laid out in front of us, and each of us can either choose which one he wants or choose a little bit of each and make some new syncretic picture. Then we will get meaning into our life. But Heidegger's point is that once our concerns have become mind sets, they have lost their meaning and authority, and whether we pick one of them or make up a collage out of the "best" elements of each, we cannot get back any meaning. The most one might get is something interesting, but there is a big difference between something interesting and something important. That is what I meant when I said at the start that talking about "human values" is part of the problem. Once we see that we posit values we can equally "unposit" them. As long as we think in terms of explicit value-objects rather than implicit shared concerns, we cannot find anything that has authority for us and elicits our commitment. Thus, finally, belief in values is the last stage of a tradition that begins with theory and ends with nihilism.

PARADIGMS AND PRACTICES

Once Heidegger helps us see how a symposium on human values such as this one runs the risk of illustrating rather than combating nihilism, it is time to turn to another aspect of his thought, which gives us, if not aid in overcoming nihilism, at least a way to avoid being part of the problem. What we need, as Douglas Sloan has said, is a total transformation in our way of knowing. That would be, I take it, a new understanding of what knowing is. We would have to reject the view we inherited from Plato that knowing is "knowing-that"— that what I know is true theories that correspond to the way things really are. Luckily, we also inherit a deeper understanding of what knowing is than that handed down by our philosophical tradition. This more commonsense account affirms that knowing is an ability to cope with things—an ability that resides in our bodies more than in our minds. It is a kind of *knowing-how* rather than a knowing-that. At the deepest level such knowing is embodied in our cultural skills and practices, rather than in our concepts, our beliefs, and our values. This cultural know-how has nothing to do with consciousness or the subconscious, let alone the unconscious. To get a sense of what this means, take a very simple case. Each person stands a different distance from an interlocutor when chatting than when engaging in business or courtship. Likewise, we adopt different distances when we deal with intimates, colleagues, strangers, children. Each culture embodies an incredibly subtle shared pattern of social distancing. No one explicitly taught this pattern to each of us. Our parents could not possibly have consciously instructed us since they do not know the pattern of responses explicitly any more than we do. We do not even know we have such know-how until we go to another culture and find, for example, that in North Africa strangers seem to be breathing down our necks while in Scandinavia our friends seem to be standing halfway across the room—or so it feels to us. This makes us very uneasy, and we cannot help moving closer or backing away. That is how we got this know-how in the first place. As small children, when we began to interact with other people, we sometimes got the distances wrong. This made our parents and friends uneasy and they either pushed us away or got closer so that we gradually picked up the whole pattern. It never was made explicit. It is probably not something like a set of rules that *could* be made explicit.[6] It is certainly not anything that anybody was ever conscious of, yet it already embodies rudiments of an understanding of what it is to be human and how to relate to human beings.

Now practices like how far to stand from people are not all that is passed on by training and imitation. Our everyday manipulative know-how involves an understanding of what it is to be a thing, a natural object, a plant, an animal, and so forth. Our understanding of animals these days, for example, is in part embodied in our skill in buying pieces of them, taking off their plastic wrapping, and cooking them in microwave ovens. A thing is best exemplified by a styrofoam cup—to be used and thrown away. Our social practices thus not only transmit an implicit understanding of what it is to be a person, an animal, or an object, but, finally, an understanding of what it is for anything to be at all. This implicit understanding of the meaning of being is what interests Heidegger. He calls attention to (without, of course, trying to make explicit) the implicit understanding of being in terms of which we relate to everything: the public, the private, the social, the cultural, scientific objects, nature, people, and so forth.

Our cultural practices and the meaning of being in them work to direct our activities and to make our lives meaningful only insofar as they are and stay implicit, that is, stay the horizon in terms of which we live. The more our know-how is formulated and objectified as knowing-that, the more it is called up for critical questioning, the more it loses its grip on us. That is how our understanding of being has gradually been eroded during the 2,000 years since Plato. Fortunately, however, our meaning-bearing practices cannot be made completely explicit so they cannot be completely destroyed. As Heidegger notes, even the practices that make technology possible are not explicit and therefore are not subject to technological control. This fact reveals something very important: Just having nonobjectifiable practices is by no means in itself the answer to nihilism. We are now formed by nonobjectifiable technological practices, but this does not save us from nihilism since these practices, while nonobjectifiable, are nonetheless *objectifying*.

The crucial question for those concerned with nihilism thus becomes: Is there still left in our practices some remnant of the *nonobjectifying* practices that were presumably extant in fifth-century Athens before the cultural collapse that is expressed and furthered by Socrates and Plato? It is an open question for Heidegger whether there is anything left of these earlier meaningful practices and, if so, where they are to be found. The strongest argument that some must be left is that without some remnant of nonobjectified concern we would not be distressed by technology and nihilism. Heidegger says in his essay on technology that we must foster the saving power of little things, presumably a sense of the simple life handed down from the early Greeks. (Bob Dylan says on one of his recent records that we must "strengthen the things that remain"—presumably some aspect of our Christian practices.) But the difficult question is: What little things and what Christian practices still have saving power?

This question is too difficult for us or even for Heidegger. All he can say is that if we are to resist nihilism we must get back in touch with our heritage of nonobjectifying practices whatever and wherever they are. One thing should be clear, however: The worst thing we can do is to try to make our saving practices explicit in our attempt to preserve them. To strengthen what remains of our heritage we must resist the Platonic temptation to come here and make a list of our values, since that would just turn whatever still has a grip on us into more meaningless objects.

So, what *can* we do? Well, how have people in the past managed to live in terms of the shared meanings in their practices? How have they shared this meaning and furthered it without attempting to make the meaning explicit as beliefs and values and so destroy their cultural commitments? Is there a way in which meaning can be focused and preserved without becoming explicit as beliefs? There was. In our pre-Platonic past and in other cultures, meaning has been focused in what I am going to call a paradigm. I mentioned in the case of Euthyphro that when grilled by Socrates and pushed to define piety he answered by offering paradigmatic cases. Euthyphro presumably tried to be helpful to Socrates by holding up perspicuous examples of piety from the practices of his day and the myths of the past, so that Socrates would get a sense of what piety was and so be able to imitate these examples. (Why not read a little wisdom into Euthyphro since everybody else reads so much wisdom into Socrates?) It is as if Euthyphro knew that by spelling out what piety was he would bring about the end of piety, which, thanks to Socrates, is exactly what happened. Of the five virtues accepted by Socrates' contemporaries (wisdom, courage, temperance, justice, and piety), Plato recognizes only four: courage, wisdom, temperance, and justice—piety, respect for the tradition, was destroyed by dialectics.

There are, as far as I know, only three thinkers in the history of philosophy—or in what might more appropriately be called the history of antiphilosophy—who discuss paradigms and their importance for focusing the implicit practices that make serious, meaningful human action possible. They are Søren Kierkegaard, Martin Heidegger, and Thomas Kuhn. I want to say something about each because they have very different, somewhat complementary notions concerning paradigms. It helps to start with Kuhn since he gives us the most detailed account of what a paradigm is and how it functions. Indeed, although Kierkegaard used the term "paradigm" or "pattern" to describe the God-man and Wittgenstein used it occasionally in his discussion of understanding, Kuhn is the first to have thematized it as his guiding notion. In his book *The Structure of Scientific Revolutions,* Kuhn shows that scientists engaged in what he calls "normal science" operate in terms of a paradigm—an outstanding example of a good piece of work.[7] The paradigm for modern science is Newton's *Principia.* Newton saw the right problems, he gave the right solutions (he did the right experiments insofar as he did any experiments), and, in any case, he gave the right sort of justifications for his claims. Thus, for over two centuries natural scientists knew that, insofar as they did something similar to the work of Newton, they were doing science.

The Newtonian paradigm was later replaced by the Einsteinian paradigm. Such a paradigm shift constitutes a scientific revolution. After such a revolution scientists *see* and *do* different things. They also *believe* different things but this is less important. Kuhn is quite clear that it is the paradigm that guides the practices and the paradigm cannot be rationalized as beliefs. One cannot spell out a set of explicit beliefs and values that scientists in a certain epoch share. As Kuhn notes: "That scientists do not usually ask or debate what makes a particular problem or solution legitimate tempts us to suppose that, at least intuitively, they know the answer. But it may only indicate that neither the question nor the answer is felt to be relevant to their research. Paradigms may be prior to, more binding, and more complete than any set of rules for research that could be unequivocally abstracted from them."[8]

A shared paradigm preserves and perpetuates what Kuhn calls the "disciplinary matrix." In the Postscript to the second edition of *The Structure of Scientific Revolutions,* Kuhn says that his original use of paradigm confused two complementary notions: the paradigm as *exemplar* and the paradigm as *disciplinary matrix.* According to Kuhn, the disciplinary matrix is the practices involved in doing a particular science that the young scientist picks up through training, just the way children pick up correct distancing. More specifically, the required know-how is acquired by working out examples that are variations on the dominant paradigm. Thus, paradigms and practices work together to set up, preserve, and perpetuate normal science.

This does not contradict my claim that science, when idolized, is nihilistic. Science is theory and theory is always objectifying. But that is not the point here. My point is that scientists learn certain kinds of objectifying, decontextualizing practices, but even these practices are not and cannot be objectified and decontextualized. They are implicit and contextual as are all social practices. Yet these particular practices enable the scientists to produce or isolate a kind of reality that is objective and decontextualized. Thus, one must distinguish, as Kuhn realizes and as Michael Polanyi[9] has stressed, between what the scientist *does* and the kind of reality that the scientist's activities reveal to us. One is thus led to see that science cannot account for its own possibility, that is, its disciplinary matrix of practices cannot be explained in terms of the decontextualized objects such practices isolate as reality.

Kierkegaard has a different notion of paradigm. He understood nihilism very well. In his book *The Present Age*,[10] written in 1846, he gave a prophetic Bellah-like description of how all authority was disappearing, all concrete differences were being leveled, everything was becoming indifferent, giving rise to alternate fits of lethargy and energy. His whole life was devoted to the question: How can we get meaning and commitment back into our lives once we have gotten into the reflective or analytic attitude we are now in? Obviously one cannot appeal to anything in the Greek tradition. If you believe, as Heidegger and Kierkegaard do, that our humanistic tradition has got us into this state, there is no point in going back to theory or wonder or quality to oppose nihilism, since these were all just stages in getting to where we are. If you try to go backward on the historical escalator, you will simply arrive back here again.

So, you need something new. On my reading, Kierkegaard's new idea is what I call a "defining relation"—that is, an unconditional commitment to someone or to some cause. Only such an absolute commitment can produce meaningful difference in a person's life. If you can commit yourself unconditionally, in love for instance, then that becomes a focus for your whole sense of reality. Things stand out or recede into insignificance on the basis of that ultimate concern. One does not discover a significance that is already there. There is no recognition of objective quality. There is no basis for this commitment in the cosmos. One does not find his place in a preexistent totality. Indeed, such a commitment is exactly the opposite of identification with some undifferentiated whole. You are called by one individual, either a person or a cause, and when you define yourself in your dedication to that individual, you get meaning, seriousness, and significance in your world.

This sort of commitment, like any commitment, must be unconditional. You cannot say, as David Bohm would like to say about our commitments, that they are fixed until further notice. Such flexibility is gained at the expense of seriousness. You cannot love somebody or serve some cause in a way that is fixed until further notice. The commitment, if it is a true commitment, must be experienced as fixed for all time. Of course, it is not, but you must take the risk of grief and of the collapse of your world if you lose your defining person or your cause fails. If you go into a commitment as if it were fixed until further notice—always ready to switch to another—you can avoid grief because you are prepared for failure, but you also avoid meaning. Openness to the meaning of everything means loss of the meaning of any one particular thing. The only way to get meaning is to let your involvement become definitive of reality for you and what is definitive of reality for you is not something that is in any way provisional—though it certainly is vulnerable. That is why, according to Kierkegaard, once a society becomes reflective such total commitments are rarely made.

So far I have described Kuhn's scientific paradigm and Kierkegaard's individual paradigms. But for us what is most important is that there are also *cultural paradigms*. Heidegger has developed this idea in his essay "The Origin of the Work of Art."[11] He calls the establishment of a shared cultural exemplar "truth setting itself to work." A work of art is for him an example of truth setting itself to work. When a work of art works, some object focuses and collects the scattered practices of a culture, unifies them into a coherent possibility for acting, and holds them up to the people who can then act and relate to each other in terms of this exemplar. We can take Aeschylus's *Oresteia* as an example of what Heidegger is getting at. Aeschylus wanted to show the Athenians what they stood for. He did not want to state propositions or justify their beliefs. The last thing he wanted to do was to tell the Athenians their values. So he produced a drama in which they were participants—he presented his fellow citizens with a pageant, a ritual, a paradigm of their way of life. And in doing that he helped focus and preserve the practices of his age.

Heidegger himself describes the Greek temple as an instance of truth setting itself to work in art. He says, "It is the temple work that first fits together and at the same time gathers around itself the unity of those paths and relations in which birth and death, disaster and blessing, victory and disgrace, endurance and decline, acquire the shape of destiny for human beings. The all-governing expanse of this open relational context is the world of this historical people."[12] According to Heidegger the paradigm sets up history by focusing meanings already scattered in the people's language and practices. Thus, Homer already set up a way of acting for the Greeks. The temple focuses these practices in such a way that the serious issues in the practices are publicly displayed. There can then be serious disagreement and thus history begins.

According to Heidegger, the modern paradigm that focuses our current understanding of being is the hydroelectric power station. It takes the river and turns it into power, which it organizes into a total power grid that puts the power at the disposition of everyone. We can use the electricity to satisfy whatever desires we happen to have, and we can completely forget it when we are not using it. Our culture, then, lives in terms of a technological paradigm that focuses, preserves, and furthers our current understanding of the meaning or, rather, meaninglessness of being.

This technological paradigm is like a Kuhnian scientific paradigm. According to Kuhn, a science becomes normal when the practitioners in a certain area all agree that a particular piece of work identifies the important problems in a field and demonstrates how certain of these problems can be successfully solved. Thus, a scientific paradigm, although meaningless in itself, sets up normal science as an activity of puzzle solving. It is the job of normal science to eliminate anomalies by showing how they fit into the total theory the paradigm sketches out in advance. In a similar way, the technological paradigm embodies and furthers our technological understanding of being according to which what does not fit in with the paradigm, that is, that which is not yet at our disposal (e.g., the wilderness and the stars) will finally be brought under our control. The Greek temple, on the other hand, is not a totalizing paradigm. It shows people not only what they stand for but also that there is something about our practices that withdraws and is hidden, something Heidegger calls the "earth." The true paradigm sets forth the earth. The Platonic/technological paradigm conceals the earth. It tries to show that everything can be objectified, made explicit, decontextualized, totalized, and brought under our control.

We can now see why having nonobjectifiable practices does not guarantee any meaning in our lives, and how having paradigms of total control such as the technological one is compatible with—indeed, can even further—nihilism. What can we do, then, to get whatever there is that is still nontechnological in our practices in focus in a nonnihilistic kind of paradigm? Once one sees the problem, one also sees that there is not much anyone can do about it. Heidegger said in a posthumously published interview, "Only a god can save us."[13] By that he meant that (1) given that our culture has gone as far as it has, whether there could ever again be another non-nihilistic paradigm is something of which we cannot be sure, and (2) a new version of the Greek temple or another God-man—something that grips us so much that we cannot treat it as a value or belief or mind set, something that shows forth the earth and cannot be made explicit, something all can point to but none can objectify—is not something we can bring about by will, choice, and planning.

What then *is* up to us? All we can do is to act and to teach (there are certainly implications for education here) in such a way as not to contribute to the problem. That is, we must try to preserve what shared, historical, cultural concerns have survived. We must resist retreating into private experiences, instincts, individual creativity, energy, Jungian archetypes, and the like. We must not further the nihilistic dichotomy between subjective experience and objective reality—the destructive distinction between the inner and the outer. It furthers nihilism to convey in our teaching that we need not worry about the fact that the outer public world has become completely meaningless as long as there is a world within. Everyone who believes that the only values left are these of the inner life contributes to the spread of nihilism. If we write off the public practices, if we do not even notice them anymore and retreat to the "meaning" of the inner life, then we become part of the problem.

What can we do that is positive? One of the things we can do is to get in the right relation to theory and science, since theory and science were the cause of the problem. There is no doubt that they are here to stay, so we had better learn to use them to our advantage but not to contribute to their nihilistic possibilities. The real danger, it should be obvious by now, is not science and technology. It is a certain attitude toward science and technology, which unfortunately we all share. This meeting has demonstrated once again that we all worship science and technology as our religion. Science is our religion in the very important sense that we think science tells us what reality is. If we say "Thank God science now tells us that reality is energy, reality is process, reality is wholeness," then we are part of the problem. If, on the other hand, we think of science as just a special discipline that has had the interesting and important luck to stumble on a certain kind of objectifying practice that is able to deconceptualize entities and recontextualize them in such a way as to give us control of a certain part of our environment, then we can use the fruits of technology. We can even allow that science gives us insight into a certain kind of reality, namely meaningless physical reality. We can then stop worrying about whether that reality is wonderful or not. It does not matter, when nihilism is the issue, whether scientists have felt awe and wonder in the fact of the cosmos (as Plato and Einstein did) or have tried ruthlessly to exploit it as do our modern technologists. As soon as we think theoretically of *our* having an attitude in the face of some independent reality, the damage is already done. The moral should be obvious by now: If we accept the view of reality implicit in theory and science then we will get objectification, we will get a reality independent of our interests and concerns, independent of our everyday context, and therefore intrinsically and necessarily meaningless. There is nothing wrong with science, nothing wrong with scientists. It is admirable to be able to make a part of reality meaningless and thereby get so much theoretical understanding and power from it. It is our fault if we decide that this meaningless realm is ultimate reality and let it make our lives meaningless as well. So, again, let us not be part of the problem. Let us not teach theory and nihilism. Let us not seek new values. Let us rather try to understand what theory and nihilism are, so that we can save what meaning— if any—remains in our historical, cultural, linguistic practices, and we can be ready for a new paradigm should one be granted to us.

Footnotes

1   Martin Heidegger, "The Word of Nietzsche: 'God is Dead,'" in his *The Question Concerning Technology*, trans. William Lovitt (New York: Harper & Row, 1977), pp. 62, 63.

2   Frederich Nietzsche, *Twilight of the Idols* (New York: Penguin Books, 1968).

3   Heidegger, "The Word of Neitzsche," p. 65.

4   Plato, *Euthyphro*, Library of Liberal Arts (1956), p. 7.

5   Plato, *Apology*, Library of Liberal Arts (1956), p. 27.

6   For an argument that such practices cannot be made explicit and the consequences of this limitation for social science and cognitive science respectively, see my article "Holism and Hermeneutics," *Review of Metaphysics*, September 1980, and my book *What Computers Can't Do* (New York: Harper & Row, 1979).

7   Thomas Kuhn, *The Structure of Scientific Revolutions*, 2nd ed. (Chicago: University of Chicago Press, 1970).

8   Ibid., p. 46.

9   Michael Polanyi, *Personal Knowledge* (London: Routledge & Kegan Paul, 1958).

10   Søren Kierkegaard, *The Present Age* (New York: Harper & Row, 1962).

11   Martin Heidegger, "The Origin of the Work of Art," in his *Poetry, Language, Thought* (New York: Harper & Row, 1971).

12   Ibid., p. 42.

13   "Only a God Can Save Us," from an interview with Heidegger published in *Der Spiegel*, May 31, 1976.

Limits in the Use
of Computer Technology:
Need for a Man-Centered Science

JOSEPH WEIZENBAUM
Massachusetts Institute of Technology

The computer has become so powerful an instrument that its power seems unlimited to many people. But surely, one is tempted to retort, this apparent omnipotence of the computer must be an illusion affecting only those whose knowledge of computers and computation is at best casual. Unfortunately, this is not so, for the general public's belief in the omnipotence of the computer is based firmly on the public and private pronouncements of some of the most prestigious and visible computer scientists.

All of us have been trained to suspend our normal skepticism when an authority (in a branch of science in which we are ourselves not experts) speaks. What critical faculties are we, after all, to bring to bear when, for example, a physicist announces that the mysteries surrounding the interaction of elementary particles may be explained by "the eight-fold way"? Can the layman who knows next to nothing about computers do anything other than to prepare himself for the "visible future [in which] the range of problems [computers] can handle will be coextensive with the range to which the human mind has been applied"? (Simon and Newell, 1958). It is simply a fact, and a tragic one, that the spokesmen for the computing community have communicated an outrageously distorted image of computers and computation both to their colleagues and to the outside world. By so doing, consistently and over a long period of time, they have created a need for responsible people to think and speak about limits to computing.

Where does the power of computers come from? This question needs to be answered on several different levels. As seen from an elementary point of view, computers gain their power from the fact that computer programs may be made to take alternative computational paths depending on the outcome of intermediate computations. One can, in other words, write a set of instruc-

In lieu of the speech delivered at the symposium by Joseph Weizenbaum, which is not available in manuscript form, we are reprinting this closely related article by him. It is reprinted by permission of the author and the publisher from *Toward a Man-Centered Medical Science*, eds. Karl E. Schaefer, Herbert Hensel, and Ronald Brady (Mt. Kisco, N.Y.: Futura Publishing Co., 1977), pp. 83–97.

tions for a computer which the computer is to execute in the sequence given and such that each instruction leaves a result which, unless overwritten by following computations, is available as data to subsequent instructions. A crucial property of such programs is that some instructions can alter the order in which instructions are executed on the basis of a test on a previously computed result. Thus a so-called branching instruction can effectively order the computer to skip the, say, next ten instructions in sequence if a certain previously computed number is, say, less than zero. This simple property of computers, together with the fact that programs are themselves stored in the computer and may therefore be manipulated as data, gives the computer the power to execute programs which are arbitrarily large and complex decision networks. Of course, something has to be said about the primitive instructions built into the computer as well as the alphabet of symbols the computer can manipulate directly. Suffice it to note here that a quite small inventory of instructions and primitive symbols lends a computer all the power any computer can possibly have.

The above account explains, at least roughly, how it is that a computer can be made to carry out even the most complex processes. But, on another level, more needs to be said to justify the assertion that any computer with a quite small but appropriate instruction set and alphabet has the computational power of essentially any other, possibly much more richly endowed, computer. That remarkable result is due to A. M. Turing, an English mathematician, who designed an almost ridiculously simple computer (actually a class of abstract machines) and proved that given a description of any other computer in a certain class, it could *imitate* that other computer. This simple computer is today called a *Turing machine*.

It has to be added that a number of other logicians have described formal computing systems that appear radically different from Turing's. Yet each that has been shown to be as equally powerful as Turing's system has also been shown to be equivalent to his. Mathematicians believe there to be an absolute notion of effective computability and that Turing machines exemplify it. However, this thesis can in principle not be proven. The implications of Turing's result are enormously far-reaching. For our purposes we note only that Turing's machine can be "described" to virtually every modern computer, i.e., in the form of a program. Therefore, every modern computer can be made to imitate a Turing machine and hence every other modern computer. In that sense then every modern computer is "universal" and, of course, equally as powerful as every other. Another way of putting this is to say that any program written for computer A can be converted into a program for a different computer B by concatenating it with a program describing computer A in a symbolism suitable to B. This implies that, beyond a certain point, there is no necessary logical distinction between programs and computers. To program a computer is to logically redesign and rebuild it.

We can design instruction sets for computers, which is to say programming languages, of arbitrary complexity, providing only that we can also set up precise and unambiguous procedures for translating our artificially created languages into instruction sets primitive to the computer we intend to actually use. In a formal sense each such translating procedure (technically an interpreter or a compiler) constitutes a description of an abstract machine which transforms an actual machine into one that has the complex language we have designed as its built-in instruction repertoire. Such "machines," i.e., programming languages, are typically designed to serve specially selected problem domains and are usually given alphabets also specially chosen to be appropriate to the special problem domains. Thus a programming language intended for use as, for example, a natural language manipulator will typically have letters, words, and even sentence structures as primitive objects which may be manipulated as easily in that language as numbers, say, may be manipulated in a language designed for arithmetic processes.

In effect then, computer languages can be designed as collections of pieces (data structures) out of which models in the desired problem domain are to be built and collections of devices for sticking the pieces together (instruction sets). Just as we may find wooden sticks, tissue paper, and glue appropriate for building model airplanes and the quite different pieces supplied in a child's Mechano set appropriate for building models of cranes and Ferris wheels, so languages may differ in the sorts of data structures and instruction sets they supply to various model builders. Thus, another source of the power of computers is that they are highly specific modeling kits.

We may say that a construction M is a model of a system S if some theory of the behavior of M is also a theory of the behavior of S. The theory of the modeled system S need not be complete. Indeed, model building is most often useful when no complete theory of S is known. If M behaves exactly like S *in all essentials*, then the study of M, which may be much easier to pursue than a corresponding study of S, may yield the insights necessary to form a more nearly complete theory of S. This, in general, is the purpose of modeling. The computer, because of its universality, can be made to be an environment within which any system can be modeled that is capable of being formally modeled at all. Moreover, and this is very important, computer models can be made to *behave*. (They are often called performance models.) The computer thus provides a unique bridge between theory and model.

Normally, we speak of a model as *satisfying* but not as *being* a theory. A theory is a text, generally in natural language, that explains or accounts for the behavior of some aspect of the world on the basis of a set of posited concepts. But it is left to the reader of a theory to deduce its behavioral consequences. Even mathematical models, say in the form of differential equations, provide only static snapshots of the behavior of the systems they describe. A computer model is also a text. It may be read and understood by sufficiently indoctrinated specialists. For them its discursive description as theory in the ordinary sense would be completely redundant. Theory and model are then the same. What has been gained is that the playing out of the consequences of the theory is no longer an exercise for readers whose understanding of natural language is idiosyncratic, but for a patient and completely determinate agent, a computer.

But now we come to a cautionary observation: we recall that a model behaves exactly like the system it models *in all its essentials.* And that means that it may otherwise behave quite differently than its real-world counterpart. A model airplane may melt in a rain through which a real one flies without hazard. When models become very complex and exhibit enormously complex behaviors, how does one determine what parts of their behaviors may be identified as corresponding to possible behaviors of the systems they represent? This question is closely related to the one that asks what it is about a real-world system that is essential. Essential to what?

It is largely, so it seems to me, the failure on the part of computer scientists and others using computers in modeling activities to appreciate that question and all it implies that accounts for their enormous hubris. They succeed in modeling certain aspects of human cognitive functions and believe, and announce to the world, that their techniques are sufficient to constitute a hypothetical basis for understanding "the whole man." Thus H. A. Simon (1969) follows a discussion of how fundamentally simple a computer is and how it may be used to explore "the consequences of alternative organizational assumptions for human behavior" with the assertion:

> A man viewed as a behaving system is quite simple. The apparent complexity of his behavior over time is largely a reflection of the environment in which he finds himself. . . . I believe that this hypothesis holds even for the whole man. (Simon, 1969)

Simon must believe that the data structures he uses and the instructional repertoires that manipulate them—plus those like them that are likely to be invented "in the visible future"—in short, such abstract machines—are all that is essential to an understanding of the whole man. Professor Marvin Minsky of M.I.T., another leading authority in the computer field, expresses an analogous perception when he says: "The brain is merely a meat machine."

Fortunately, it is not necessary to be able to say what the essence of man is in order to refute this simplistic view. It is only required that it be shown that such a view leaves out something that must inevitably be a part of what it means to be human. My own view is that an organism, be it a man or an ant, is in its essence defined by the problems with which it must cope. The biological structure of the human organism determines that the infant human must cope with the trauma of birth, i.e., the initial separation from the mother, and immediately thereafter with its dependence on other humans for its very survival. A human, to be socialized as a human, must be perceived as and treated as a human by other humans. By the time his physical survival is no longer a physiological question, he may still die for lack of psychological nurturing. The story of the socialization of the human is a long one. Suffice it to say here that the problems humans face, problems that are the very determinants of their humanity, are not and can logically not be problems with which a machine can be confronted. For example, only humans can be confronted with the problems that tormented Faust or Hamlet.

When, therefore, Simon speaks of the "range [of problems] to which the human mind has been applied" as being in the future coextensive with "the range of problems computers can handle," he must be engaging in a pun on the word "problem." The same pun appears in the title of a book recently published by Newell and Simon, namely *Human Problem Solving*. This work reports perhaps twenty years' work on computer simulations of certain kinds of human problems completed by the two authors and their students. I would characterize the kinds of problems they discuss as *"bounded" problems*. By a bounded problem I mean one for which one may suggest a solution and a mechanism, e.g., a suitably programmed computer, for applying the suggested solution to the problem such that the actual solving of the problem leaves all but that mechanism unchanged. All mathematical problems are examples of bounded problems.

The authors' own definition of "problem" is as follows:

> To have a problem implies (at least) that certain information is given to the problem solver: information about what is desired, under what conditions, by means of what tools and operations, starting with what initial information, and with access to what resources. The problem solver has an interpretation of this information—exactly that interpretation which lets us label some part of it as a *goal*, another part as *side conditions*, and so on. Consequently, if we provide a representation for this information (in symbol structures), and assume that the interpretation of these structures is implicit in the program of the information processing system, then we have defined a problem. (Newell and Simon, 1972)

But when ordinary men speak of human problems generally, they also mean examples such as:

How to serve truth and yet be a university professor

Maintaining good relations with one's children

The world pollution problem

How to reduce tensions in one's neighborhood

One may ask about these problems: what information is given to the problem solver? What is "desired," and what does it mean to speak of "conditions" at all? Is the fact that much of the world is corrupt and filled with greed and hate a "condition" in a sense intended by the authors? What "tools and operations" are available to the problem solver, *a priori* in any of these kinds of problems? What is the "initial information" with respect to any of these problems? Perhaps most crucially, is it not a gigantic and entirely unwarranted leap to assume that interpretations of any information connected with the problems I have mentioned can be sufficiently explicated to enable them to be represented in computer manipulatable symbol structures?

No, not all human problem solving fits into the neat categories given us by Newell and Simon. The kinds of problems I have cited here are *unbounded* in the sense that the very attempt to apply "solutions" to them changes them, the environments in which they are imbedded, and indeed the problem solver himself. They cannot be "solved" (by man *or* by machine) in the sense that "answers" can be found that forever dispose of them and all their consequences. Surely that is elementary and obvious to everyone.

Or not?!

Some years ago I wrote a program that simulated the verbal behavior of a psychiatrist conducting a psychiatric interview (Weizenbaum, 1966). Dr. K. M. Colby, a psychoanalyst at Stanford University, wrote of it:

> If the method proves beneficial, then it would provide a therapeutic tool which can be made widely available to mental hospitals and psychiatric centers suffering a shortage of therapists . . . several hundred patients an hour could be handled by a computer designed for this purpose. (Colby et al., 1966)

I had thought that an absolutely essential prerequisite to the very possibility of one person's helping another to learn to cope with his emotional problems is that the helper himself participate in the other's experience of those problems and, in large part by way of his own empathic recognition of them, come to understand them. There are undoubtedly many *techniques* to facilitate this, the therapist's imaginative projection into the patient's inner life. But that it was possible for even one practicing psychiatrist to advocate the entire supplantation of this crucial component of the therapeutic process by pure technique, that is hard to imagine! The elementary and obvious distinction between bounded and unbounded problems is not clearly appreciated by everyone. What must a psychiatrist who makes such suggestions think he is doing while treating a patient, that he can view the simplest mechanical parody of a single interviewing technique as having captured anything of the essence of a human encounter? Perhaps Colby gives us the required clue when he writes:

> A human therapist can be viewed as an information processor and decision maker with a set of decision rules which are closely linked to short-range and long-range goals. . . . He is guided in these decisions by rough em-

piric rules telling him what is appropriate to say and not to say in certain contexts. To incorporate these processes, to the degree possessed by a human therapist, in the program would be a considerable undertaking, but we are attempting to move in this direction. (Colby et al., 1966)

What can the psychiatrist's image of his patient be when he sees himself *qua* therapist, not as an engaged human being acting as a healer, but as an information processor following rules, etc.? In this passage we see a feature of reality that a model may actually share with reality, namely that aspect of a human therapist which *is* an information processor, extrapolated to the point where *everything* that is true of information processors must be true of the real person, the human psychotherapist, and *nothing* else can be true. The patient's problems have been transformed into bounded problems that can be solved by the application of empiric rules.

Another pun that sheds light on what I am trying to say here is one committed, quite unconsciously, by Professor Minsky in his book *Semantic Information Processing*. He writes:

To write really good music or draw highly meaningful pictures [by computer program] will of course require better semantic models in these areas. That these are not available is not so much a reflection on the state of heuristic programs, as on the traditionally disgraceful state of analytic criticism in the arts—a cultural consequence of the fact that most esthetic analysts wax indignant when it is suggested that it might be possible to understand what they are trying to understand. (Minsky, 1968, p. 12)

The last sentence contains a very deep pun on the word "understand." What Minsky does not understand, and I have discussed this with him, is that when an esthetician—or, for that matter, an ordinary person—speaks of understanding a piece of music or a "highly meaningful picture," he means an understanding involving him as a whole man. Such an understanding rests on a person's entire experience of becoming the socialized human he is at the moment of groping for understanding. But Minsky equates this with an understanding of the presumed rules which generated the formal aspects of the work of art in question. It is as if the majesty of an eagle's flight, a poem celebrating it, and the aerodynamic laws governing it were all one and the same. The ability to make this pun in all innocence, so to speak, and completely unconscious of the fact that it is a pun reveals a fundamental attitude that, I am afraid, is shared by almost all scientists and technologists, if not by nearly everyone. This is that scientific understanding is the only legitimate way of understanding anything at all about the world. And from this it follows, in the common wisdom, that all of life is computable.

I want to say explicitly, even though it may not be necessary, that I *do not* believe all of life to be computable. I *do not* believe that whatever moved Käthe Kollwitz to draw her picture of a child begging its mother for food is computable. I *do not* believe that what happens inside me when I hear the word "Treblinka" spoken is computable. Nor is whatever happens in an infant who feels his mother's breast in his mouth and her warm body surrounding him computable.

But perhaps it *is* necessary to say these things after all. For when we are discussing the limits in the use of computer technology, we are in reality wrestling with precisely these assertions as *open questions*. No, more than that! Many of my colleagues in computer science, and certainly almost all in that branch of it called artificial intelligence, believe that no human mental capacity is beyond realization by machine. Note again that Simon sees machines ranging over the whole set of problems that man has thought about in all the centuries of his existence—and also those of the "visible future"! The enormity of that idea is simply staggering. What can one say to it?

Nor must those of us who are genuinely devoted to the idea of a man-centered culture and hence a man-centered science permit ourselves the comfort of believing that only a few mad computer scientists operate on the basis of the principles to which I have here alluded, namely the essentially equivalent ones that

Science is the only path to knowledge of the world

The brain is merely a meat machine

Computers will soon range over the entire domain of human thought

All of these are restatements of the position that rationality (and I mean here to include imaginativeness in all its forms) is equivalent to logicality. Professor John McCarthy of Stanford University stated this position in perhaps its rawest form when he said that we do not yet have a generalized machine intelligence only because of a *defect* in current versions of mathematical logic that has prevented us from writing a complete formulation of what the world is like. Of course, he and his students are working to repair that "defect." In practice, these principles are widely held, not only among computer specialists, but among people who proudly identify themselves as technologists in virtually every field of human conduct.

Surely, much of what we today regard as good and useful, as well as much of what we would call knowledge and wisdom, we owe to science. But then science may also be seen as an addictive drug. Not only has our "unbounded" feeding on science caused us to become dependent on it, but, as happens with many other drugs taken in increasing dosages, modern science has been gradually converted to a slow-acting poison. Beginning perhaps with Francis Bacon's misreading of the genuine promise of science, man has been seduced into wishing and working for the establishment of an age of rationality, but with his vision of rationality tragically twisted so as to equate it with logicality.

Thus have we very nearly come to the point where almost every genuine human dilemma is seen as a mere paradox—a merely apparent contradiction that is thought capable of being untangled by judicious applications of cold logic derived from a higher standpoint. Even murderous wars have come to be perceived as mere problems to be solved by hordes of professional problem solvers. Hannah Arendt says of the makers and executors of policy of recent tenure in the Pentagon:

> They were not just intelligent, but prided themselves on being 'rational'. . . . They were eager to find formulas, preferably expressed in a pseudo-mathematical language, that would unify the most disparate phenomena with which reality presented them; that is, they were eager to discover *laws* by which to explain and predict political and historical facts as though they were as necessary, and thus as reliable, as the physicists once believed natural phenomena to be. . . . [they] did not *judge*; they calculated. . . . an utterly irrational confidence in the calculability of reality [became] the leitmotif of the decision making. (Arendt, 1972)

I have tried here to show that the fundamental attitude of the leadership of the artificial intelligence community—of the artificial intelligencia—namely, that every aspect of human life is computable, is shared by large and powerful segments of society quite far removed from computer science as such. Indeed, I believe it constitutes a zeitgeist, perhaps even a dominant one. Hence questions about the possible uses of computers and computation should not be seen as mere speculations about what computers can or cannot do in principle or in some distant future. Instead they are, and should be so seen, questions directly relating to the bases on which our society makes decisions today. Professor Fredkin, head of M.I.T.'s Project MAC, sees the danger of using computers as decision makers in human affairs in terms of the possibility that computer programs may have bugs, i.e., technical errors. He believes that danger will be overcome by advances in automatic programming, i.e., by the increasing ability of computers to understand people's *intentions* and then to program themselves accordingly. This rests squarely on the kind of perception of what human problems are that I have mentioned and that Arendt correctly attributes to people in the Pentagon. It supposes that people have exactly one intention with respect to any given social problem and that technicians, or even computers alone, can divine that intention. The solving of social problems then becomes a merely technical exercise in which, to be sure, one has to take care that no technical errors are committed.

We can, therefore, see that the commitment of a large segment of our society, especially of the artificial intelligence leadership, to the rationality-logicality equation, i.e., to the current technological "zeitgeist," is a profoundly political one. It presupposes a politically homogenous society, one in which there are no genuinely conflicting interests or points of view. There have, throughout history, been many attempts to create exactly such societies by direct political means. They have all failed, often at the cost of great human sacrifice. Will the subtle temptations offered by modern science and technology lure us into the nightmare we have so dearly paid to avoid?

References

Arendt, Hannah (1972): *Crisis of the Republic*. Harcourt Brace Jovanovich, Inc., Harvest Ed., New York, pp. 11 et seq.

Colby, K. M. et al. (1966): A computer method of psychotherapy: Preliminary communications. *J. Nerv. Ment. Dis.*, **142**: 148–152.

Minsky, M. (Ed.) (1968): *Semantic Information Processing*. M.I.T. Press, Cambridge, Mass.

Newell, A. and Simon, H. A. (1972): *Human Problem Solving*. Prentice-Hall, Englewood Cliffs, N.J., p. 73.

Simon, H. A. (1969): *The Sciences of the Artificial*. M.I.T. Press, Cambridge, Mass.

Simon, H. A. and Newell, A. (1958): Euristic problem solving: The next advance in operations research. *Operations Res.*, **6**: 61.

Weizenbaum, J. (1966): Eliza, a computer method for the study of natural language communications between man and machine. *Comm. A.C.M.*, **9**: 36–45.

CONTRIBUTORS

PETER ABBS is lecturer in art, philosophy, and education at Sussex University. He was editor of *Tract* and among his books are *The Art of English, Reclamations: Essays on Culture, Mass-Culture and the Curriculum, Root and Blossom: Essays on the Philosophy, Practice and Politics of English Teaching, Autobiography in Education,* and with Graham Carey, *Proposal for a New College.*

OWEN BARFIELD graduated in English with first class Honours at Wadham College, Oxford, in 1921. In later life he practiced the law for thirty years. Among his numerous books are included *Poetic Diction: A Study in Meaning, Romanticism Comes of Age, Saving the Appearances: A Study in Idolatry, Worlds Apart, History in English Words, What Coleridge Thought, The Rediscovery of Meaning,* and *History, Guilt, and Habit.*

ROBERT N. BELLAH is Ford Professor of Sociology and Comparative Studies and chairman of the Center for Japanese and Korean Studies at the University of California, Berkeley. Among his books are *Beyond Belief: Essays on Religion in a Post-Traditional World, The Broken Covenant: American Civil Religion in Time of Trial, Tokugawa Religion,* and with Charles Glock is editor of *The New Religious Consciousness.*

DAVID BOHM has taught at Princeton University, Universidade de Sao Paulo (Brazil), and Technion, Haifa, Israel. Since 1961 he has been professor of theoretical physics at Birkbeck College, University of London. His main interests have been in plasma theory, in the fundamentals of relativity and quantum theory, and, especially, in their significance for philosophy, and more broadly, for general notions current in life as a whole. He is also deeply interested in psychology, education, and related fields. He is author of *Causality and Chance in Modern Physics, Special Theory of Relativity: Its Origins, Meanings, and Implications, Fragmentation and Wholeness: An Inquiry into the Function of Language and Thought,* numerous articles on theoretical physics, and a new book, just published by Routledge & Kegan Paul, *Wholeness and the Implicate Order.*

HUBERT L. DREYFUS is professor of philosophy at the University of California, Berkeley. His philosophical interests have been in phenomenology and existentialism and in the issues of artificial intelligence. He is author of *What Computers Can't Do: The Limits of Artificial Intelligence.*

SIR JOHN CAREW ECCLES is Distinguished Emeritus Professor at the State University of New York in Buffalo. A research neurophysiologist, he received the Nobel prize for medicine in 1963. He has been a distinguished lecturer and research fellow at many universities around the world and was the Gifford lecturer at Edinburgh University in 1977 and 1978. Among his many publications are included most recently, *Facing Reality: Philosophical Adventures of a Brain Scientist, Understanding the Brain, Physiology of Synapses,* and *The Self and Its Brain* co-authored with Karl Popper, and the Gifford Lectures, *The Human Mystery* and *The Human Psyche.*

KATHLEEN RAINE is from Great Britain and is a poet, scholar, critic, and philosopher. She has written eight books of poetry, a three-volume autobiography, and a number of books of scholarly and philosophical criticism. She is a fellow of Girton College, Cambridge, and is a leading authority on Blake. Among her works are, in addition to her poetry, *William Blake, Yeats: The Tarot and the Golden Dawn, The Letters of Samuel Taylor Coleridge, Blake and the New Age, From Blake to a Vision, Thomas Taylor; The Platonist, Blake and Antiquity*, and the three-volume autobiography, *Farewell, Happy Fields: Memories of Children, The Land Unknown: Further Chapters of Autobiography*, and *The Lion's Mouth: Concluding Chapters of Autobiography.*

HUSTON SMITH is Hanna Professor of Philosophy at Hamline University in St. Paul. Previously he was Thomas J. Watson Professor of Religion and adjunct professor of philosophy at Syracuse University. He is author of *Condemned to Meaning*, the John Dewey Lectures for 1964, *The Purposes of Higher Education, Religion of Man, Dialogue on Science, Forgotten Truth: The Primordial Tradition*, and *Beyond the Post-Modern Mind.*

JOSEPH WEIZENBAUM is professor of computer sciences at M.I.T. and is currently a guest professor at the University of Hamburg in Germany. He is author of *Computer Power and Human Reason: From Judgment to Calculation*, and with W. Handler is editor of *Display Use for Man-Machine Dialogue.*

INDEX